MW00990138

HERBERT W. McBRIDE
*Captain, 21st Battalion
Canadian Expeditionary Force*

A Rifleman Went To War

By

Herbert W. McBride
Captain

Twenty-first Battalion
Canadian Expeditionary Force

and

United States Army

Being a narrative of the author's experiences and observations while
with the Canadian Corps in France and Belgium, September 1915-
April 1917. With particular emphasis upon the use of the
military rifle in sniping, its place in modern armament,
and the work of the individual soldier.

Lancer Militaria
Mt. Ida, Arkansas

Originally published by
Small-Arms Technical Publishing Co., 1935

Printed in the United States of America

Library of Congress Catalog Card Number 87-81974

ISBN 0-935856-01-3

Lancer Militaria
P.O. Box 886
Mt. Ida, Arkansas 71957
USA

0 9 8 7 6 5 4 3 2 1

PROLOGUE

The reprinting of this splendid work has been long
awaited by everyone who knows about it. It is not only a
true classic; it is also, to the best of my knowledge and
belief, unique—the only thing of its kind.

The title is self-explanatory to those who read it
accurately, but perhaps there are those who will not.
While it would be good if all soldiers were riflemen, only
a few really merit that title. The true rifleman is an
enthusiast, an artist, an *aficionado*. He loves his weapon,
he loves to shoot, and he usually learns to shoot long
before he puts on a uniform. For a rifleman to go to war,
therefore, is not for a young man to be called from the
pursuits of happiness, thrown into the military
establishment, handed a weapon, trained to use it, and
then sent reluctantly into the fearful crucible of battle; it
is rather for a dedicated practitioner gladly to set forth in
search of his chosen practice.

Men like to fight. They do not like to suffer, to fear, to
grieve, or to die, but there is a lot more to fighting than
just misery. There is challenge, skill, self-control, self-
realization, and a transcendent exhilaration found in no
other activity. In 1914 McBride was no raw recruit, he
was already a captain in the Indiana National Guard. But
his country was not at war, so he split to Canada—for the
other reason. He relinquished his earned rank and joined
the Canadian Army as a private. And thus he, a true
rifleman, went to war.

He fought all the way through it, in the trenches of the Western Front. His original outfit suffered eighty percent casualties. He refused promotion again and again, because he was essentially a *rifleman*—a shooter—and he preferred shooting to commanding. It would not be strictly true to say that he loved every minute of it, but he certainly enjoyed the fighting, as is strikingly evident from his narrative. Thousands of authors have told us how hellish infantry action is, but McBride is perhaps the only one to show us its other "side".

As a young marine I read McBride carefully and enthusiastically, and I learned more about my business from his work than from any other single source. I hope it is not true that I got *all* my ideas about fighting from him, as has been suggested, but I certainly got a lot of them.

Times change, and weapons change, and the human spirit seems to lose its luster, but there will always be stout-hearted men on whom Herbert McBride's story will not be wasted.

Here it is. Amen!

Jeff Cooper

Gunsite, 1987

An Appreciation

Ottawa, Canada,
November 9, 1935.

The author of this book—the late Herbert W. McBride—served in my Battalion as private, non-commissioned officer and officer. He was one of the best fighting men I knew and was promoted and decorated on my recommendations.

He was considered one of the best "Machine Gunners" in the Allied Army. Also one of the best shots with a rifle.

Herbert W. McBride was outstanding as a fighting man, fearless, untiring, a genius for invention, and always seeking authority to be given the opportunity of damaging the enemy. I had the greatest admiration for Captain McBride as a soldier, and with an army of such men it would be an easy matter to win against any troops. It was such fighting ability that enabled my 21st Battalion to come home with the record of never having been given a black eye in over four years of active participation in the war. They never went after anything they did not take, and they never gave up anything they captured. Of the original 1058, less than 150 are now alive, most of them buried in Flanders' Fields and in the Somme.

W. S. HUGHES,

Brigd. General.

DEDICATION

This book is dedicated to all those members of the *original* Twenty-first Battalion, Canadian Expeditionary Force, who served in the Machine Gun Section during the time I had the honor to belong to that unit.

The following list, made from memory and such meager records as I possess, may, possibly, omit some of them. If so, I tender my most sincere apologies. I would not, intentionally, slight any member of that gallant Section.

*Allen	*Gray	Parker
Baldson	Hart	Paudash
Booker	Harvey	*Peverelle
*Bouchard	Jackson	Redpath
*Brooks	*Jendon	Rothwell
*Castleman	†Johnstone	*Russell
*Charles	Laidlaw	Shangrow
*Clark	*Lanning	Shepard
†Currie	Lee, Cecil	Smith
*Deegan	Lee, Jack	Southgate
*DeLisle	Lynch	*Stillman
*Dupuis	†McBride	*Tinkess
Endersby	McFarlin	*Toms
Esdon	McGinness	*Wendt
Flannigan	McNab	†Williams
*Freeman	Mangan	*Wilson
Gillette	Meeks	
*Gordon	†*Norton-Taylor	

Those marked with an asterisk were killed in action.
All the others were wounded.
Those marked with a "†" were commissioned.

HERBERT W. McBRIDE.

An Explanation and An Introduction

It fell to the lot of the author of this narrative to serve as a member of the British Army in some of the battles it fought during the not-so-recent Great War. Ever since my return to the United States I have been asked countless questions by hundreds, yes thousand, of friends and acquaintances relative to my personal experiences in that conflict. The great majority of these questioners happened to be riflemen or soldiers of our own U. S. Army who did not have the "luck" (as they expressed it) to serve in battle, or to have ever used their military rifles for the purpose for which they were designed. Yet—like myself at the beginning of that great conflict—they felt fully qualified and were eager to face the common enemy and do their bit. Moreover, like any qualified workman, they had the true craftsman's intense interest in any and all questions of work, tools or technique relating to even the most minute phase of their chosen profession—riflecraft.

It is for the edification of individuals such as these that I have been persuaded to write these pages. In doing so, I have purposely avoided the fields of strategy, applied tactics, military movements and, yes, even history; because, strange to say, nobody asked me anything about these general subjects of war; not, I take it, because they have been treated in so many other accounts, but because they are academic, theoretical—meaningless until they have been made to "tick", have been taken off paper and shown on the battlefield; and here it is soon discovered that what makes them go is MEN. And this is just what my inquirers have been asking about. Their questions have been of seemingly insignificant things, which, when they are all answered, give one some sort of a picture of MEN at WAR.

Hence—and as the proper preparations for the defense of my Country are yet a vital matter with myself—I have tried to the best of my humble ability to give, in the chapters which follow, the honest answer to many of these questions regarding such small and human matters—the most important of all matters however, because they relate directly and particularly to the individual man, with whom battles are always won.

In describing these incidents and experiences and in making the observations given, I have carefully tried to stick to the straight and narrow path of truth, and tell the story as things really happened—with fictitious "sob stuff" and dramatics left out. Hence, if you do not find enough material about rifle shooting, or about scouting, or some other phase of warfare upon which you particularly wanted information, please be lenient with the old man and remember that I did not make the war. I did only my own little bit in it and must tell of the things which actually *did* happen and just how they happened. This I have done and this only.

* * * * * * *

I have often said that a soldier can and does outlie a fisherman and I still say it, but now I have come to the conclusion that he is not entirely to blame in the matter. The truth is that the public—*his* public—demands it. The average citizen: man, woman or child, has such peculiar notions as to actual modern battle conditions that it is impossible to make them understand anything beyond the fact that it is a fight; and fighting, as they visualize it, means a stand up and knock down, hand-to-hand struggle. They think that, because a man was in the Army, in France, and took part in some of the great battles—the Argonne, for instance—that he must have shot, bayonetted or otherwise killed off innumerable Germans and are inclined to doubt the veracity of any honest-minded soul who tries to tell them a true and straightforward story of events as they really happened. They just cannot understand that, out of the million or so of soldiers who actually did their bit in that great offensive, probably not ten per cent ever saw a German until he came back through the lines, a prisoner. The soldier, or ex-soldier soon learns this and to relieve himself of the necessity of long and tedious explanations, he simply starts in to invent a lot of blood-curdling, spectacular tales; whereupon everybody is satisfied. Man believes what he wants to believe and that is the kind of stuff they want to hear. It coincides with their already formed ideas of what a battle ought to be like.

The same thing applies to the "popular" war stories and pictures. In cases where these stories and pictures are from the pens of men who actually served as soldiers, the authors know full well that they are ridiculously exaggerated and distorted, but they also know that the plain, unvarnished truth would not be accepted by the public or, what is more important to them, by the publishers, so they proceed to manufacture thrills to order. This I have not done.

Closely akin to this situation is the idea, prevalent among the populace of the United States at large, that the nation is safely and sufficiently protected because, in the event of foreign invasion or aggression, millions of men would immediately "spring to arms," as the late Mr. Bryan expressed it. Even with the disastrous example of the last war still fresh, they just cannot or will not accept the truth that the ordinary citizen cannot be made into a trained soldier by the simple expedient of placing a weapon in his hands. Soldiers themselves; those who have "gone through the mill," know all about it, but who pays much attention to a soldier—in time of peace? It's Kipling's "Tommy Atkins" all over again:

"Oh, it's Tommy this and Tommy that,
  And Tommy go away.
But it's 'Thank you, Mister Atkins,'
  When the Band begins to play."

* * * * * * *

Probably no other single thing in the soldiering game is so little understood as rifle shooting. The general impression seems to be that all that is necessary is to give a man a rifle and some cartridges and that, in some miraculous way, that man immediately becomes a perfectly good and competent rifleman, able to knock over any number of the enemy at most any range.

WE know: Those of us who have spent years and years trying to learn the game—but how are we going to pound it into the head of "the man in the street"? This writer grew up in a family of shooting men—and good ones too—and kept up his training, *all the time,* winter and summer, throughout the years, yet he was well past thirty before he really learned much about real, honest-to-goodness military rifle shooting and it took a long period of intensive training, under the best of instructors and in the stiffest of competitions before he felt that he was really entitled to be called a "rifleman."

The above is written as a partial answer to numerous queries, received from correspondents all over the country, as to whether I thought all the training and range firing and the annual competitions at Camp Perry were "worth while." The answer, most emphatically, is *yes*: not only worth while; they are absolutely essential for the proper training of military riflemen. Without the intimate knowledge of weapons, ammunition and weather conditions which can be gained in no other way, there would be no real riflemen. Every bit of information that may be picked up on the range will prove useful in war. True, it will not always—nor often—

be possible to assume the exact, orthodox positions used in competitions and there is the matter of adjusting oneself—mentally and physically—to the stress and strain of battle but, just the same, all those fundamental principles will have an important, even if sub-conscious influence, tending to increase the rifleman's effectiveness.

All the "rifle cranks" in this country are helping the cause. Their ceaseless experiments in reloading, devising new cartridges and components and designing new bullets, sights and various other mechanical improvements; their indefatigable industry in trying out everything new, both on the target range and in the hunting field; all are of incalculable value to the military rifle game. And of special value are the great National Rifle Competitions, held annually at Camp Perry, and similar meetings. Without such men, doing these things, and particularly without the continuous efforts of their splendid organization—the National Rifle Association—we would soon find ourselves far behind in the big parade of progressive nations insofar as military preparedness is concerned. And it is for these men that I have really written this narrative.

HERBERT W. McBRIDE,

Indianapolis, Indiana.

CONTENTS

Chapter 1

How Come?

A S THIS is the story of an alleged rifleman, I suppose it is fitting that I offer some evidence to support the allegation.

My experience in this line really began some fifty-odd years ago when, as a little boy, I used to sit and watch my father get his outfit ready for the annual deer hunt. We lived up in the Northeastern corner of Indiana and the hunting ground, at that time, was just a few miles out of Saginaw, Michigan. Father had two boxes, which he had made himself. One of them contained the cooking outfit— everything from reflector oven to knives, forks and spoons— all especially made to nest and fit in the chest. The other, smaller than the first, carried his guns and all the accessories. In those days you "loaded your own" so, besides the usual cleaning tools, oils and so on, there were plentiful supplies of powder, both rifle and shotgun, shot, bullet moulds, cartridge cases, both for the rifle and shotgun and all of brass (that was before the advent of the paper shotgun cartridge case), primers and a goodly supply of lead. Of course, at the start, he had a plentiful supply of loaded cartridges for both guns. At first, his deer rifle was a single shot Remington, .44 calibre, rimfire. He later had it bored out to take the .45-70 U. S. Government cartridge.

For weeks before the time of departure for the hunting

grounds, the crowd would get together every few days and pull off a shooting match, each one trying some new idea he had worked out since the last expedition. It was nothing unusual for half the merchants of the little town to shut up shop in the middle of the afternoon and, together with the lawyers, doctors and, yes, the preachers, to repair to some vacant lot and shoot impromptu matches with everything from old "pepper-boxes" to the latest rifles at that time available. At that time and in that place, practically all of the "men" were veterans of the Civil War and this shooting business was part of their gospel. Naturally, as a young boy, I became infected, and my father, believing in the idea of preparedness, gave me ample opportunities to learn the game; even to letting me shoot his heavy guns when he knew very well they would kick the stuffing out of me. He was a good and kindly man but he had no use for mollycoddles.

From time to time he bought me rifles, beginning with the little old Flobert; then a Quackenbush. Well, anyway, I remember that last one, with its heavy, round, nickel-plated barrel. When I was about twelve he had the local gunsmith make me up a *real* rifle: a muzzle loading Kentucky squirrel rifle with the barrel cut down to thirty inches and the stock likewise trimmed down to what we would nowadays call "sporter" proportions. I still have that rifle and while it looks like—well—not very much, when I was using it, it certainly delivered the goods. A hawk on a snag anywhere within one hundred yards or a woodpecker on the highest limb was certainly out of luck and the squirrel that was foolish enough to stick his head over the limb was just as good as in the pot.

I made my own powder-horn and bullet-pouch and, of course made my own bullets. The caps—"Elys"—I had to buy, as I did the powder and lead, with what money I could earn by odd jobs, one of which was the catching of rats around our premises. Father gave me five cents apiece for every rat.

Well, there you have it. Any youngster brought up in such an atmosphere is bound to develop into a rifleman. As the years rolled 'round I graduated through the different grades. My father was Captain of a company of the old Indiana Legion, as it was known before the adoption of the designation of National Guard, and I was one of the privileged boys who 'tended target for them on the range which they had improvised at the edge of town. In those days the Militia companies were self-supporting. Even after I became a full fledged "soldier" we not only bought our own uniforms, but paid armory rent and all expenses.

On some occasions, we boys were actually allowed to shoot, the older men taking our places in the pits. How those old Springfields did kick. They were wicked. I have seen many of the old timers with black-and-blue shoulders after a day's shooting and, curiously enough, I remember that most of the officers had their shoulder straps bent. That was before the idea entered anyone's head to lie at the now commonly accepted "forty-five degree" angle. They lay straight toward the target and took the whole kick right on the top of the shoulder when firing from the prone position. The back positions, which were commonly used then, were not at all bad. Either the Texas Grip or the Stevens were easy, even for us kids, but when it came to the "belly-whooping" position, well, we did it, but every shot would set us back a foot or more.

At the age of fifteen I enlisted in and for several years remained a member of the Third Regiment. During that time, my father rose to the rank of Colonel commanding, and I became a sergeant. Then I went to work in Chicago and immediately affiliated with the First Illinois Infantry—Company I—Captain Chenoweth commanding. During the summer of 1893, having been informed by a wise medico that I had T. B., I put in my time ranging around in Colorado and New Mexico, part of the time as a cow-puncher and the rest working for a coal-mining company. (That is, I was supposed to be working for them, but, as a matter of fact, I was using them simply as a meal ticket, as I spent every minute of my idle time in scouting around look-ing for something to shoot at.) I met and got acquainted with a lot of the *real* old timers: men famous during the hectic days of Abilene, Dodge and Hays City and, of course, those who had been mixed up in the various ructions in-cident to the clearing up of the famous Maxwell Land Grant, upon part of which this mine was located.

Trinidad, near the mine (Sopris), was one of the hot spots in the old days and many a bad man had met his "come-uppance" there and along the Picketwire or, as the original Spanish name has it, the Purgutoire River. From these men and from my practical shooting with them in various matches, I learned just about how good they and their erstwhile friends—and enemies—could really shoot, both with the pistol and the rifle. Bat Masterson, Jim Lee, Schwin Box and Nat Chapin, just to name the best of them, were all good shots, but the best of them never could hold a candle to the amazing performances of a lot of hither-to unknown "experts" who are continually bobbing up in the moving pictures and the sensational stories published in supposedly reputable magazines in the year of grace, 1930.

I should have included Brown—Three-finger Brown—in the above list. He was as good as the best of them although he had to do all his shooting left-handed: due to the fact that he had allowed his curiosity to over-ride his good sense in the matter of investigating the doings of a band of "Penitentes" one might and, as a result, lost the thumb and first finger of his right hand.

All these men had grown up in the West and had lived through the various "wars" and ructions which flared up every now and then, all the way from Texas to the Black Hills. They all bore the scars of combat but the very fact that they had survived was, to my notion, the best evidence that they were *good*. Those were the days of the survival of the fittest, especially in the case of men who, like all those mentioned, had occupied positions as legal guardians of the peace, all along the border.

From these men I learned many things, the most important of which was the point which they all insisted was absolutely vital: the ability to control one's own nerves and passions—in other words, *never* to get excited.

I had the opportunity to see a couple of them in action during some disturbances which came up during the Fourth of July celebration and never will forget that, while armed, they never even made a motion toward a gun: they simply walked up to the belligerent and half drunken "bad men" and disarmed them and then walked them off to the calabozo to cool off. Yes, I learned a lot from those men. That they could shoot, both quickly and accurately, is unquestioned, but the thing that had enabled them to live to a ripe middle age was not so much due to that accomplishment as to the fact that they were abundantly supplied with that commodity commonly called "guts." That was the point, above all others, that impressed me and remained with me after I had returned to the East; and, ever since, I have tried to live up to the standard of those pioneers of the shooting game.

By the time I got back, my father had been appointed to the bench of the Supreme Court and the family had removed to Indianapolis. I took up my home there and immediately joined up with Company D, of the Second Infantry—the famous old "Indianapolis Light Infantry" which, in the military tournaments from late in the Seventies, had stood at the very head of all the crack drill teams of the country. But, they could not only put on a prize-winning close order drill: they had, as officers, men who knew the value of shooting ability and, although the State and Federal authorities never appropriated a cent for the purpose, they managed to carry on target practice. Every member paid dues for the privilege of belonging to the Guard or, as it was then known, to the Indiana Legion. We bought our own uniforms and paid our own armory rent and we bought the necessary components for the ammunition which we expended on the range and which we loaded ourselves. Then we rented a part of some farmer's pasture for a range and built our own targets. The company officers were all rifle enthusiasts; but one, above all others, kept the game moving in those early days—Major (then Lieutenant) David I. McCormick, the "Grand Old Man" of military rifle shooting in Indiana.

After a hitch in the infantry, in which I attained the rank of Sergeant, I signed up with the artillery—Battery A, First Indiana—known all over the country as "The Indianapolis Light Artillery." You see, Indianapolis had both infantry and artillery organizations that ranked with the very best. Both of them had carried off the highest honors in many of the military tournaments which were held annually in those days. (I wonder if any of those old outfits still retain their original names—the Richmond Blues, the Washington Fencibles, the Chickasaw Guards?)

This Battery A was the 27th Indiana Battery in the Spanish-American War and the nucleus of the 150th Artillery (Rainbow Division) during the World War, and its then commander, Robert L. Tyndall, was the Colonel of that Regiment. (He's now a Major-General—but that's all right: he is just Bob Tyndall to his old tilicums.)

My work took me to Cincinnati and I joined Battery B of the First Ohio Artillery—Captain Hermann's Battery. Too bad they have discontinued the practice of naming the battery after its commanding officer—(and I'll bet that young lieutenant who was in Reilly's Battery in China will agree with me—even though he is now a Major-General and Chief of Staff).

Now, this Battery B was peculiar in one respect—possibly unique: it was a Gatling-gun battery. With the Indianapolis outfit, I had learned about the Rodman muzzle-loading guns and, while with the 1st Illinois, had frequently seen Lieutenant Jack Clinnin playing around with a bunch of kids and some Gatling-guns, but I had never taken these contraptions very seriously. Now, however, that was all we had to do. Of course we had pistols and sabres and all such, but our real game was to learn how to use those Gatlings to the best advantage. Captain Hermann was a very practical officer and saw to it that we had all the actual outdoor shooting that the law—and the state of the exchequer—would stand. I remember that I won a can of oysters at one of those shoots and I declare that no medal or other thing I have since won by shooting ever gave me the thrill that that did. It was probably about tenth place—we had turkeys, hams and a lot of other things for prizes—donated by patriotically inclined German-American citizens from "over the Rhine" (in Cincinnati), and I think that was what first put the machine-gun bug into my head.

During the Klondike rush, I got the gold fever and went off up there and spent more than two years in northern Canada. When I came out, or, rather, on my way out, I had the opportunity to help gather up a bunch of recruits for the Strathcona Horse, just then being mobilized for service in South Africa. I had hoped to go with them but, at that time, the regulations were such that none but British subjects were eligible. That was in 1900 and I came back to Indianapolis and again hitched up with my old outfit—Company D, 2nd Infantry.

Of course I had had considerable game shooting while in the North and had kept up pretty well on my marksmanship;

so, when I got back into the military game, I was not so rusty but that I could do a fairly good job of it, either in the gallery or on the range.   The commanding officer of the company at that time was Robert L. Moorhead, now Colonel of the 139th Field Artillery, and I am glad of this chance to make it a matter of record that he was, in my opinion, the keenest of officers and one of the first to recognize the fact that individual proficiency with the rifle was the very highest attainment of the "doughboy."

Under his direction, that company won higher figures of merit than any similar organization in the United States services, before or since—and I do not even except the Marine Corps, for the shooting ability of which I have the utmost respect.   One year we furnished, after long and arduous competition, every member of the Regimental team of twelve men and then went on to place ten out of the twelve men on the State team.   Every man in his company had to qualify as at least a marksman during his first year or get out.   In the second year, if he could not make sharpshooter, he also took the gate, and after three years, if he did not rate expert, he was no longer eligible for re-enlistment.   That was a real shootin' bunch.   From it came Scott Clark, who won the National Individual Match in 1910; Jim Hurt who, with his son, Jimmy, Junior, are well known to the present day generation of National Match shooters; Hump Evans—and a lot more who have made life miserable for the young fellows trying to get along at Camp Perry.   I became Captain, in command of this company in the early part of 1907.

I shot along with them in all the National Matches up to ⸺nd including 1911 and then my foot got to itching and I hit out again for the Northwest, where I spent something over two years, ostensibly helping to build a railroad through the Yellow Head Pass and on to Prince Rupert but really to get out somewhere so that I could shoot a rifle without having to spend a couple of months and all my money building a backstop.

Some way or another I managed to get a job that kept me out ahead of steel from a hundred and fifty to two hundred miles, so was in virgin game country all the time. Moose, caribou and bear were not only common; they were abundant. I have had moose wake me up and have to be driven away when they were rubbing their antlers on the ropes of my tent and the bears were so common around our garbage dumps that no person ever thought of harming them. Goats and sheep were easily to be found by taking a day off and going back a little way, up the mountain; in fact, I have seen bands of goats standing on a ledge of rock, not over one hundred yards above where a bunch of Swedes were putting in a blast of dynamite and have watched them scamper away when the shot was fired. Yes, I managed to keep up on my rifle practice.

Then, along in March, 1914, we heard about the disturbance down in Mexico. "Now," says I to myself, "here's where we get into something worth while. That means war and I'll be double-damned if I am going to miss it." (I did not know, at that time, nor for a long time after, what kind of an Administration we had.)

From where I was, it was 46 miles to the nearest telegraph station—back up the line. I remember now: it was St. Patrick's day—1914. Well, I got me a good feed and a bottle of Johnnie Walker and hit the trail. Ten hours later I sent a telegram to my father, asking for information. Did he think it meant war? He answered: "Seems like war, sure: hurry back." Father, you see, had been a soldier and *his* father is still buried in the United States National Cemetery in Mexico City—(he went in with the Army of Occupation, in 1847 with the 7th U. S. Infantry, and got *his* at Chapultepec).

From where I then was, it was one hundred and twenty

miles to the end of *transportation*. The steel had been laid
into Ft. George, early in the winter—temporary construction, on brush and all that, in order to get in supplies
for the winter—but the temporary roadbed had sloughed
off until, now, no trains could come farther than "Mile 90"—
and that was 120 long miles away. I made it in three
days, through and over snow most of the way. That, taken
with the 46 miles of the previous day, made 166 miles in
four days. (The old man was not so bad at that, was he?)
This Mile 90 place, by the way, is the station you will find
on the maps and in the guide books named McBride.

When I got back to Indianapolis I applied for and was at
once granted restoration to active duty. (I had been carried
on the retired officers' list all the time.) Being assigned to a
company—Co. H, 2nd Infantry—I did my best to lick them
into shape for the fight I knew was coming. We went
through the annual maneuvers at Ft. Harrison and then
sat around to wait for the call to go to Mexico. As is well
known now, it did not come; but just about that time the big
fire broke out in Europe.

When this so-called "World War" started, I was playing
golf at Riverside, Indianapolis, with Harry Cooler and Wil-
lis Nusbaum. Along late in the afternoon we came up to
the eighteenth hole. We were playing syndicate and I was
loser to the extent of four bits. It is an easy par four
hole—well, any golfer knows what that means—easy if you
hit 'em right and I had the luck to get on the green with my
second while both the others found the rough and took three
to get home, both of them, however, being outside my ball,
which was only about ten feet from the pin. Then comes
Mr. Cooler and rams down a thirty foot putt. As though
that were not enough, Nusbaum, the robber, proceeds to
do the same from about twenty-five feet. Still, the case was
not hopeless. All I had to do was to make my putt to be
even on the match. But just then a boy came running out

from the Club House, waving an armful of papers and shouting: "WAR IN EUROPE: EXTRA! EXTRA! BIG WAR IN EUROPE." I do not know, to this day, whether or not I even tried to make that putt. I suppose I paid up—I don't know—but from that minute, golf was not for me. There was a war on and I did not intend to miss it.

I am sorry I cannot say that those early stories of German atrocities, or the news of Belgium's invasion impelled me to start for Canada to enlist and offer my life in the cause of humanity. Not at all, it was just that I wanted to find out what a "real war" was like. It looked as if there was going to be a real scrap at last, and I didn't intend to miss it this time. I had "lost out" on two wars already; the Spanish-American and Boer War and now the opportunity was at hand I wanted to have a front seat. I got what I was looking for all right.

Being at that time a Captain in command of a company of the Indiana National Guard, it took some time to turn in property and get the proper clearances and to have my resignation accepted but, as soon as all this could be accomplished, I was on my way to Canada where General Sam Hughes, Minister of Militia and Defense, immediately granted me a commission as Captain, Musketry Instructor, and I was assigned (or gazetted, as they say there) to the Thirty-eighth Battalion. However, as this battalion had not yet been mobilized, I was instructed to go to Kingston and work with the Twenty-first Battalion which was in training there. The commanding officer of this (21st) Battalion was Lieutenant-Colonel William St. Pierre Hughes, brother of the Minister of Militia and Defense. He was not only a graduate of the Royal Military College but a veteran of the Northwest Rebellion of 1885. He attracted me from the start, as a real soldier. Later I was destined to know him as one of the broadest-minded and most generous men I have ever met.

Chapter 2

Canada

I SPENT a couple of months with the Twenty-first Battalion and then, returning to Ottawa to join my own outfit, I soon learned that they, the Thirty-eighth, were slated to go to Bermuda to relieve the Royal Canadian Regiment which was doing garrison duty. That was not so good. I had come over to get into a real war, and garrison duty in Bermuda did not appeal to me a bit. Had I known then, as we all know now, that the Thirty-eighth would get to France soon enough to get into all the fighting any man could ask for, I suppose it would have been different, but at that time my chief worry was that the war would be over before I could get there.

I was mad; yes, crazy mad. I went out and tried to drink all the whiskey in Ottawa and made such an ass of myself that the higher-ups were glad to get rid of me. Prior to this, however, I had wired to Colonel Hughes, at Kingston, asking if he would accept me as a private in his battalion, and he had answered: "Yes, glad to have you." My resignation was quickly accepted and I took the train for Kingston where I was sworn in next day as a private and assigned to the Machine Gun Section (The Emma Gees).

Well, there I was, a machine gunner, but machine gunners in those days also carried rifles. That was enough for

12

me. I was with an outfit that was sure to get into the war and that was enough. We trained at Kingston all winter. There was the usual routine of physical exercises, close order drill, (very little of this, however), bayonet exercises and occasional small maneuvers that would come under the head of "Minor Tactics." But the best thing we did was to march and shoot—march and shoot. There was no especial training for trench warfare—that came later, in England. Here, in Canada, the program, which was certainly laid out by an officer who knew his business (I suspect it was Colonel Hughes, himself), was one calculated to do just two things: to put the men in physical condition to endure long marches and to thoroughly train them in the use of their weapons. In the latter years of the war, I had occasion to compare this system with that laid down in hard and fast schedules for the training of the United States Armies and the more I saw of our (U.S.) system, the better I liked the Canadian.

We had route marches in all kinds of weather, and winter in Ontario is real winter. On one occasion, we marched from Kingston to Gananoque, through snow a foot deep and came back the next day—twenty-two miles each way. Another march took us to Odessa—about the same distance there and back, this time with full packs. But on one or two days of each week we went out to the Barriefield rifle range for target practice. Sometimes when we were out there shooting, one could have skated all over the place on the ice. But we surely were learning a lot and getting seasoned for the bitter days to come. Toward the latter part of this training, we had rifle competitions every week, between picked teams from the different companies and detachments. In these matches the Machine Gunners always managed to give a good account of themselves.

In the Battalion were many of the best riflemen in Canada, including Major Elmitt, (member of the Canadian

Palma team of 1907), Sergeant-Major Edwards, Sergeant Williams, (of the Machine Gun Section) and many others whose names have now escaped me. The Colonel, himself, took part in the firing as did all the other officers. I particularly remember how enthusiastic Major Bennett was about this training. He was Second in Command. I just mention these things to show how it was that this particular battalion developed into a *real* aggregation of *riflemen*. In the months and years that followed, that accomplishment, on numerous occasions, saved them from disaster such as overwhelmed certain other outfits not similarly prepared. All the patriotism, courage and determination in the world can never compensate for the lack of thorough instruction in the use of the arm with which the soldier is equipped.

We were using the Ross rifle, a splendid target weapon, and Mark VI ammunition—the old, blunt nosed bullet. Later, in England, we switched to the Mark VII with its spitzer bullet and checked up on the changes in elevation required.

Instruction in rifle shooting in the British service, which, of course, includes Canada, is, in the main, similar to that followed in the United States Army. That is, the recruit is first thoroughly grounded in the theory and practice of sighting and aiming and then put through a course of firing with reduced loads at short (gallery) ranges. When he first goes to the range for instruction with the service ammunition however, the first thing he is required to do is to shoot a "group" at one hundred yards. In this practice, the man fires five shots without any marking. It is simply a test of his ability to sight, aim and *hold* properly. After he has completed his string, the target is withdrawn and the officer in the pit proceeds to measure the group. No consideration is given to its location on the target: size only counts. To avoid delays in making this measurement, a device consisting of a series of wire circles is used, the inner circle being about four inches in diameter and the others running up to something like fifteen inches—if my memory serves me right. There is an official scale for rating the various sized groups. If the man cannot keep his group within the limits of the maximum circle, he goes back for further preliminary instruction and practice. This firing, as is all the regular slow fire practice in the British service, is done from the prone position.

While the sling on the Ross (and the Enfield, too, for that matter) is not especially designed for use in firing, by common practice and authorization it may be taken out of the butt swivel and rigged up much the same as we used to do with the old .45 Springfield and the Krag rifles.

I have said that the musketry instruction was, in the main, similar to that of the United States Army and this is true. The object of both is to instruct the man in the fundamentals of sighting, aiming, holding and firing the rifle. The weakness of both, in my opinion, lies in the lack of sufficient *practice* after the above instruction has been assimilated. All of us who are or have been in the military service are all too familiar with the "set schedules" for training in this or that branch of the soldier's educational work. The time for instruction firing is usually limited— as is the ammunition allowance—and the record firing is crammed into a few hectic days. Everything must be done just so and so.

Well, perhaps that is all right, although I cannot see it that way. My idea of training a rifleman would be to put him through the full instructional course and then give him a lot of ammunition and let him go out on the range, at odd times, and work out his own salvation. Have targets available at any time, with men to work them, but keep no records excepting those which the man would be encouraged to keep for his own private information.

Some men learn very quickly while others have to keep

hammering at any subject before the right idea gets into their noodle. The whole matter can be likened to the golf player who never goes out but that he plays a "match" with some-one or other. He never gets the same shot twice, hence has no opportunity to check up on his errors as they occur. The result is that he joins the great army of "ninety-to-one hun-dred" players and remains in that class the rest of his life. On the other hand, if he be the one in a thousand who real-izes the importance of *practice,* he will take a couple of dozen balls and a caddy and hunt up some deserted fairway and spend hours in endeavoring to master some one club. This man, given time, will be one who shoots consistently in the seventies.

Oh, yes; I know very well that such a procedure as I have suggested would be contrary to all the accepted rules in an army where every act and movement of man is sup-posed to be strictly in accordance with the plans and speci-fications ordained by a lot of "regulations" but don't you think it is about time we were cutting loose from some of those antedeluvian notions and making some practical use of the individual brains of the soldiers? For close-order drill and such matters, of course, it is necessary that each individual conform to the movements of others but when a man gets into a fight he is very much "on his own" and, unless he is qualified, by nature and training, to do a little independent thinking, he is—well—S. O. L. that's all.

During our training in Canada we used what was known as the "Oliver" equipment. This was a fearful and wonder-ful arrangement of straps and buckles. There was a place for everything, all right—in fact, so many places and so many little straps that it made one dizzy to contemplate the thing and, unless one possessed the skill and patience of a Houdini, he usually had to call upon the services of another to get into or out of it.

Later on, in England, we received the Webb equipment

which was much more satisfactory in every respect. The shoulder straps were broad and comfortable to the body; the pack-sack was large enough to carry all necessary clothing, and the haversack easily held all the little personal articles as well as a couple of days rations. The ammunition pockets were all at the front. This not only made them easier to get at but served to balance the weight of the pack on the back. The water bottle, holding a full quart —an Imperial quart, I mean—was carried on the right hip and the bayonet on the left, with the haversack just behind it. The entrenching tool was carried in the middle of the back. On the whole, I consider it the most comfortable and satisfactory equipment I have seen for foot soldiers. When going into action, the pack was detached almost instantly, and if there was plenty of time the haversack could quickly be slung in its place. If not, it remained at the side.

During our training and when we first went to Flanders, we wore a peaked cloth cap with a flat, round top, similar to that worn by the United States soldier at that time only a little larger. Later on these were replaced by another type—a soft crowned cap with side flaps which could be turned down so as to cover the ears. In addition to this we had what was called a Balaclava cap—which was nothing more nor less than the familiar "toque" worn by the Canadian woodsman.

Our uniforms were of good woolen material—in fact, every article of wearing apparel was woolen, the underwear, especially being of excellent quality. (I wish I could buy any as good now, at any price.) Heavy woolen socks were supplied in abundance by the various women's organizations back in Canada. The shoes were heavy and clumsy, of course: had to be to stand the wear, but early in 1916 we got an issue of genuine Canadian "pacs" with sixteen-inch tops and, while in the trenches, had rubber boots. We even received regular Mackintosh capes of excellent quality.

Perhaps a little thoughtful study of the above will explain why it was that, although exposed to cold and wet weather for weeks at a time—living like muskrats—there was scarcely any illness. Looking over the official record of the Twenty-first Battalion I find that, during the period from October, 1914, to April 1919, the total deaths were—killed in action and died of wounds, nine hundred and twenty— from all other causes, just twenty. As the normal strength of the Battalion was about eleven hundred, it can be seen that the death rate, exclusive of battle injuries, was not more than four to the thousand annually.

Those men were just the ordinary run of volunteers, probably no better nor worse than the average in the National Guard units of the United States Army and I attribute the fact of their greater stamina and immunity to disease to another undeniable fact, and that is that the authorities in Canada devoted all their efforts to the task of keeping their soldiers warm and comfortable, indoors and out, using any and all available supplies to that purpose— regardless of whether or not it was "uniform."

And right here is a good place to mention a matter that did not come up until three years later. During the fall and winter of 1917, I was in command of a battalion of machine gunners at Camp Shelby, Mississippi. I say machine gunners: well, that was what they were destined to be although, at that time, we had no guns of any kind. That winter, as many will remember, was very severe and even in November we had freezing weather away down there in Mississippi. There had been no provision for heating the tents and most of the organizations there were but poorly equipped for that kind of weather. My outfit, which had been a part of the 4th Indiana Infantry, had only the cotton khaki uniforms which they had bought and paid for out of their own pockets because our Uncle Sam had none to issue them. Most of them, however, had sweaters of various hues, which they had either brought with them or had received from loving mothers or sweethearts—personally knitted with good, honest wool yarn.

On a particularly cold morning (away below freezing) I had them out for a practice march and happened to pass the Brigade Headquarters, both going and coming. By the time we came back it was near noon and the sun had warmed things up a bit and most of the men had shed their sweaters and were carrying them, in various fashions, across their shoulders.

No sooner had we reached our quarters than I was called upon by a young officer whom I well knew—an Aide to the General—and informed that the General wanted to see me at once. It was only about one hundred yards from my quarters to his, so I was there within a couple of minutes. It was General G—, so far as I know, a very able officer, according to the standards at that time in effect in the United States Army—but what he did not know about common sense, as applied to the care and comforts of troops was a plenty. He bawled me out for allowing my men to go out on parade wearing all those nondescript sweaters when every article of clothing they wore, from their B. V. D.'s out had been bought and paid for with their own money. At that time there was not a nickel's worth of clothing or equipment in that whole battalion that had not been privately purchased.

Well; I had just lately come from a war, out of an inferno which can never be adequately described: and this damned poppycock seemed so trivial and childish—so far from the realities of war—that I was first a bit sickened, and then mad. In that frame of mind, is it reasonable to suppose that I would be unduly worried by the unreasonable and senseless tirade of an officer who, so far as I knew, didn't know a damn thing about war—certainly not about this latest edition of the game.

Anyway; I told him what I thought of his speech and, incidentally, of the whole General Staff at Washington. Before the incident was closed, I had occasion to say the same things, with elaborations, (I had time to think them up), to the General in command of the Division—the 38th —General Sage, I think it was. (They changed so fast I never could keep track of them.)

I suppose they thought I ought to be taken out and shot. I do not know, to this day, why they did not take some summary action for I told them plainly that no General officer, not even the President himself, could prevent me from doing my best to promote and preserve the health and comfort of the troops under my command. Dodging the direct issue, the Division Commander called me to task for wearing a Sam Brown belt. Well, that was the only one I had (part of my Canadian equipment), so I just remarked that they would all be wearing them before long and let it go at that. I got away with my life and my self-respect but had to make my men put their sweaters on inside their shirts after that.

This was but one of the asinine regulations that our Higher Command promulgated. Had they spent one-tenth of the time in trying to teach the newly-made soldiers something of the real and practical side of warfare, there would not be so many graves over there for the Mothers to visit.

Canada was fortunate in having General Sam Hughes at the head of her Militia Bureau—Minister of Militia and Defense—when the war started. Few men would have had the courage to do what he did. From the very start, he seemed to realize that this was to be a great war—greater than the world had ever seen—and he proceeded accordingly. The Gordian knot of red tape he cut with one slash of his pen and proceeded to apply the practical, common sense methods of industry. He authorized the purchase of necessary materials and equipment wherever they could be found. He built, at ValCartier, one of the greatest training camps and rifle ranges the world had ever seen. From one end of Canada to the other, he ranged back and forth with but the one thought—to make the Canadian Expeditionary Force thoroughly and practically efficient as fighting soldiers. The records show that he was eminently successful.

Throughout my whole service with the Canadians, covering more than two years, I had less trouble and bother regarding paper work and reports than any company commander in the United States Army encounters in a week— any week of any month of any year. If our Army, (U. S.), would adopt the systematic methods of any of our large manufacturing concerns, they could either cut off half the amount of money they are now expending or use that much additional for practical training purposes. Just in the matter of pay-rolls, alone, a saving of thousands of dollars and innumerable hours could be saved. In the Canadian service, each man had his "pay-book," in which was recorded the date of his enlistment and, following that, entries showing when he was promoted to another grade. Subsequent pages were for the use of the paymaster. A soldier could go to any Field paymaster and, upon showing his book, receive whatever money he needed—within the limits of his credit, which was always shown in the book. Officers never had to turn their hands over to get theirs. Upon being commissioned, they were presented with a bank book and a cheque book. If they had been commissioned from the ranks, the amount due them as an enlisted man was shown to their credit and if during the war and overseas, an additional credit of fifty pounds (about $250.00) for uniform and equipment was advanced. From that time on, all the officer had to do was to keep track of his checks. On the 27th of each month his monthly salary was deposited to his credit. No vouchers or anything required.

The Second Division, to which we belonged, was particularly fortunate in having had some six months time for training in Canada and an additional four months in England. The First Division and the "Pats" had been hastily mobilized and sent over as quickly as possible, but as they were largely made up of old, seasoned soldiers, they did not require much training. It was different when it came to the Third Division and the Fourth. By the time they were mobilized it was necessary to get them over as quickly as possible, and, as they comprised a large percentage of men who had had no previous military training, many of them never had any chance to learn how to shoot. Some, I am told, had fired only ten shots before going into action. The experience of the United States vividly emphasizes this same point. Many men of our National Army went into action without having ever fired a shot from their rifles. And yet, we have men and women in this country—fathers and mothers, too—who oppose the idea of training our young men in the use of arms. They know—they *must* know, that in case of war their sons will go whether they like it or not, yet they refuse to give the boys a chance to learn something about the game. It would be futile to speculate on how many of the little white crosses would not now decorate the graves overseas had the men whose names appear thereon been given the opportunity to learn how to shoot straight. But it is certain that the number is great.

On all our marches, we were accompanied by our bands. Yes, I said bands because we had two, a Bagpipe band and a Bugle band. And they were good. I never saw any, outside the Scots Guards band that could compare with our Pipe band and the Bugle band was equally good. They would alternate in leading the march, the other either bringing up the rear or marching in the middle of the battalion. One of them was always playing. By some system of signalling or by pre-arrangement, the instant one ceased to play, the other struck up. Bugles and drums—pipes and drums—but always the drums; aye, that's the music for the soldier. Coming into town after a hard and gruelling march, when those "Scotties" would start "The Cock 'o the North" (which was our own regimental air), you could see the chins come up and the shoulders square away and the command would stride along as though just coming from breakfast. The old fife and drum bands of Civil War days, and which were still common in my youth, were equally inspiring and I have never been able to understand why they were discontinued as "Field Music" in the United States Army. That's marching music and fighting music, I want to tell you.

Throughout the winter and early spring, we marched and we shot and we drilled. The close order drill in the British service is much simpler than that of the U. S. Army—yet they seem to be able to get to the desired spot and in the required formation just as easily and quickly. But we had but little of that, anyway. What we did mostly was to get out and march anywhere from ten to twenty miles and back again, learning to keep "closed up" at all times. When on the road, a column of British soldiers is as compact as a snake. There are no file-closers and no officers wandering around outside the column of "fours." Officers and N. C. O.'s simply slip in and fill up the blank files or form extra ranks at the head or tail of their own organizations. Often, from some hill-top, I have looked forward (or back) and marveled at the appearance of that long, smooth column. In all my experience, both before the war and since, I have never seen any large unit of the United States services that could equal it in march discipline.

We were quartered in two separate buildings, about a mile or more apart: the "Right half," comprising Companies A and B, at the Armouries, where the Headquarters was also located and the "Left half," Companies C and D, in what had been a large cereal mill. The Machine Gun Section was with the latter. As the mobilization for all parades or maneuvers was at the headquarters, we of the left half had the benefit (?) of that extra march, both going and coming, each day.

There were special courses of instruction for officers and non-commissioned officers—days of sport and recreation and, every Sunday, the inevitable church parade. About the only thing I remember about these latter is that we always sang: "Onward Christian Soldiers." We went to various churches, as that is one point on which the British army authorities are particular. When a man enlists or is commissioned, he must specify his religion—denomination: Whether Church of England, Methodist or whatever it happens to be and if you do not belong to any of the recognized sects you either choose one or are summarily attached to the C. E. (Church of England). The Catholics always had their own party, under one of their own officers. While I never went with that bunch, I'll bet they also sang "Onward Christian Soldiers."

The Army and Navy Veterans Association of Kingston presented the Battalion with handsome "Colours," with appropriate ceremonies. These were deposited in the custody of the Canadian High Commissioner, in London prior to our departure for France.

After many false alarms, we finally received orders to move and on the evening of May 5th, we entrained for Montreal. The citizens of Kingston gave us a grand send-off. At other towns and cities along the way rousing demonstrations were staged for our benefit. There was no mistaking the temper of those people. We had just recently received the reports of the fighting at Ypres and the hideous savagery of the enemy in using poison gas against the Canadians of the First Division. Hundreds of casualties were being posted daily—names of many from these very towns—and we were to go over and clean up on the savages.

Well, we finally did out bit, but it was a long time before we had the chance.

We sailed, from Montreal, May 6, 1915, and landed at Plymouth (Devonport Dock) on the 14th. That is really all that need be said about our crossing, looking at it from the vantage point of fifteen years, but, at the time, it was not quite so uneventful. Before we were out of the St. Lawrence we heard of the sinking of the *Lusitania*. It was really unbelievable. While the news was undoubtedly authentic, we could not conceive how any nation that pretended to be civilized could perpetrate such an atrocious deed. It gave us Americans (there were several in the battalion) something to think about. I remember, it occurred to me that if the report were true, it was a certainty that the United States would be in the war tomorrow. That being the case, my old outfit would be right in it. Had I remained at home I would go over in command of my old company—perhaps with even higher rank. But I quickly dismissed the thought. I had sworn to defend "King and Country" for the duration of the war and was in with an organization which I had come to love. Officers and men were my friends and, come what might, I would stick with them. It never occurred to any of us that there was any possibility that the United States would not declare war immediately. No use talking any more about what really did happen. It is too well known.

We had aboard, besides our battalion, hospital detachments from both Queens and McGill Hospitals, including about one hundred and fifty Nursing Sisters—"Blue Birds" we called them from their natty blue uniforms. They wear the two stars of the First Lieutenant, which rank they hold, and believe me, they rate it too. Many's the man on that boat who later had cause to bless those same bluebirds in the hospitals of France and England. It later happened that I was one of these.

When we got word by wireless that the *Lusitania* had really been torpedoed an effort was made to suppress the news, but it soon made its way throughout the entire ship. Having had plenty of experience with soldier rumors coming in over the grapevine, which start from nowhere and amount to nothing, I personally did not believe the story. But next morning, when we of the Machine Gun Section got orders to go down into the hold, get our guns and mount them on deck I began to think differently. We then had six guns, two more than the usual quota to a battalion, as two Colt guns had been presented to our Commanding Officer by old friends in Canada just a few days before our departure.

The Machine Gunners got up all six of the guns and mounted them in advantageous positions around the upper deck and on the bridge and we remained on duty throughout the rest of the voyage. I think all our crowd realized how futile would be any efforts of ours to stop a submarine but, in a psychological way, it was probably justified as it gave the others on board, especially the women, a feeling of security. At any rate, it gave us an opportunity for some valuable target practice, for we were continually firing bursts at sea birds or any other objects that offered any kind of target—estimating ranges and all that.

I was stationed with the two forward guns and as we ran into several days of really rough weather it was a cold and wet job. The ship changed direction several times a day and the wireless was continually crackling and sputtering. We saw very few boats on the way across and had no convoying warships, until one night about nine o'clock several dark and slim shadows came slipping out of the gloom and establishing themselves all around us. Boy! what a grand and glorious feeling that moment was, one of the really big thrills of the war to me. And the sigh of relief that went up from those gun crews was loud and sincere. Those

British destroyers showed no lights and we could barely discern their outlines as they slipped silently along with us. This was a bit of the real thing I had come to see.

News that the Brtish destroyers were about us soon reached throughout the entire ship. I forgot to mention that one of the advantages of sitting watch on those machine guns for the past several days was that we Machine Gunners and the ship's crew were the only ones permitted on decks. When the rest of the battalion learned the news the grapevine started working overtime and the wise guys gave out just which port we were heading for; some said Liverpool, some Bristol and some even had the ship headed straight for France. However, just before sunrise we dropped anchor inside Plymouth breakwater. But no one made any kick then, any port looked good at that time. A few hours more and the ship moved into the harbor and tied up at Devonport Dock.

We lay there at the dock and unloaded cargo and supplies all that day. It rained too, but then it usually rains down on soldiers every time they change station, or move up to battle. Right alongside our ship was another big transport, loaded with troops and supplies for the Dardanelles. The troops were the Dublin Fusiliers and they gave us a great cheer that morning as our ship came in. Poor devils, they were in for a rough time of it down there.

It kept raining all day, but we gradually got all our stuff off the ship and loaded on the trains and about dark we pulled out. Not a soul knew where we were going. The only training camp we had heard of in England was Salisbury Plain, where the First Canadian Division had trained. The reports they sent home had been anything but encouraging so we hoped for some other place than that. We were told off eight men to a compartment, equipment and all, and we traveled all night long in those stuffy little carriages. Soon after daylight the train stopped and we were told to get out. The name of the station was Westerhanger, which meant nothing at all to us. Westerhanger, it soon developed, was in Kent, and after a march of some three miles we found ourselves in West Sandling Camp, our home for four more months.

We had quite a parade from the station on out to camp and the roads were lined with soldiers who cheered and cheered as we came marching along. Some more of the old Lion's Cubs coming back to line up shoulder to shoulder in defense of the Empire. How proudly we marched up that long hill and past the Brigade Headquarters, the pipers skirling their heartiest and our drummers laying it on as never before, two beats to the step. We were on exhibition and we knew it. The loads were heavy, the mud was deep and we were all tired, but not a man in that column would have traded his place for anything. And our "Rifleman," who is now telling all this, held his shoulders just as square and put his feet down just as hard as anybody in that column. It was grand.

There did come a day when we hated that hill and that camp as the devil hates holy water, but on that Sunday morning, as we marched into a British camp, with British soldiers cheering like mad all around us, everybody felt that we ought to go right on across the channel and clean up Kaiser Bill. Say, the meanest private in the Twenty-first Canadians felt able to do it single handed.

Chapter 3

England

OUR camp at West Sandling was some three miles from the famous Hythe rifle ranges—home of the Hythe School of Musketry. We took up a course of training which covered many features of modern warfare which we had omitted in our Canadian training. Trench construction, signalling, bombing, all came in for attention but we kept up the old practice of marching and shooting. We spent many days down on the Hythe range. For several weeks, our range practice was confined to the same sort of program we had followed back in Canada. That is, it was practice shooting, pure and simple. At the last, however, we did fire through the full course for qualification and I can certify that it was a tough one. The targets for a large part of this course are not bull's-eyes but dull-colored silhouettes of the head and shoulders of a man. They are not black, like the silhouettes used in the U. S. Army, but of a greenish-khaki color, extremely difficult to pick out against a neutral-colored background. Most of the shooting at these targets was at rapid fire—fifteen shots to the minute—and, with the wind whipping in from the Channel (the range is right along the beach) and swirling in and out among the old Martello towers which line the shore, it is no cinch for any-one to put two successive shots in the same place. But our crowd had, by that time, become so familiar with their rifles that we managed to make a very creditable showing, qualifying a goodly number of Marksmen and two or three attained the very highest rating of Marksman-Distinguished.

A part of the course is fired with the bayonet fixed, and, during one afternoon's shooting, I had occasion to replace three rifles which had become disabled due to the bayonet coming loose and swinging around in such a way as to obstruct the muzzle.   This, I believe, was afterward corrected by a modification of the bayonet-catch but I cannot be real sure about that.   I never after that fired a rifle with the bayonet on it.   Even during a battle, if I wanted to do any shooting, I first removed the bayonet.   I know and knew then, that this was contrary to all rules, regulations and orders, but we got away with it—that is, those of us who believed in using the rifle as a weapon of precision, in deliberate, aimed fire.

During all this time, the Machine Gunners, in addition to going through the whole infantry course, had covered the full course of instruction and firing as prescribed for machine guns, at that time.   We afterward learned a lot more about that particular game and made our own rules accordingly.

Our four months in England was not entirely a period of work and worry.   We followed a carefully planned schedule of strictly military work but this same schedule allowed ample time for the diversions and recreation which the High Command deemed necessary for the well-being of the soldier.   The idea that the wars of England have been won on the cricket fields at home, has not entirely died out and I hope it never will be allowed to perish.   My later experiences in some of the training camps in the United States— in 1917—where every officer and man was kept busy at something or other from dawn to late at night, and then allowed Saturday afternoon for recreation, have convinced me that *that* system is wrong.   The *work* is administered in too large doses.   Six hours a day is quite sufficient for the strenuous training work—as much, in fact, as the average man can stand and derive any profit from the instruction. To drive men for from twelve to fourteen hours, as was done at Camp Shelby—just to mention one camp, which I suppose was typical—is a mistake. No doubt they can stand it, *physically,* but not mentally. A short day of carefully planned instruction, with several hours of absolute freedom for rest, recreation or study, will bring results far more quickly.

That was the way we worked it. I doubt if we ever put in more than six hours actual *work* in any day—with the exception of the times when we were out on maneuvers or on the rifle range and in both those cases there was ample time for rest and relaxation. Sunday was all our own and many of us took advantage of that day to visit many of the places of historic importance along the Kentish Coast. Our very camp was on ground that had been occupied by Caesar's Roman Legions and there were ruins of old Roman works scattered all over that region. Saltwood and Lympne Castles still show the remnants of their work and all the main roads in that part of England were built by those same Romans.

We had only been at Sandling about a week when a couple of the members of the Machine Gun Section developed fine cases of measels. Well, that was fine. They quarantined the whole bunch of us—wouldn't allow us to go out and march around with the rest of the battalion. At first we were ordered confined to our hut, but a few well-directed suggestions to our Medical Officer brought permission for us to go out for exercise every day, only we must go in a body and stay away from the other troops. Can you imagine anything nicer?

We would start out in the morning and climb up to the top of Tolsford Hill and take a look at France. Then we would scout down the other side and see what we could

find in the way of live things—birds, bugs, snakes—anything. I always have been a sort of nut on all natural
history subjects, so was able to boost the game along.

Redpath caught two young rooks which he took back and
tamed so that they would fly to him whenever he called.
McFarlin had a hedgehog for a while—a small and harmless edition of the porcupine. We found a wood pigeon's
nest and also some young lapwings. One day a couple of
the boys brought me a snake. As most boys would do,
they had killed it. Now, I do not approve of the promiscuous killing of snakes and was about to tell them so, when
I happened to take a good look at the reptile—and held
my peace. It was an adder, so far as I know, the only
venomous snake found in the British Isles. I opened the
mouth and showed them the fangs and also explained how
they could tell a poisonous snake from a harmless one. Yes;
we had great times during that quarantine period. If we
got tired or the weather was inclement, we stayed in the
hut and played poker. Hard lines for the poor soldier, eh,
what?

But there was one thing about which we had a real griev-
ance and that was the food. The time we spent in England
was the only period during my Canadian service when we
did not have *plenty* of good food. In Canada, and later in
Flanders and France, we had an abundance and of the best
quality, but while in England we had to put up with what
the people there were accustomed to. It was pretty tough
but some of us managed to get money from home and used
it to supplement the meager fare. You see, the United
States and Canada—and possibly the other British Colonies
—have a standard of living that is undreamed of in Europe.
We are just spoiled, that's all. People can live and live
comfortably, on much less than what we think is absolutely
necessary. Anyway, we survived—and none the worse for it.

While we were in England many of the men were granted

leave to visit relatives in various parts of the British Isles. As I had no relatives that I knew of and as I had no particular desire to go anywhere, I stayed at the camp. I had spent a good deal of time in England and Scotland, on previous visits, and had seen most of the prominent points of interest. I *did* enjoy the little trips to points along the Channel coast, however. Much of the history of England is written there, from the time of the raids of the first sea rovers, on through the era of Roman domination and to the Conquest by the Normans. Nor does it end there, for all along the shore are the remains of the huge, stone towers, the Martello towers, erected as a defense against the threatened invasion by the French under Napoleon.

Then, Sandling Camp was located in the midst of a lot of the old and interesting places which have figured in the early history of England. Saltwood Castle, built in 499 by the Romans and enlarged later by the Normans, was about a mile from the camp. Here was where the conspirators met and planned the assassination of Thomas à Becket at Canterbury, which was only some sixteen miles away and which I visited many times. Hythe, one of the old "cinque ports" was only a few miles distant, and in it was the old church which dated from the time of Ethelbert, King of Kent. In this old church crypt lie the bones of hundreds of persons which have been there since the time of the Crusades, and in the church there were the arms and armour of some of those old-timers who had been on those same Crusades. But to me, the most interesting of all was a tablet on the wall, "To the memory of Captain Robert Furnis, Commanding H. M. S. *Queen Charlotte*. Killed at the Battle of Lake Erie: 1813." Perry's famous victory, and Camp Perry, so far away, both came to mind as I stood before it.

Only three or four miles away was Monk's Horton, Horton Park and Horton Priory. This latter church dates from the twelfth century and looks just about as it did when built. There also was Lympne Castle, one of the old Roman strongholds, and Caesar's Plain, and Caesar's Camp, where Julius Caesar is supposed to have spent his time on that memorable expedition to England. Also there was Hastings and Battle Abbey, where William the Conqueror defeated Harold and conquered England. Many of the roads over which we marched had been built by the Romans and every town and village we came to had its history running back for centuries. To me it was all very interesting and for those who did not care for ancient history there were Sunday trips to Ramsgate, Margate, Deal, and Dover.

But we were all getting impatient. Hearing the rumble of the heavy guns, as we could often do—especially at night —and seeing the fast-increasing number of convalescent wounded who were domiciled in various establishments in our vicinity, we were anxious to get over there and get in it.

Along in September, we had a series of "Reviews." The King looked us over, as did Lord Kitchener, and I believe we did it again for the benefit of someone or other— darned if I know who. It got rather monotonous after a while but the first time we went through the performance it was quite impressive. As a starter, every company was "sized up," to give the appearance of uniformity in height. Then we marched to the reviewing field, which, in our case, was some three miles distant. The whole division was massed in one great field, the infantry in front and the artillery and trains following. All were massed as closely as possible and the spectacle of that great body of men, marching in column of companies, with no interval between the front rank of one company and the rear rank of the other, reminded me of nothing so much as a vast field of grain, bowing to the wind, as, on all such occasions, bayonets are fixed and rifles are carried at the slope.

By this time we knew that we were just about due to

"shove off" for some unknown destination. We machine gunners got orders to load up every belt with a new lot of the Mark VII ammunition and we had a merry time that day. It takes quite a while to load eighty-four belts—even with the loading machines—and we put in the whole day at it. We had fourteen boxes, each holding a belt of 250 rounds, for each of our six guns. In addition to this, we drew ten thousand rounds, in boxes, for each gun. Then we got one hundred and twenty rounds per man for our rifles. In all, we had about ninety thousand rounds in the section. We took our bayonets over to the Armourer and had him sharpen them on his grindstone—and drew an issue of files with which to keep them sharp in the future.

The next orders were to pack up all surplus clothing and equipment, to be stored against the time of our return. (I have often wondered if anyone in that outfit ever got back there to claim the things he had left.)

We were to take, in addition to our guns, rifles, ammunition and such equipment, one ground sheet (a rubber sheet, similar to a poncho but without the hole in it), one extra suit of underwear, one extra pair of socks, one overcoat (great coat, they call it), and the numerous small articles that go to make up the kit. It was *permitted* to take one blanket. I am not sure whether or not any of our crowd did this. I know I did not, nor did any of the others with whom I was closely associated. We took no extra shoes and it was with regret that I left two pairs behind.

Then we got our "transport." I will not tell you how many waggons we had. (Get that double g.) At any rate, the stuff we piled into the little limbers soon filled them to the top. We had to *make* our own drivers but, fortunately, had plenty of men who were familiar with horses.

Now, all these things were done during one day and the ensuing night and it was near morning when we had finished packing and loading. We had breakfast and then the orders came to move out. Everybody was jubilant. Here we were, on our way, at last. We formed on our own parade ground and then moved out on to the road. But, what the hell? Instead of turning toward the right and so on to Folkestone, we turned to the left. Oh, well, just some maneuver to get the division straightened out, we thought. Huh: we had another think coming—in fact, several thinks. We hiked all that day and camped in a great park (Hatch Park) with the deer scampering all around us. I say we camped. We simply lay down in formation and slept a few hours. If anyone cares to look it up, he will find that there was a beautiful, full moon at that time for I remember lying on my back and wondering what was up there, for an hour or so before going to sleep. That was about the 10th day of September, 1915.

Well, sir, we marched all over Southern Kent for three days. Of course it is plain now that this was simply to get the whole division licked into shape so that they could take the road over in France without using up the space that was needed for an army corps, but we could not fathom it at that time.

On the third night we arrived back at our Sandling camp but only halted for a short time—only until it became real dark, in fact—then moved out again. This time we *did* head for the coast and, after the usual confusion and delays, found ourselves aboard a train—going somewhere. By this time all hands were tired enough to sleep anywhere and in any position, so it was not until the next morning that we discovered that we (the Emma Gee Section) had the train to ourselves. Our horses and waggons, (again, don't forget that extra g; that's the English of it) were loaded in freight cars—and, by the way, *they* are called *waggons,* too, so, I guess we will have to call our conveyances carts or limbers from now on—and we, the men, were in the usual second class carriages.

We travelled all that day and the next night, going by a very devious and roundabout way—probably to deceive any spies who might be trying to keep track of our movements— and finally arrived at Southampton, just about daybreak. There we were required to keep to the docks and, as much as possible, under cover during the day. Our ship (I never did know the name of it) was snug up against the side of one of the covered docks and we were able to load all our gear and horses without going outside. Right alongside was another ship on which some British troops were embarking. They said they were going to the Dardanelles, so we figured that we were probably slated for the same place.

Most of our crowd wrote letters and posted them here. I had no writing materials handy but noticed a box on the dock which contained a lot of post cards, placed there, as an inscription on the box related, by the "Missions to Seamen." On the off chance that it *might* go through, I addressed one of them to my mother in Indianapolis and told her that we "don't know where we're going, but are on our way." Without any stamp, but with the magic letters: "O. H. M. S." (On His Majesty's Service), it went straight through to her.

It was a cold and drizzly night when we pulled out, or, as I should say, "shoved off." We had carefully stowed all our guns down in the hold of the ship, but no sooner had we cleared the harbor than a couple of us had to go down and dig out two of them and bring them up and mount them on the deck. For my sins I was one of the two and Sandy MacNab, because he was not so good either, was the other. Oh, well, what the hell! We were all so glad to be out and going somewhere that we did not worry about a little thing like that. There were "subs" in the Channel and they had been sinking everything on sight—even shooting up the crews in the small boats after torpedoing the transports, so there was a chance that we might be able to take a few "Huns" with us if they did get us with a torpedo.

So as I have said, Sandy and I finally got two machine guns and some ammunition on deck, and by dark we had them mounted, mine to starboard and Sandy's to port. Then the ship steamed out of the harbor and we two "stood to" until daybreak, expecting anything or nothing to happen. After a few hours, we didn't care which.

Everything was in pitch darkness, not a light showing aboard ship or elsewhere and the trip passed uneventful until about the middle of the night. Then I saw a bright glow on the horizon, just dead ahead. It was mighty puzzling, but the ship's lookouts said or did nothing and I did likewise. I had about decided that it must be a ship afire, and was wondering what we would do about it; but the thing gradually kept taking on the appearance of an immense Christmas tree and I began to think that the English booze was sure holding up for a long time. Finally I could stand it no longer, so I sneaked over to MacNab's side to see if he saw what I saw. He did, but we were both too bewildered to ask any questions so we waited, and a Red Cross *hospital ship,* lighted from stem to stern and from waterline to truck with hundreds of electric lights, swept past. There were flood lights sweeping downward to show the green stripe along its side as prescribed by the Geneva Convention, and the ship could not possibly have been mistaken for anything else in the world—yet the Germans sank all of these "Castle" liners before the war was over. Sandy MacNab, who stood by my side that night, came back on one of these ships within a month and I took my first ride to Blighty on the *Carisbrook Castle* a year or so later.

About daybreak we picked up a string of colored lights and dropped anchor. When daylight came on we could see that it was the harbor of Le Havre we were in; I had been there before and recognized it immediately. Then and there we knew that it was France we were headed for and that the Dardanelles was not to be our destination.

We waited around a bit for the tide to rise, and then a few tugs pushed us in against the dock and we tied up. The Promised Land at last. The docks were swarming with men, practically all in uniform and all very busy. Most of the French soldiers were still wearing that old uniform of red and blue, the new "horizon blue" not having yet been adopted. Many elderly English soldiers were about, from the so-called "Navvie's Battalions." But the most puzzling of all were some whose uniform was the subject of much speculation, until we happened to notice that they always kept in groups and that a *poilu* invariably followed them with a rifle and fixed bayonet. It was our first sight of German prisoners and it was one of the real genuine thrills of the war, which was getting closer and closer all the time.

That disembarkment was nothing but common, every-day, hard labor accompanied by an unusual amount of confusion and cussing. Occasionally we were relieved by the antics of some horse which did not want to come down the steep and narrow gangway; it had been a devil of a job to get them aboard in the first place and was even harder to get them to go ashore. But finally, about noon we got everything off, the waggons loaded and teams hitched and made our way through the city and moved into a so-called "rest camp." Just about time for a shave and wash-up. Then a biscuit, but mighty little rest we got, as we started again at dark, in a driving rain as usual, and marched for miles across the city.

That rain never let up until after we had entrained, and it was a night of horrors. Sloshing through the mud, over unknown streets and roads, soaked to one's skin and then loading our train for the Front. The English language is not adequate to describe the loading of that train; getting all those waggons on those dinky little flat cars and then

the horses aboard. At that the horses fared better than
we did because they were only eight to the car while we
had to cram in forty or more, and in the very same car too—
the Forty and Eights. *Chevaux huite; Hommes quarante*—
that's what is said on the side of each car.

While we had been loading the cars, our cooks had somehow managed to make up a mess of good hot tea, and that
helped a lot. Then we got an issue of cheese, bully and
biscuits which we took into the car with us. There were
fifty-six in our section at that time, but we all managed to
get into one of the things. There was no room to lie down
or even to sit down without piling up two or three deep but
we managed, somehow or other, to get along. We were
soaked to the hide and all our equipment was in the same
condition, but what do you suppose those birds did? Commenced to *sing;* yes they did, and kept it up all day long.
We had some cheese and bully-beef and a few chunks of
bread, so we made out nicely.

On the way up to the front, we passed through some of
the most historical parts of France, but then all of France
is an historical pageant. Here we were landing at Harfleur,
which other British armies had done centuries earlier, then
through Rouen with its memories of Jeanne d'Arc, Rollo
the Norman, Duke William and Harold, all of whom had
their walk across history's pages. Although we went right
through Rouen without stopping we could see the wonderful cathedral and the hospice on the river. After crossing
the river one has a brief glimpse of the village of St. Adrien,
with the curious church in the face of the cliff where
maidens come to pray Saint Bonaventure for a husband
within the year.

Then past the field of Crecy, where, several centuries
earlier, another British army had made history, and on
across the Somme which later on was to become such an
experience to many of us. At Abbeville we joined the rest

of the battalion. They had come directly across from Folkestone to Boulogne. From Abbeville the entire battalion rode on together and about three o'clock the next morning we pulled into St. Omer, at that time the British Headquarters in France. It had taken almost a year to make it, but the war was just around the corner at last.

There was no loafing at St. Omer; we immediately detrained and before daylight were on the march—headed eastward. Stopping for a couple of hours at some little town to make tea, we then headed on. This was the hardest day we had had, and that march was just about as tough an experience as I have ever endured—and I was pretty tough, myself, at that time. It was *hot* and we were loaded down with our packs and ammunition, everyone being overloaded, as a new soldier always is. Moreover, our packs and clothing had not dried out and we were carrying about twenty or thirty pounds of water in addition to the regulation sixty-some pounds of equipment. The roads were *pavé,* of Belgian blocks, or cobbles, as we would call them, and our iron-shod soles slipped on them as though they were ice. On the hard smooth roads of England we would not have minded it, but this sort of going was new to us; our ankles were continually turning, our feet eternally slipping. All in all I consider this the hardest march I have ever made in my life, and I have made as much as forty-eight miles in one day over the snow of the Northwest in my time.

So far as I can remember, none of our crowd dropped out on this march, but I am sure that every one of us would have liked to. We kept going on our nerve after we were worn out physically and whenever we did stop for a short rest every man was asleep in less time than it took to lie down. About dark we halted at a farm and the word went out that we would bivouac and probably be there for a week or more. There was a large barn there with plenty of clean straw in it, and we machine gunners promptly took possession of this while the rest of the battalion were standing about waiting for the Quartermaster to assign them somewheres. This called for a fight with the signallers and scouts who were finally assigned to the barn; we compromised and let them use the poorer part of the place. There were names, inscribed on the beams, of earlier organizations who had stopped in that barn, amongst them being the Princess Pats. However, we read all those the next day, that night we were too tired to even eat and everyone just dropped into the straw and slept. We got just one ·day's rest here and were as good as new for it—astonishing how quickly healthy, active men can recuperate.

Next morning, everybody got busy and cleaned up or dried out his kit, in anticipation of that promised week's rest. But about four o'clock that afternoon we formed up and were marched some two or three miles distant for a review and talk by General Alderson, the Commander-in-Chief of the Canadians. We arrived at the reviewing ground a bit ahead of time and while lying about waiting we had our first sight of real war. It was high up in the air and well away from us, but it was a thrilling sight just the same. A couple of German planes were being shelled by some of our own anti-aircraft guns, and we held our breath expecting to see them come tumbling down at any minute, as the shells were apparently bursting right alongside the Germans. But none was hit and they went on their way. We soon learned that it was a rare thing indeed for a plane to be brought down by a gun on the ground. Later on I saw thousands of shots fired at them and never saw one hit by an "Archie" and only one hit by machine-gun fire from the ground. Most of the planes which are shot down are hit by machine-gun fire from another plane while in combat.

Generals are always late in keeping their appointments, but this one finally came. He looked us over and then gave the usual bit of hooey about what a splendid lot of men we were, glorious spirit, and all that, and then went on to say that as a reward for our magnificent appearance and maneuvering he was going to let us go right on up into the front line, instead of putting the battalion through the usual procedure in reserve and support. We got all swelled up about this, but later on learned the truth—that the British Army was about to start the big offensive known as the Battle of Loos and that at that time they did not have enough troops in France to be able to keep any reserve. However, that day we merely swung back to billets and spent a busy night getting our belongings together and packed, as we were to march at daybreak.

We moved out at dawn and had another stiff march of it, the weather having turned very hot again. Through Hazebrouck and many small villages we went, stopping at Bailleul for an hour's rest. The Machine Gun Section halted right in the market square, so we had a splendid chance to see the main points of interest in this ancient town: the Hotel de Ville with its twelfth century trimmings and the Hotel Faucon, which latter I particularly remember owing to the excellence of its cold beer.

After our rest we continued on our way and as we advanced towards the east, we commenced to observe an increasing number of the scars of war. The first German push, in August, 1914, had carried them well into France but their repulse at the Marne had been so sudden and unexpected that they had no time to do much in the way of pillaging. Live stock was killed or driven off and the inhabitants had to stand for many indignities but, so far as we heard, there were no atrocities such as were reported from Belgium.

One of the boys pointed out a house which had a hole through it big enough for a cow to jump through, and we all realized, without a word being spoken, that it had been made by a shell. That was the first one, as we went along these signs increased and multiplied. Soldiers of the Pioneer Corps were busily engaged in repairing the roads, and in this work they were assisted by detachments of German prisoners, each wearing on his back the conspicuous P G (Prisonnier de Guerre). We had seen some of these prisoners before, at work on the docks at Havre.

Naturally, all these things helped to keep us going—even after we should have been utterly exhausted. At one place, I remember, we halted for a few minutes just opposite where an old timer of the Pioneers was shovelling the accumulated mud and debris out of the ditch alongside the road. As he dug up each shovelful, he deposited it on a little mound alongside the ditch and patted it down, accompanying the action with a flow of words such as: "There ye are, me laddie buck: rest aisy": and a lot of other things which I dare not write.

Curiosity impelled one of us to ask him what in hell he was doing: whereupon he turned about and took the two or three steps necessary to bring him to our position. He reached in his tunic pocket and pulled out a lot of buttons and a belt buckle which bore the inscription: "Gott Mit Uns" and told us: " 'E was a Oolan, 'e was. I dug the blighter up in the ditch an' 'e was fair ripe, 'e was. 'ow about a bob for the buckle an' a tanner apiece for the buttons—oo wants 'em?"

Some of our bunch bought the whole lot. That was the start of the souvenir-hunting craze. From trifles picked up in this manner, to various objects found in the ruins of the houses and the many types of fuses or, as we called them, "nosecaps," we gathered and hoarded everything. When we finally commenced to get live prisoners we had perceptibly slowed down on this game. We had found that, although we might gather and accumulate the most wonderful collection of these trophies, whenever we made a move, it was necessary to ditch the whole lot. Personally, I buried several cart loads of junk in various parts of West Flanders, in the hope that I might, sometime, get back to dig it up.

As we continued, the signs of war increased. More houses and out-buildings wrecked by shell fire, more graves alongside the road, each surmounted by a cross. Airplanes were continually in sight—both ours and those of the enemy. When we first watched the bursts of the "Archie" shells around an enemy plane, we were sure that it had been hit. A dozen—yes, a hundred shells might be exploded around it, but, so far as we knew, never a plane was brought down in this manner. To the observer on the ground it might appear that all the shell-bursts were very close to the plane, while, as a matter of fact, they might have been—and usually were—hundreds of feet away.

Dranoutre, which was our last stopping place before going into the line, was a small village of possibly five hundred inhabitants before the war. Now it had more than twice that population, due to the refugees who had come in from the East in advance of the German occupation. For some reason or other, this town had escaped any shelling, although every town, city and hamlet in the vicinity had been literally *razed* to the ground. The reason, of course, was that the Germans had some good spies domiciled in the place. I do not know whether or not our Intelligence ever found them out but I have been told that, later in the war—in 1918—the Boche did shoot up the town.

We bivouacked in a field adjacent to the village and were allowed to ramble about and visit in the town itself. Very few of us had money enough to do much in the way of celebrating, however, so it was a very tame proceeding. About the only real excitement I saw there was when some of the boys, taking a bath in the town fish pond, stumbled on to a pike about two feet long. After a mad scramble, in which at least a hundred engaged, the fish was caught— and I suppose someone ate it.

We only spent one day and night at Dranoutre: that is, the Machine Gun Section. Next day, September 19, 1915, the "Number ones" of each gun crew went in to locate the positions of the guns of the Surreys and the East Kents (The Buffs), whom we were relieving. The remainder of the gun crews came in that night and the infantry next day.

As we made our way, that Sunday morning, by a round-about route through Locre and way stations, the signs of war became more and more evident until, at last, we came to the village of Wulvergheim. I say "village." It had been that and probably a prosperous one; but now it was nothing but a ruin. No person lived there, every building having been utterly destroyed by German shells. Even the church had been destroyed, only one side of the clock tower remaining. The hands of the clock on this side were hanging limply in the position of about six-thirty. As though angered that even this small remnant should survive, the enemy persisted in shelling the ruined edifice every day while we were there. Thousands of shells were wasted on that little place. We never had a man in it, and when we left, the clock was still there.

Now, our little crowd was just an average bit of the long fringe of British soldiers who were at that time holding back the flower of the German Army. No better, no worse than the rest of them, and what I have to tell of them is going to be the *truth,* in spite of all the objurgations of the thousand and one people who insist that I should put a little more of the "sob-stuff" or, as some of them call it, the "human-interest" element into it.

Why; damn you and God bless you; there was nothing of the kind in evidence. We probably had our inner feelings—I know I was particularly interested in a strange bird which I could not identify—but, so far as all this business of showing your emotions by facial contortions is concerned; well, there was no such thing. All that "blah" was invented in the movie studios of Hollywood and thereabouts. I recently spent a very uncomfortable hour and more, watching and listening to what was advertised as the Best War Picture. As it is so well known, I can see no reason for not naming it—"All Quiet on the Western Front." The parts which dealt with actual battle were excellent. The properties—uniforms, and all that—were accurately portrayed and the depiction of shell-bursts the best I have ever seen. It was only in the portrayal of the individual *men* that I had any reason to find fault—but that was quite enough to sicken me of the whole show. Why; confound it, man; men do not act like that whether in war or in peace. One can almost hear some Director shouting to this one or that one: "Register HORROR" or something like that. Damn it; they just don't do it. Of course, I do not know anything about the young German soldiers, but I am giving them the benefit of the doubt and assuming that they were just as good in that respect as the soldiers of other nations.

I have seen a brother bringing his twin out of the line, ripped from shoulder to buttocks by a steel shard from a "wooly bear" shell. Did he look like anything I have seen in the pictures? He did not. He bore the uncertain but hopeful expression which any of us would probably show if one of our blood brethren should be knocked down by a "hit and run" driver. "Got to get Bob out; he's hit pretty bad," was all he said.

"Here, son; a jolt of rum won't do either one of you any harm right now," says I. Both of these boys were teetotalers and the star athletic performers of our Battalion. The blonde one, he was doing the carrying, spoke to his brother. What they said, I do not know. The other was very seriously hurt and was losing blood at an alarming rate.

"All right," he said: "let us have it."

I poured each of them a generous slug of rum and made

them swallow it at one gulp. *"Medicine,"* I said, "take it all at once."

And they did. And I am glad to say that both of them are now living although they have two *blesse* stripes apiece.

If any of us felt any particular emotion on that day when we first went into the line, it was very successfully concealed under the usual "grousing" and joshing. "Bet I get the first shot," was George Paudash's last word to me. "Like hell, you will," says I. That's about all the sentiment or "heart-throb" stuff you could find in that outfit.

Chapter 4

Flanders

OUR Battalion Headquarters was in an old cabaret along the road leading from Neuve Eglise to Ploegsteert (corrupted to "Plugstreet" by the soldiers) and the way from there up to the front line was through a communication trench known as "Surrey Lane," as it had been constructed by the Surrey Regiment whom we were relieving. The entrance to the trench was in a little orchard, just behind the cabaret. Just as we were about to start into the trench, a man from the "Buffs" came over and was talking to one of our men when *sput*—he looked around in a vague, questioning sort of manner and dropped to the ground, groped around with his hands, then straightened out—and died. A stray bullet had hit him, right through the heart. Another of the Buffs, who were being relieved the same day, ran over and dragged the body back to the shelter of the building. "There goes Will," he said, "out since Mons and never did learn to take cover; w'y 'e was arskin' for it, I s'y."

That was our first experience in seeing a man actually killed in war but, curiously enough, it did not seem to affect our men very much. We had seen so many wounded men in England and listened to their stories of how things were going at the front that this was about what we expected.

So, we went in. It was a long way to the front line but nothing else happened to disturb us excepting the faint whis-

49

per of big shells, coming from miles behind our lines and consigned to points equally distant in "Germany." Only the machine guns went in this day (it was a Sunday) and the infantry "took over" the next day. This was common practice and for very good reasons. The enemy was, at all times, very well informed as to our movements as the people of that part of Flanders were largely German sympathizers and had many and devious methods of conveying information across the lines. The machine guns, wherever we had anything like permanent trenches, were so situated as to cover all the ground in no-man's-land and, as long as the guns were in position, they offered a pretty stiff obstacle to any attempted raid. If the infantry and Emma Gees were changing at the same time, it might offer an opening for an attack, but by first changing the guns, while the infantry stood watch, and then changing the infantry, after the new guns were in position, this menace was averted.

When we arrived at the front line, we were welcomed by the M. G. crews of the Surreys and, glory be—they had tea and biscuits and *jam* ready for us. Bless those boys. They were of the Old Contemptibles—the original Surreys, who had been right in the thick of things for more than a year and they knew we would be hungry after our long march. We had been moving so fast since leaving England that we had not had much time for eating and we were very thankful, indeed.

While sipping a can of tea, I was curiously watching a man who was standing against the parapet, looking through a large periscope which was built up against the wall, with the top cleverly concealed in the ragged edges of the sand-bags. After a while he moved over a few feet and took hold of a queer contraption which looked like a rifle stock, and a moment later I heard a shot. I then saw that the thing he was holding was, in reality, a skeleton rifle to which was attached a real rifle which was laid across the top of the parapet, the muzzle wrapped in a piece of sandbag and concealed, as was the periscope, by the irregular arrangement of the sandbags. Going over to him, I soon learned all about it. These things were common thereafter but that was the first time I had ever seen one. It was simply a device by which one could aim and fire over the parapet without exposing anything but the rifle itself. The sighting was done through a miniature periscope, the upper end of which was directly behind the bolt of the rifle and aligned with the sights, and the lower end in the position that would ordinarily be occupied by the rear sight. Connecting rods hooked up the dummy trigger on the skeleton frame with the trigger of the real rifle and a sort of crank arrangement was connected with the bolt.

The rifleman, seeing that I was interested, invited me to take a shot, first taking me over to the large periscope which he used for observation purposes and explaining to me that, "Them Wurtembergers over there are trying to fix up their parapet which our artillery knocked down this morning, and if you watch carefully you can get sight of a head now and then." Taking out my binoculars, I applied them to the periscope. This was evidently a new one to the Surrey man, and when I turned the glasses over to him he was wildly enthusiastic and called to several of his companions to come and take a look. Field glasses or telescopes are just as useful when used in connection with a periscope as anywhere else but it had evidently never occurred to those fellows. With the glasses, we could see every movement over the top of the enemy trench, some three hundred yards across the way. For the most part, all we could see was the sand-bag coming up on top of the half rebuilt wall, but every now and then a head would be visible for an instant. At the others' invitation, I took the rifle and, holding a careful aim on the point where we expected the next sand-bag to come up, I awaited his word. He was at the big periscope, with

the binoculars and when he called out, "Now," I shot. He
said I hit the sand-bag. I don't know about that but I am
very sure that that was the first shot actually fired at an
enemy by any member of the Twenty-first Battalion.

That was the start of our "rifleman in war."

The first casualty in the Battalion occurred that night,
when a scout named Boyer was killed on his initial trip out
into no-man's-land. Then the next day one Starkey decided
that he could not see well enough with a periscope, so he
took a look-see over the parapet. We buried the two of
them in a garden back of the lines, where many others from
the best and most famous British Line Regiments also lay.

Things had been very quiet in that sector before we came
along, but just as soon as our infantry had taken over the
position the Germans decided to give us a welcome. They
knew just who we were and when we had taken positions,
to an hour, as the rear was full of their spies. There had
not been a bombardment at this point for several weeks,
but the day after our infantry came in they put over a
furious barrage of shells of both 77 m/m "whiz-bangs" and
5.9 (150 m/m) "crumps." Considerable damage was done
to our parapets and several men were seriously wounded.
While this shelling was nothing compared to the bombard-
ments they put over later on, we were deeply impressed at
the time and it gave us an opportunity to make the acquaintance of the sound and effect of the various kinds of shells.
But our trenches were shot up badly, necessitating much
work with pick and shovel for the next few days, a thing
which never went well with Canadians. I might say at this
time that when we took over those trenches from the Buffs
and Surreys, they were clean and dry and comfortable, as
much work had been spent on them that summer. I am
afraid we did not appreciate it at that time, but as I think
back over the many trenches we held afterward, I must
admit that this was the very finest one we ever occupied.

The Machine Gun Section came through these first few days in great shape, having but one man seriously wounded, he was an old U. S. Army man named Mangan who had served in the Philippines. After eight days of it, we were relieved by the Twentieth Battalion and we went back to Dranoutre for our first "rest." We soon learned to dread these rests and would have much preferred to stay in the trenches, as it was then customary to move out everything, including one's ammunition supplies. A month's stay in the trench would have been preferable to having to lug all that stuff in and out so often.

During our first month or so in the trenches there was no time or occasion to do much with the rifle on my part. We were too busy with our machine gun work and it was not until along in October when we moved up into the Ypres Salient that the opportunity came to test my skill with both rifle and machine gun.

That first month was taken up almost entirely with our becoming acquainted with "strafing" work with our two Colt guns. The Machine Gun Officer of the Surreys, whom we had relieved, had established two strafing positions, well behind the front lines, and it was my fortune to be assigned to this position. I say *this* position because, although there were two different emplacements for the guns, they were used alternately—one at night and the other during the day-time. This latter position—which I afterwards changed— was for aircraft strafing. At that time the enemy planes came over at an elevation of fifteen hundred feet or less and they made fine targets. We finally got one and then they kept up so high we could no longer reach them.

The other, the real, permanent gun position, was so situ-ated that we could fire over our own front lines and harass the enemy ration parties as they came up at night. We cer-tainly made life miserable for Heinie from that place. One morning, after one of our strafing parties, we could see, through our glasses, at least a dozen men and as many horses piled up at a place called The Barricade—the end of the road down to the German trenches across the valley. That was as far as they could come with their field kitchens which were hauled by horses. After that they only came as far as the top of the ridge, at a place right behind the Hospice. We named this place "Cookers Halt." That was about twenty-two hundred yards from our position but, by bringing up our reserve guns and giving them the whole dose, we were able to convince them that they better stay back behind the hill. I'll bet a lot of Fritzes cursed us aplenty when they had to pack all their stuff for a mile or two. That's where the fun comes in—just to know that you have stung the other fellow.

One of our strafing positions was about a hundred and fifty yards to the front of a group of wrecked buildings and from this position on two occasions we caught large working parties in broad daylight and cut them up badly. Our fire coming from the line of buildings naturally led the Germans to believe we were using the buildings for cover, and they shelled those buildings steadily but never put anything close enough to our real hideout to do us any damage. This taught me a good lesson which I put into operation later on in my sniping, as will be duly told.

Up to this time, we had no instruments of our own for working up the firing data other than what we had borrowed from our artillery. Just for the edification of some of our mathematical sharks (in the United States Army, I mean—they are all my friends), I will tell how we sometimes found our targets *without the aid of a mil scale*.

We had a lot of little playthings, just like the "string and gadget with a hole in it." Hell, yes: we had all that and the "graticules" on our binoculars—and range finders! Say, folks; I have seen more of those expensive instruments lying alongside the road than you could carry in a two-ton truck. We tried our best to make some practical use of all these things, but it was out of the question—so we ditched them and went back to the old system of figuring things by degrees and minutes of angle. We had, of course, good maps of the whole terrain over which we were fighting. The only thing necessary to know was exactly where *we* were located on that map. Having ascertained this, we were in position to deliver fire on any other area shown on the same map or any other which joined up with it.

Were we? Well; yes—maybe. Here we are at "B-4-6-21" —the enemy we want to straff is at "A-2-6." "Un-ha; now how we going to catch him? Got a good compass and the map says that the magnetic deviation (or declination) is 24 degrees. Well; that's all right, so far; what do we do from here? What to do—what to do? That's what I thought. Here we are and there he is but how in hell am I to lay these guns so they will drop their bullets in the right spot?

At that time we had no clinometers (quadrants) for proving the angle of elevation—but we did have *carpenters;* in our Pioneer Section; and these carpenters had squares and levels and at least one of them knew the ratio of angles on his square. Perhaps I have not expressed this in the proper mathematical way, but neither have I put in the technical language of the textbooks that come from Ft. Sill or Benning. I'm just telling you how we worked it out. To make a short story out of what might drag out into an all-night discussion, we figured the thing out *and got results.*

The Battle of Loos opened on the 25th of September and lasted about a week. We were outside the immediate sphere of the action but were called upon to stage a demonstration to prevent the taking of reinforcements from our front to the scene of the big battle. The Nineteenth Battalion of our Brigade (the 4th) carried out the feint, the others simply standing by to take care of any counter-attacks. All the machine guns of the Brigade took active part in the show and we were kept busy for some twenty minutes or so, laying a barrage along the line of the enemy parapet to cover the advance of the infantry who only went far enough to throw a few grenades into Heinie's trench and then retired.

The casualties on our side were light and I suppose the same was true of the enemy but the performance accomplished the desired result; keeping our enemy on the *qui vive* and preventing the dispatch of reinforcements to the embattled troops to the south where the combined British and French attack was gaining headway every hour. Unfortunately, at that time, as in several subsequent attacks, our High Command had evidently underestimated the strength of the enemy artillery and our batteries ran out of ammunition, necessitating a retirement to the original lines. Had the supply of shells for our guns been adequate, I think it quite probable that the battle would have resulted in a decisive victory for the allied cause. However, it was to be long, weary months later before the allies *did* catch up with the Germans in the number of guns and the supply of fodder for them and by that time they had suffered such enormous losses of men that the advent of the United States, with its fresh divisions was most welcome. No, I do not think the United States won the war but they certainly did a good job of shortening it. If, in a major battle, a commanding officer holds back a substantial reserve until the critical point of the action and then hurls them in to overcome the weakened and tired enemy, thus winning the battle, it could hardly be said that these reserves won it. Those who took the shock of the earlier stages of the struggle are, in my opinion, entitled to something more than half the credit.

Those of us who were operating the machine guns during the little show above mentioned, simply took them back of our front line to slightly higher ground in the rear, to insure safe clearance over the heads of our advancing infantry and just set them up, right up in the open. It was at night and we were safe from observation but fully exposed to the rifle and machine gun fire. It was our first experience of the kind. The bullets were cracking all around us, exactly as it sounds in the pits at Camp Perry during a stage of rapid fire during the National Matches—the only difference being that we were right up on top of the parapet instead of down behind a concrete wall. Neither I nor my No. 2 man, who was feeding in the belts, were hit. He was just a kid, about seventeen, and the little rascal kept shouting and laughing in high glee so, of course, I could not do less, even had I wanted to. As a matter of fact, I *did* rather enjoy the performance. The fact that I might be hit never occurred to me. The whole show was over within about a half hour, but in that short time we had learned a thing which can be learned in no other manner—that it is possible for thousands of bullets to pass by or come close to you without doing any harm.

During those last few days in September, we had beautiful Indian Summer weather. I remember one afternoon when, things being quiet, Bouchard and I sneaked away for a look around to see what we could find in the way of souvenirs. At that stage of the game, we were all souvenir hounds. We never gave a thought to the matter of disposing of our finds or how we could get them out of there. It was only the men of the other services who had any chance to take anything home. The infantryman and the machine gunner had enough to do to carry their own equipment, but that did not prevent us picking up this and that and gloating over it until the time came to make a move, when we regretfully turned it over to some artilleryman, transport man or medico.

We had worked our way around to where we were on a

hillside, well behind our lines and a mile or more from the Ridge (Messines) when we suddenly came upon a great patch of blackberries, growing along a hedge, and there we spent the rest of the afternoon.

The warm glow of the westering sun beat gently upon us as we sat there behind the hedge. It was late September, but the autumn was tardy that year and the gentle breeze carried the warmth of summer. I was idly sketching the landscape across the wide valley, the boy busily picking and eating the luscious big berries.

After a while, the youngster ransacked the haversack which he was carrying and dug up a piece of bread and the remnant of a can of jam. Prying loose the top of the can with a big knife, he proceeded to scrape out the contents and spread it on the bread. As if by magic, dozens, hundreds, yes thousands of "yellow-jackets" appeared and fastened themselves on to the sweet-tasting stuff. He would spread some jam on the bread and, before he could get it to his mouth, it would be literally covered with the little, tiger-striped insects. After several ineffectual attempts to get a square bite, he gave it up and then, with some of the grim perversity that had enabled his ancestors to conquer the wilds of Quebec, he went in to clean up on the robbers, who had spoiled his meal. Bending the lid of the can (tin, they call it over there), he left just enough opening for the little jokers to crawl in. Within a few minutes the thing was literally crammed full of the little sugar-hunting bees.

I had just finished the sketching, which was a preliminary part of a range chart which I was making for our machine gun work when "Bou" called to me, "Now I got 'em, what the hell am I goin' to do with 'em?" He had squeezed down the lid of the can—or "tin," if you happen to be English, and was holding it toward me, perhaps three or four feet away when—"wheet" comes a bullet and very nicely decided the matter. It took the can and its contents and it also snipped out a slice of Bou's finger—just like that. "W'at ta hell," says Bouchard—and I just laughed.

We tied up the finger and that was that. Smoking a cigarette (that is, he did, I always stuck to my pipe), we lay there and looked out over the valley which separated us from the Messines-Wyschaette ridge. That was Germany. Stray bullets, like that which had hit the jam tin (by golly, I got it right, that time), were drifting in now and then all around us and, while we watched, several salvoes of whiz-bang shrapnel were poured into a communication trench, just in front of us. It seems incomprehensible to me, after a lapse of over fifteen years, but, as a matter of fact, we did not pay the least bit of attention to them other than to idly wonder if they "got anyone." Right now, I would be scared stiff if a shell burst near me. I know I would but, somehow or other, in those days, when we all took it as a matter of course that we were going to be bumped off most any time—well, we just didn't worry about it at all.

Blackberries and bullets—that is the way I always remember that afternoon. Lazing there in the sunshine, looking away across the valley, for all the world like somewhere in southern Indiana, sketching in prominent points on the sky-line (to be used as aiming points for future machine gun strafing) while all the time the kid was picking the delicious blackberries and, every now and then, bringing me a handful, shells winging their way overhead, some going and some coming and occasionally bursting within a hundred yards or so and the frequent whisper or *sput* of a bullet close alongside—well, I tell you, folks, that is something worth living for—or dying for, if it's your turn.

Chapter 5

The Trenches

THE Battle of Loos occurred during what turned out to be our last tour in those trenches at Ploegsteert. When we came out again, we marched, that very night, away off to the northward. The word went up and down the line that we were bound for "Wipers" and after the usual hard march in the rain we stopped about daylight, at the town of LaClytte which turned out to be our billeting place for many months afterwards. The infantry remained there and rested for a few days but we machine gunners went right on in and took over some support positions along the Ypres-Neuve Eglise road and at Groot Vierstraat, relieving the King Edward Horse who, like all the cavalry, had been acting as infantry.

Early in October the rains started, rains that were to continue, with few interruptions, until the following April. We have read of how the Duke of Wellington's soldiers "swore at the mud in Flanders." No doubt but what they did but I'll bet, if some of those old timers had heard the things we said while on that march up from Dranoutre to LaClytte, they would have hung their heads in shame. Swearing, like most everything else, has improved with time and our modern vocabulary is much more comprehensive than that of our ancestors. The rain was just going good when we received our orders to move. It was night, of course. There was no chance to move about on the roads in daylight. We went via Kemmel, as I well remember,

for it was in that village that we made a short halt for
rest and I simply "flopped" on my back, in the middle of
the road; my head on my pack, and was sound asleep,
instantly. I was not the only one; most of the others did
the same. I suppose the halt may have been for as much
as ten minutes but, during that time, I got a good night's
rest, not "singin' in the rain" but sleeping in the rain. Then
up and away.

Our position, when we all finally got there, was at the
angle at the southeast "corner" of the Ypres Salient, our
left opposite the village of St. Eloi and our frontage, about
eleven hundred yards for the Battalion, extending to the
Voormezeele-Wyschaette road. On our right was the Nineteenth Battalion with about the same frontage. Directly
opposite us was the *Bois Quarante,* along the front of
which were the German front line trenches. The distance
between our lines varied from about seventy yards on the
right, to something over two hundred at the left where the
Germans held a dominating hill called (on our maps)
"Piccadilly Farm" which merged with the high ground in
the village of St. Eloi which was designated as "the Mound."
Back of our front line, at a distance varying from four hundred to six hundred yards, was our support line, which
was not, really a *line* at all, but merely a series of redoubts
or, as we called them, "Strong Points," with, here and there,
a bit of completed trench. These redoubts were concealed
among the trees of the *Bois Carré* and other woods the
names of which I have forgotten. Back of that, ranging
from eight hundred to twelve hundred yards, was what was
known as the G. H. Q. (General Headquarters) line, which
was our last defense. This line was unoccupied during the
time I was there but was the place where the Germans were
stopped at the time of their big "push" in March 1918.
Just back of this was Ridgewood, a considerable forest,
where Battalion Headquarters was located and where we

established a cemetery. I go into detail about these things because, as we made our home in this place for eight months, I shall have occasion to refer to these locations from time to time as we go along.

The Twentieth and Twenty-first Battalions worked together, alternating between front line and support and the Eighteenth and Nineteenth did the same on our right. These four battalions comprised the Fourth Brigade, Second Division, Canadian Expeditionary Force (Canadian Army Corps).

For the first few days, after moving into this new territory, the machine guns were located in detached buildings (I should say, ruins) just back of the G. H. Q. line, where we relieved detachments of the King Edward Horse. At that time I was a Number One, with the honorary rank of Lance-Corporal and in charge of one of the guns. Our gun was stationed in the ruins of a group of farm buildings which, on our maps, was designated "Captain's Post." Several good machine gun emplacements had been constructed inside the ruins and, though we were often severely shelled, we had no casualties there. During the following months, in fact as long as we remained in that sector, we used this as a resting place, preferring to go there rather than back to the village of LaClytte, where the outfit had a so-called "Rest Camp." What a joke that was. The most arduous work we ever had to do was done while back in those rest camps. True, there was a chance for a bath and some clean clothes, but we soon fixed up our own bath house there in Captain's Post and managed to do our own washing. Some of the boys would go to town but several of us preferred to stay "at home," even though it was subjected to pretty severe shellings at odd intervals.

At this point we will digress a moment while I tell something about the German spy system as we encountered it in the field.

The Belgium of today is made up of a conglomeration
of peoples. From the time of Caesar, who mentions the
Belgae as among the most fierce and warlike of all the
tribes which he encountered in his conquest of Gaul, this
particular region has been a sort of free-for-all battlefield.
It has been held by Romans, Germans, Spaniards, English
and French, in whole or in part, off and on, for nearly
two thousand years, so it is easy to understand that the
race is somewhat mixed. However, we may ignore all of
them but two, as the Kingdom as we now know it, is
composed of but the two really definite races—the Flemings,
akin to the Dutch of Holland, who occupy the country
along the Northern coast, known as East Flanders and
West Flanders, and the inhabitants of Brabant and the other
provinces to the South. These latter all speak the French
language, while the Flemings stick to their own Flemish.

During the war it was soon learned that, while the people
of French-speaking Belgium were, for the most part, intensely loyal to their country, a large portion of the inhabitants of Flanders were, either secretly or openly, friendly
to the German cause.

As we, the Canadians, spent a year or more up in that
part of the country, we had ample opportunity to verify
this. The demeanor of the people was usually sullen and
unfriendly toward us. Information was difficult to obtain
and was often deliberately false. Back of the lines, where
some of them operated estaminets (Herbergs, they called
them) they were keen enough to gather in all of our money
they could get, just as did the French when we moved down
into Picardy, but the Flemings never showed a trace of the
real friendliness with which the French greeted us.

One night I was with a crowd in an estaminet, in the
village of LaClytte. A sergeant in our party bought a
round of drinks and, as he pulled out a handful of silver
coins to make payment, noticed one particularly bright new

coin. It was a Belgian franc and, as he passed the change over the bar to the proprietor, he called attention to the new coin, which bore the likeness of King Albert. The man took the coin, looked at it and then deliberately spat on it, at the same time almost shouting, "Bah, he make the war, the —————."

Well, there were four of us in our party, all standing close together and if ever there was unanimous and synchronized action, it was right there. The man who had passed the money, being a little closer, hit him first but all hands got at least one good crack before the bar went down. Several other natives joined in and a good time was had by all until the military police came in and took charge. The whole place was a wreck and I suspect that many a Canadian soldier went back to billets that night with a bottle or two which he managed to grab during the fracas. The M. P.'s on being informed as to the circumstances decided that the fellow had only got what was coming to him and took no action whatever.

That is just an instance, to illustrate the temper of these people. The whole region was a nest of spies, some of whom were detected from time to time, but probably the majority of them went all through the war without being discovered. It was pretty generally believed that the Germans had been for many years, "planting" spies in that neighborhood, in fact I think there is no doubt at all that they did the same thing all over France, too.

No one knows how many schemes these people had for getting information across the lines. For a while, they made use of the wind-mills—spelling out messages, in code, by manipulation of the sails. After this was discovered, all the mills were required to keep the sails at exactly a certain angle when not running. That they made use of pigeons was well known but, for a long time, it was a puzzle as to how they brought the birds over from "Germany."

When one of our men happened to see a small parachute coming down out of the sky, well in back of the lines, just after dusk one evening, that puzzle was solved, for in a cage attached to the parachute were four pigeons. These were turned in to our Intelligence Department, and if they did not make good use of them they were not as intelligent as I give them credit for being. A chance like that, to send over misleading information, would hardly be overlooked.

At another place, near Wulvergheim, we found, in the old shell of a wrecked farm building, a giant periscope which extended from the ground floor up through the chimney, which was still standing. With such a device, it was a simple matter to send over a message by simply using a flash-light at the bottom mirror.

Doubtless there were certain men who made it their regular business to go to and fro between the lines. Not nearly so difficult as it might seem, at that. Disguised as one of our men, they could walk right up into the front line and wander along until they found a likely looking spot and simply crawl over. We had a few who did the same thing—going the other way, but not so many, I believe, as the enemy, as these fellows were right at home and knew every inch of the ground.

One morning, just after "stand-to," I *captured* a German who deliberately climbed over our parapet. He said he was a Canadian officer but, as he was dressed in full German uniform, I did not take his word for it but sent him back under guard. He swore that he would have some awful things done to me but they never materialized.

Soldiers at the front seldom have any opportunity to hear of the underground work of the Intelligence System, as most of their work is done away behind the lines. As a matter of fact, it is a waste of time for any spy to search for information from the men in the front line. They don't know a damn thing beyond the fact that they are there—

and wish they were somewhere else. The contour of the lines themselves and the building of any new defensive works can almost invariably be detected from the airplane pictures which both sides are constantly making. No, the spy gets in his work back around the Headquarters. Of course he may pick up some minor information as to when such and such an outfit is going back into the lines, from any more or less befuddled soldier in some estaminet, but seldom is this of much value for, like as not, the soldier did not know anything about it and was just talking for another drink.

That we had some spies in our own ranks is undeniable. One such, whom I knew, was a sergeant in charge of a line of trucks which brought supplies up from the base at St. Omer. I say he was a spy. Well, he was in the pay of the enemy, anyway, but his principal job was to carry messages from the real spies back at Headquarters and transmit them to other operatives at the end of his route, which was, at that time, the village of LaClytte, where our Battalion had billets when not in the lines. He was a fine looking, upstanding chap and very popular with all ranks. I will not mention his name, as he was detected, long after, down in France and I suppose they did the usual thing to him although I never heard anything definite about the matter after he was arrested and taken away. The worst of it was that he was really a native born Canadian, which makes it all the harder to understand how he happened to "get that way." Thank God, he was not a member of *our* Battalion.

We had good, first-hand evidence that the enemy was well informed as to our movements, as they greeted us, by the number of our battalions, the very first time we went into the line—and quite frequently afterward. I doubt if our side ever did equal them in this respect. It was almost a hopeless case, where most of the population was against us and for the other fellow. Perhaps that is one reason why they did not attempt the trench raids—for prisoners—as we did. That was the only way we could find out what troops were opposing us. They (the Germans) did take up the trench raiding business in earnest down in France and it may be that it was because they did not have such a good native espionage system down there.

However, back to our story about the doings at Captain's Post. One morning, soon after we took over the position there, I was up in the hay loft with Bouchard, looking over the country, when we heard a shot, evidently fired from nearby, and then heard an outcry from a trench a short distance to our right (it was a communication trench called Poppy Lane) and saw several men carrying another out into the roadway. Bou grabbed me by the arm and said, "There he is, Mac, that's the fellow that shot him, get the son of a ————— something or other." I looked where he was pointing and, sure enough, a slinking figure was coming down along a hedge which concealed him from the men over at Poppy Lane but exposed him to plain view from our position. I took my glasses and could see that he was not in uniform, but he had a rifle and certainly was trying to escape notice. He kept looking over to where the group was gathered around the trench entrance, and, while I was watching him, stuck the rifle under a bunch of litter and bushes which grew alongside the hedge and then started to crawl away toward the woods—Maple Copse, I think it was called. I did not have time to do much thinking but simply acted on impulse. Taking deliberate aim, I shot him through the middle and he dropped.

Then I commenced to feel a little bit shaky. Down in my heart, I knew that I was right but the whole thing came up so quickly and was so queer all round that, for a few moments, I was at loss as to what to do. The result was that I swore Bouchard to secrecy and we went down and joined the rest of the bunch at breakfast. Later in the day, Norton-Taylor came around. He was a sergeant at that time, but he was a good soldier and my personal friend, so I told him all about it and, as soon as it began to get dark, we went out to have a look. We found the fellow dead, of course. He was dressed in the usual costume of the farmers thereabouts and had not a single thing on his person but his clothing. I soon found the rifle which he had cached and it was a regulation French Lebel. He had never even ejected the empty cartridge case, and the magazine contained three other cartridges. Hughie, that is, Norton-Taylor, agreed with me that the less said about the matter the better, so we just rolled the body over under the hedge and left it there, together with the rifle. From that day to this I have never mentioned that affair to anyone. During the succeeding days there were numerous instances of such murderous sniping behind our lines, and several of the culprits were caught and executed, *toute de suite*.

On the fifteenth of October, the entire Battalion moved on up into the front line (I remember that date, because it was my birthday), and next day I was delegated to pick out a good strafing position from whence we could harass the enemy with machine-gun fire. This phase of machine-gun work was new then, having been developed by the Canadians within the last few months. It soon became the regular procedure and every machine-gun section maintained one or two strafing guns wherever they happened to be located, if within range of the enemy.

I had located a good sniping nest in the ruins of an old farm building which was known as Sniper's Barn. I suppose the name was given it because when we first went there we found the body of a French soldier lying with the muzzle of his rifle poked through a small hole in the brick wall and eight dead Germans lying out in front. They finally got him but he certainly had a good balance to his credit before they did it. This place, like all the farm buildings in that part of the country, was a substantially built brick house or, rather, group of buildings, consisting of the dwelling house, stables, barns and everything else, all connected and built around a sort of court-yard—the open space or court being the depository for the manure. From the frequent shellings it had endured it was apparent that the Germans believed that it was and had been continuously used by our troops, while as a matter of fact, for nearly a year it had not been occupied at all. So when they told me to select a good position from which to operate a strafing gun, I decided that Sniper's Barn was a pretty good place. It was only about four hundred yards behind our front line and less than five hundred from Germany, but across a narrow valley, which put it on a level with and, in some places, a few meters above the enemy line. It was an ideal observation post, as from there we could see at least a mile of the terrain behind the other fellow's line, while, from our front line, we could see nothing beyond the narrow strip of no-man's-land between the two trenches.

While I was first inspecting the place, the Germans gave it what we afterward came to know as their "daily hate." That is, they put some fifteen or twenty shells into the place. Well, that did not look so good, but, after a little scouting around I noticed that, while the buildings bore the signs of frequent and severe shelling, the ground in front of them was almost entirely innocent of shell-holes. Carefully crawling down to a line of hedge which surrounded a garden patch in front of the house, I quickly decided that that was the place for the gun. Prior to this, at Messines, I had noticed that when we had a strafing post out in front of a group of buildings, the enemy had persistently shelled the buildings but never, excepting in case of a "short" did a shell burst near us.

There was at least a hundred yards between this hedge and the nearest of the buildings and the way those Dutchmen were shooting, those days, that was a-plenty. They could come pretty near to placing every shell into a five foot trench if they wanted to.

We dug in a little and built up a little, just behind the hedge and made a nice little nest, big enough for two men and the gun. (No use putting a half dozen in one spot where one shell might clean out the whole bunch.)

Beside the machine gun, I always had a rifle at hand, and spent a lot of time checking up on ranges to various points behind the enemy line. I did this with the machine gun too. There were innumerable shell holes filled with water, and it was a simple matter to shoot until the splash showed a hit. One had to be careful, though, and pick his time. Early morning was no good, for two reasons; we were shooting toward the east and the light was very bad and, as a general thing, the air was cool enough to cause a puff of vapor to appear at the muzzle—just like light smoke. As the enemy undoubtedly had good observers, it would have resulted in their blowing us out of there. But, during the afternoons, with the light in our favor and moderate tem-perature, we did very well.

From the start of this tour of duty we could see plenty of individuals and now and then a group of men. Some-times, in the latter case, we would give them a burst from the gun, and, perhaps two or three times a day, would take a crack at a single man, with the rifle but we made no attempt to start a regular campaign of sniping at that time for the reason that our front line was in a sad state of disrepair and our men, necessarily had to expose them-selves in moving up or down the line and, as the enemy appeared to take it easy, we did the same. At night how-ever, we regularly shot up the cross-roads, main line trenches and dumps which our daily observation showed were regularly used. As our position was in plain sight from the enemy line, it was necessary to devise some means to conceal the flash of the gun. At first, we simply hung up a sand-bag screen about two feet in front of the muzzle but this was not very satisfactory as the bullets soon cut a hole large enough for some sparks to go through. Then our ordnance people had a lot of contrivances made which looked (and were) very much like the ordinary mufflers used on gas engines. They stopped the flash, all right, but were so heavy that, mounted on the muzzle of the gun, they not only changed all our elevations but rendered the guns very inaccurate. I had some ideas of my own and found time to slip back, now and then, to our armourer's shop and do some experimenting and, eventually, turned out a gadget that worked perfectly. It was a crude bit of work but it did the business.

I made it from a French 75 case. I first cut a strip some two inches wide out of one side—extending from the base to the mouth—then riveted a narrow strip of sheet steel along the opposite side, this strip extending out over the mouth of the case and being formed into a regular bayonet-lock, such as used on the Civil War muskets. I cut a hole, about one inch in diameter in the base of the shell, directly in line with the muzzle of the gun. I then riveted three flanges inside the case, curved from the top toward the front and downward, these projected about one-half inch. That was all there was to it at first. No flash showed from the front but we found that occasionally one of the sparks, which were deflected downward and out the open bottom of the thing, would give a faint twinkle. I then added two small hooks, riveted onto the front (base) of the shell case and hung a strip of wet sand bag on them, drawing the corners back and attaching them to the legs of the tripod. With this device, I have sat up on top of our parapet within seventy-five yards of Heinie's line and fired to my heart's content. It was not heavy enough to impair accuracy and had but a slight effect on elevations and we very soon checked up on that. I do not know whether or not any more were ever made. Our Colonel came up one night with a party of officers to see it work and they gave it their approval.

For about a month after we occupied the front lines about Captain's Post things went along in their usual way. At one time there was a sort of general attack along our front to give the higher command a chance to try out some new smoke bombs and smoke shells. This, I believe, was about the first time the smoke screen was used. Our battalion got into the lines and stood by in case a counter attack should be made, while we gunners took the machine guns and set them up to cover our infantry's advance if necessary. It turned out that we were not needed so we sat there and watched as pretty a show as has ever been seen. At the proper signal, every gun back of our lines commenced dropping these new smoke shells in a continuous row along the top of the German parapet; as each shell struck it burst and sent out a dense cloud of smoke which soon became a dense wall through which no one could see at all. Our bombers then advanced and threw some hand grenades over into the enemy trenches and then retired, no attempt being made to take any part of the line or prisoners.

Everything seemed to go fine with our side, but the Germans naturally expected a general attack to commence, so they socked shells all over our trenches and tore things apart in general. It was about as bad a bombardment as we had encountered and it sure busted up those trenches, which had been none too good in the first place. The rain had set in for keeps just about this time and there was nothing but mud—mud—mud everywhere. Those trenches just oozed away like melting butter and it was a continual job to barricade them up with sand bags. Then to top it off, the Germans held the higher ground and there were places where they could dam up the water, holding it until an unusually hard rain would come, whereupon they would open the gates and give us the full benefit of the whole dose. I have seen them turn six or seven feet of water into our trenches in less than an hour and at places in our communication trenches it would be over a man's head, a man being drowned in it one night.

Under such conditions it was an impossibility for us to dig and the best we could do was to construct sand-bag barricades or parapets. These gave some protection from bullets and small fragments but were no use against direct hits of any kind of shells, even a little whiz-bang would tear right through or blow them apart. At one time, for more than two weeks, more than two hundred yards of our front line parapet was down and we could not get it built up again. The result was, that when a man had to move about he had to do it exposed to full view of the German snipers and even at night we were continually having men hit by stray bullets. In the day time it was a sure bet someone was going to get hit, as the Germans had some good snipers who watched for just such opportunities.

Despite all this hard luck, our men managed to finally get up some sort of screen, and behind it, assisted by the engineers, they constructed a new line of trenches slightly in the rear of the old one, which was then abandoned except for a listening post and two or three machine-gun positions. We also got some pretty good barbed wire strung out in front. The German also had his share of hard luck about this time and at nights did not bother us so much, which allowed all this construction to be finished. But we always got a few shells and rifle grenades in the daytime, and some high-angle bombs, but with these the mud was actually our friend as it blanketed the effect of the shell bursts and unless one fell right on top of you it did no harm.

The most trying thing about all this digging was that the entire trench system here was nothing more or less than one continuous grave, and it was difficult to dig anywhere without uncovering bodies. Many of these graves had been marked by crosses put up by comrades to give name, date of death and organization, but hundreds had merely an un-inscribed cross or were unmarked. One of our sergeants discovered the grave of his brother, who had served in the King's Royal Rifles, and I ran across a grave marked with the name of Meyers, Indianapolis, Indiana, who was with the Princess Pats and said to have been the first man killed in action. There was a string of old English and French trenches, both in front and behind our lines, and all more or less filled with bodies that had never been properly buried. Also there were plenty of Germans mixed up amongst them. Whenever possible, we gave these bodies a proper burial, but with many of them nothing could be done without incurring unnecessary further losses in men.

However, we spent a month more or less in getting all this mess cleaned up and trenches that would again shelter us, and just about the end of it an incident occurred which changed my ideas regarding the war. Up until this time I had taken the war as a more or less impersonal affair and had not gone out of my way to look for trouble or for someone to kill. But on November 14th, a German sniper killed Charlie Wendt, one of my own boys. This put me on the warpath right.

During October the only casualties amongst the machine gunners had been three wounded; MacNab, Redpath and Lee all being hit on the same day and all three being in-valided back to Blighty. At that stage of the game it was not considered the sporting thing to be carried out if one could by any means "carry on," and all three of these chaps put up a great howl when they found they would have to leave the outfit. Later on, this attitude changed and a "Blighty" was just about the very finest thing a man could imagine or want, and the loss of a hand or a foot was not considered a bit too much to pay to get out of the hell one was going through. None of us thought very much about our casualties up to this time.

The weather was setting in bad and during the worse spells of it very little sniping went on, so we often went in and out of the lines by the "overland" route in broad daylight. This November 14th came on Sunday and it was just such an occasion for overland travel. The rain delayed the Twentieth Battalion from relieving us until about noon time. The trenches were crowded with troops and the going so bad that I talked it over with my crowd and we decided to save several hours time by going out down the open road. All hands voted for it, so I started first and had the others follow at fifty-yard intervals. Our route was in plain sight of the German lines, and we got well out under cover of a small hill without a single shot being fired at us. From here on out, we were practically safe, as the ground was partially screened with bushes and trees, so the bulk of the party went right on out across this covered ground. But Charlie Wendt and I stopped at this small hill to arrange about the relief of a gun crew I had stationed there. Charlie stayed with me a few minutes and then went on by himself, saying he would meet me at the redoubt farther out. I continued my talk with Endersby, the man in charge of the gun, and all at once heard Charlie calling "Oh, Mac," and looked out to see him lying on the ground about a hundred yards off, shot through the abdomen.

Endersby and I both ran to him and while he ran back and telephoned for stretcher bearers, I bandaged the wound. Charlie Wendt was a very strong, clean living young man, and I really thought that despite the serious nature of the wound he would pull through. He did not think so, but did not make the slightest outcry, merely kept saying that "everything is all right." Finally he asked me to get about ten of them for him and I told him that I would do it.

Meanwhile, this sniper kept up a continuous fire at us, hitting everything in the neighborhood but what he was shooting at. It was a miserable exhibition of shooting, too; the range was only about 500 yards and in clear daylight, and I told Charlie I would be ashamed to have such a rotten shot in our outfit. The shot which had hit Charlie was undoubtedly just a lucky one. At last I tried to drag him into a depression and out of sight, but it hurt him so I gave up and waited for the stretcher bearers. As they came up I made them crawl to us and we managed to get Charlie where they could change him to a long litter and carry him out right. The last thing he said to me was that everything was all right and not to worry. And on the way out that German kept slamming away at me as long as I was in sight, and missing by twenty or thirty feet most of the time.

Next day we learned that Charlie had died and was buried down at Bailleul. He was the first one we had killed out of the Machine Gun Section and was one of the most popular men we had. All hands felt very much depressed at his death and I got a permit and went down to Bailleul to see that he had been properly buried. Within five minutes the Graves Registration Commission had me alongside his grave.

I want to add a little more to this personal history of Charlie Wendt. His name would seem to indicate that either himself or his forbears came from some place over the Rhine. That may be true. His next of kin lived, at that time, at Niagara Falls, Ontario. For Charlie, himself, I can only say that no man ever showed more sincere loyalty to King and Country than he. He inscribed a large Maple Leaf in our quarters at Captain's Post. He must have been an artist or, at least, a stone mason with artistic tendencies. He chiseled that token in the stone and bricks of that wall—and I wish I could have it now, in my own house: for, of all the names inscribed thereon, mine is the only one of a living person.

I came back from the visit to Charlie's grave and began to plan ways and means of "getting" those ten Germans I had promised him. Up to that time I had been taking the war as a sort of a lark. Keenly interested as I was in every phase of warfare, I was really enjoying the experience. Now, the matter had become personal. My particular gun crew was made up entirely of youngsters; some of them had enlisted at sixteen and not one of them was of voting age. And now they had killed one of them. It was fair enough, this shooting of Charlie. We had elected to go out overland, rather than take a long, roundabout course where we would have had the protection of trenches, and he had been hit. Fair enough. But that did not prevent me from going out to collect a few scalps to, as the Indians say, "cover his grave." So, although we were going back to the reserve line for a week, I had no difficulty in getting permission to stay up there and go to work on them. As a matter of fact, I was allowed to do just about as I liked in those days.

And just about that time, actually it happened on the 27th of the month, this same sniper—at any rate I took it to be the same—shot down several of our unarmed stretcher bearers. At this time, our ration parties had been going out before daylight, as we could not use the communication trench and they had to cross the open and exposed ground behind our line. This morning, the two men who comprised the ration party, Dupuis and Lanning, were a bit late, so it was light when they got started. About fifty yards to our rear was a bend in the road called Devil's Elbow and from this point on they were in plain sight of the Germans. As soon as they reached this bend, the sniper fired and shot Lanning through the lungs. Dupuis got down to assist him and was then shot through the head, being instantly killed. So far, all right, these fellows had taken their chance and lost.

But some stretcher bearers from our pipe band were only a few yards away and as the second man went down one of these Scotties rushed out to carry them in. He was instantly shot down, as were the next three who promptly went out to do their duty. Then an officer got there and stopped anyone else from going out; he finally, by crawling down a shallow ditch managed to pull the bodies under cover. Four were dead and two wounded, one of the latter dying a few hours later. Six hits at a range of about one hundred yards, from which distance it was easy to see the broad white brassard of the Red Cross conspicuously displayed on the sleeves of those four bandsmen-stretcher-bearers.

Then and there I made a solemn vow that Charlie Wendt and these men:

> "should go to their God in State:
> With fifty file of Germans,
> to open them Heaven's gate."

Chapter 6

Record Scores

DURING the time we had been in training in Canada and England I had never seen a telescope sight or known of any definite attempt to train men in its use. Nor had I known of any school for deliberate sniping. But one day in September I was scouting around in back of our lines opposite Messines Ridge looking for suitable places to install strafing posts for our machine guns, and I ran into a sniping post, manned by an officer and two snipers from the Buffs. This was the first I had known of any attempt on our part at sniping, and being highly interested in anything of that sort I naturally stuck around. I stayed there for a couple of hours, but what I saw being done did not get me any too highly excited over that type of sniping.

These fellows from the Buffs were using the ordinary, short Lee-Enfield rifles, upon which they had mounted telescopes made by "Stanley-London." These scopes were short, brass tubes, about ten inches long and three-quarters inch diameter; they had a device for changing elevation, but no method of making lateral corrections, and for windage you simply had to hold off. I do not happen to remember the power, but recollect that the field was very limited although visibility was excellent. As they were so far behind our lines, it had not been necessary for them to construct any elaborate shelter nor to exercise any particular care to avoid observation. All they had done was

79

to dig a chamber out of one of the sides of an old disused communication trench and throw a few boughs over the top.

This outfit they were using may have been very good for reasonable ranges, but these chaps were so far in back of the line that it was hopeless for them to think of doing any definite or accurate shooting. The nearest enemy targets were at least eleven or twelve hundred yards away, but they were doing most of their shooting at targets well over on Messines Ridge and I knew the range to these points was about two thousand yards. Now, with a machine gun, it is possible to put a burst on a target or group of men at such ranges and break them up and possibly hit one or two. But my personal experience has been that the firing of single shots, at individual targets, at ranges of more than 1000 yards is just a waste of time and ammunition. I have tried it myself and seen many others try it, but never saw any indications that the target had been hit.

But this sniping outfit from the Buffs was deadly serious in their efforts to damage something over there in "Germany" and I just had to admire their spirit even though their judgment was bad. I talked with the Lieutenant, who had just been transferred from the Territorials, and he told me he had been a competitor at Bisley, and I suppose he was really a good rifle shot; the two enlisted men were also good shots probably. When I told them that I was also a rifleman and had shot at Camp Perry, they invited me to try my hand. They handed me a rifle which they said was already sighted in right and told me to take a crack at something within the German lines about 1200 yards away. They had two very fine spotting scopes and the men watched while I fired. There was no wind at the time so I held right on one of the demolished brick buildings, just to get the hang of the thing, and touched off. The shot brought forth much congratulation and applause from my onlookers, I had actually "hit the side of a house."

Then I took one of the spotting scopes and observed while the others fired. It was generally possible to pick up the strike of the bullet when they fired at the closest targets, as those brick walls gave out an appreciable "splash" when hit. But none of us were able to pick up any indications as to the location of the long hits fired across the valley. They just shot into space at those ranges. Having become pretty well acquainted with the crowd by this time, I ventured to ask the officer if he thought it was worth while to shoot away at targets located a mile or more off, and he replied they were acting under orders. That was typical of the "Imperials," just do as you are told and think nothing about it. So I came on away then, and I imagine that outfit hung around there for many more days engaged in such useless work.

I remembered about this sniping post and those "specialists" after Charlie Wendt and the stretcher bearers were killed, and then commenced inquiring around. I soon learned that an authorized school for snipers was being organized and that specially sighted rifles and equipment were available for those who were detailed to and passed through this school. So I went to our Colonel, and after telling him my qualifications as a rifleman obtained a requisition for the regulation "outfit" without the "training." I convinced them that I already had the latter, and as by this time the German snipers opposite our front were becoming a really serious menace I had no trouble in getting an immediate start towards abating the nuisance.

In order to get this rifle and special sniping equipment, I went, with the permission of Colonel Hughes, back to a newly-organized Sniping School, near the village of La-Clytte. There I was issued a Ross rifle—one of the lot made for and used by the members of the Canadian Palma Team at Camp Perry, in 1913.

As all the old timers will remember, that team came near

to cleaning up against all comers at Perry, that year. In fact they did a good job of it in the individual Palma—which was won by Major Hart MacHarg who was afterward killed at Langemarck. The only reason they did not also win the team match was that they took a chance and started experimenting with a new bullet which did not stand up so well in the wind.

These Ross rifles were exceptionally accurate and dependable with the Mark VII ammunition we were then using. For short and mid-range work, I am not so sure yet but that they were superior to our Springfield because of the longer barrel and better sights.

With the rifle I got a telescope sight. It was one of the type—new at that time—made by the Warner & Swasey Company. Prismatic and mounted on the left side of the rifle, it might not rate so high now but, at that time, it was better than any other I had ever used. One of the best features was that it could be mounted and used without interfering with the iron sights. I had a little trouble in getting it securely mounted so that it would not jar loose but finally, by using a wedge—made of a piece of safety-razor blade—and salt water, got her on so tight that I came near being court martialled when I finally turned it in. The armourer could not get it off.

I also got a fine spotting 'scope and a tripod for the same. The spotting 'scope was pretty high magnification—about 36-power I believe. Each article—sight, telescope and tripod—had its separate sole-leather carrying case, with convenient straps for slinging them over the shoulder.

Each rifle had been fitted with a particular sight and was thoroughly tried out in Canada before being sent over for issue. I happened to draw rifle No. 140 and sight No. 49. A very few shots fired at the improvised sighting range made me familiar with the scope adjustments and permitted me to check in the scope against the iron sight settings. Now, I have heard a lot of unfavorable comments against this Warner & Swasey sight, in fact, I cannot recall ever hearing a good word spoken for it. However, it is my opinion, that when compared to the others we had at that date and time, it was a pretty good sight. Naturally, it might not compare with the scope sights of today, as much progress has been made in these since the war. The one I used gave very good results, and was fully as accurate and reliable as the Winchester A-5 type. This latter model was particularly hard to keep "lined up." So, late in November, 1915 I came back from LaClytte with as good and reliable a sniping outfit as was available at that time, and for the next two months I proceeded to "check off" that "fifty file of Germans" which I had mentally promised my dead comrades. I did it and with plenty to spare.

I first picked out my observer, and this is an important half of any sniping team. For reasons which will be given later, I am not much in favor of the "lone" sniper. A man on his own will not do half as well as a properly paired team of two. For my choice, I selected a particular friend, a lad named Bouchard, of whom you will hear much later on in this story. Bouchard was the closest friend I had in the Canadian forces and in addition he possessed the qualifications which made him a good observer. So I picked him to do the observing while I worked the rifle.

We already had available an ideal location for a main sniping post in an old barn located some five hundred yards to the rear of our front line. This place was the farmhouse before mentioned. It had every desired advantage, even to name and precedent. When the British forces first settled down in this spot they found eight dead Germans lying in front of this building, while inside was a dead French soldier, who, they figured out, had accounted for the eight before they got him. So they called the place Sniper's Barn. My Machine Gun Section had already made some use of this place and we had a position in a small hedge which ran across the old orchard in front of the barn, on the side towards the enemy.

At first glance it may have looked rather foolhardy to place a machine gun post so close to a building which was in plain sight of the German lines and only some five hundred yards off at the nearest point. But I had remembered our experience at our first strafing place down at Messines where we were located about a hundred yards in front of some buildings which the Germans shelled industriously in the belief we were located inside them, with never a shell put anywheres near where we actually were. So I depended upon Heinie to run true to form again, and it worked. We kept both a machine gun and sniping post in front of Sniper's Barn for almost six months, and while the Germans shot up the barn regularly during all that time, there was never a shell apparently directed at our position, except for an occasional short or two which burst near us. We fixed up a fine little sniper's nest in that hedge.

Sometimes we would shoot from the hedge but more often from the barn, as it was slightly higher and gave a correspondingly greater command of the country across the way. I soon learned that, while they shelled the place every day, there were a few corners which appeared to be fairly well protected from the fire of the 77 mm whiz-bangs, which seemed to be the only sized guns that were working on that particular target. This was due to the fact that there were two very substantial brick walls dividing the different sections of the building which were almost, but not quite, perpendicular to the line of fire of these guns, and, by getting in close alongside one of these walls, one was fairly safe from a direct hit. We often were splattered with pieces of brick and stone, sometimes caught a few small shell splinters and, one time, by some freak of luck, a shrapnel shell struck an adjoining wall and ricochetted in such a way as to spill the whole charge right on top of us. Fortunately, although the shrapnel bullets cut off two legs of the tripod and one buried itself in the stock of my rifle, neither one of us was actually hit although we both had one or more holes through our caps and tunics. That was before the advent of the tin hat. We were all the time working on new "nests" and, eventually, had six, all well concealed and offering good fields of fire.

Every time we built a new sniping nest, we would immediately proceed to sight in and find the range to all the various prominent objects which could be fired upon in that particular sector of fire. Sometimes, these sectors were decidedly limited and were just as apt to be off to one side as to the front. In fact, it is generally safer to do one's shooting at an angle to the front lines, as the danger from observation and stray shots is much less. Once a "firing point" was decided upon and arranged, we would determine all the possible ranges by means of trial shots and observation, and then I would proceed to jot all this data down in a little memoranda book I had, just the same as I had done many a time before in my regular score book on the Camp Perry and Sea Girt ranges. Only, at the targets I now fired at, there were no sighters allowed and in general there were no markers unless you happened to catch a target out in the open and could see it fall.

This first sighting-in for ranges was merely to get the approximate distances so we could come close enough to the targets to properly sight in upon any occasion when we again used that particular nest for future sniping. Upon taking up a position for the day in any prepared location, it is always necessary to first fire a few sighting shots at available "self-marking" targets and make certain the scope sight has not moved or become disarranged since last used. You pick out a small pool of water, or a piece of brick or stone upon which the effect of a hit can clearly be seen, and then two or three trial shots will suffice to determine sight settings or correct range. This is where it pays to have both iron and 'scope sights mounted so either may be used independently of the other; many times you can check the 'scope setting against the iron sights without ever firing a shot. If the range at which you are going to work is close, it will not pay to do much firing to sight in; fact is it is often impossible or inadvisable to do *any* preliminary firing and you must come prepared to make the first shot *hit*. But it generally happens that individual rifle shots are continually being let off up and down the line and no close attention will be paid to your few sighters. A word of caution to the novice here may not be amiss; be *particular* just what you pick out for a target on these sighters. Don't go firing at any petrol cans, or empty boxes which may be lying around the top of the enemy trenches; they may possibly have been placed there to invite just such shots in order to "sight back" through the bullet holes and locate your position. I shall mention this trick farther along.

We had some wonderful shooting. By sighting in on various water-filled shell holes and bits of brick wall, both with the scope and iron sights, we could shoot in almost any kind of weather. Sometimes it was too foggy to see and sometimes, in the early morning, as we were shooting toward the east it would be almost as bad. (It reminded me of the times when I have been out of luck and caught the early relays at Sea Girt.) But, we managed to do pretty well. We certainly got our hundred—and then some. I have a little memorandum book in which I recorded, day by day, the various shots and, as nearly as we could tell, the results. I had intended to incorporate it, *verabatim,* in this story but, for various reasons, have decided not to do so. However, here are a few extracts:

December 1st. Hazy—Near leaning tree. 1 shot 750. Fell and they pulled him in. Two shots at helpers—got one.

December 2nd-3rd-4th. Rain. N. G.

December 6th. North of leaning tree, crouching, cutting wood. 1 shot. Got him.

December 7th. Brt. & clear. Fresh S. W. wind. Near 92. Twice men showed themselves. Three shots, sure of one. 50 yards R. one man—one shot. R of 02 our artillery blew down M. G. emplacement showing open end of covered trench. Men trying to get out—4 shots—2 known hits. Thirty yards left, 1 man, one shot. Got him. (This was a good day.)

December 8th. Rainy A. M. Hazy P. M. Piccadilly Farm. 5 good chances and three known hits.

December 9th. Hazy, cool. 1 at leaning tree, standing straight up. *Tué*. (If you don't know what that means, ask someone.) 2 shots at group back of 92. N. O. (That means no observation.) One fifty yards right. Fell across log. Shot three successive helpers, (all soldiers), all four lying in sight at dark.

Dec. 10. Rain: N. G.

Dec. 11. Misty. One shot—Piccadilly. Probably missed.

Dec. 16. Clear. Fine hunting. 16 good shots—7 known hits and feel sure of at least four more.

That's the way it went. The above are copied, exactly as I wrote them at the time. The references—92—leaning tree, etc., simply referred to our range chart which covered every foot of the enemy territory within rifle range. The remarks in parentheses have been added to explain certain things that might not be otherwise understood by the reader.

Yes; we got them when and where we could get them and we damned their souls to hell, every one of them. They had started the dirty work but we finished it and I am here to say that I have never regretted it. The boy who was working with me (Bouchard) was killed later on, and all the rest of my best friends, but they played the game and took their medicine like men, although they were, most of them, just boys who should have been in school. May they R. I. P.

Early one morning Bou and I were stretched out in our little hole, he with the big telescope and I with my binoculars, scrutinizing the German line, about five hundred yards away. Suddenly the kid says, "There he is, Mac, right in front of that big tree just to the right of No. 4 post, see him?" I shifted my glasses a little and, sure enough; there was a man, evidently an officer, at the point he mentioned, standing upright, with a big tree behind him, and looking out over our lines through his glasses. (By the way, here's a tip: if it ever becomes necessary for *you* to look out over a landscape where you have reason to believe that an enemy is on the lookout, choose a good sized tree and stand up right in front of it—and keep still.) Only the kid's keen eyesight discovered that fellow. I had passed him over several times, but, when my attention was called to it, I saw him quite plainly—through my glasses. When I tried to pick him up through the sight, however, I had considerable difficulty in locating him, but, finally, by noting certain prominent features of the surrounding background, I managed to find the right tree and got him centered in the sight and cut loose. I got him.

We lay there quite a while, very well pleased with ourselves and looking for something else to shoot at when, all of a sudden, a bullet came smacking into our little nest. It did not hit either of us and we took it for just one of the strays that were always floating around looking for some place to light; but when, just a moment later, another one came along and ripped through my cap—just missing any meat—and right after, another one breezes along and hits the kid, it began to look as though it might be serious. The boy squirmed around and looked at me kinda funny and I thought, for an instant, that he was done for. Only for an instant, however, for he quickly "came to" and said: "Jesus Christ, Mac (at the same time crossing himself—he was a

Catholic), they near got me that time." He was hit, all
right: I could see that, but, as the doctors say, a move was
indicated; so we proceeded to get out of there, *muy pronto*.
By carefully crawling backward, we managed to gain the
protection of a group of ruined buildings and I took a look
at the kid's injuries. The bullet had just nicked him in
several places. It had scraped the side of his head and his
shoulder and had taken quite a bit of skin off the calf of his
leg. I wanted him to go back to the dressing station but he
said: "Wat t'ell Mac? They got to hit me harder than that
before I quit." That little son-of-a-gun never would quit.
I saw him nicked several times after that but until he was
absolutely blown to Heaven, down on the Somme, that boy
never did quit.

Well, anyway, we had to hunt up another place from
which to carry on with our day's shooting, so we cautiously
made our way around behind the group of demolished buildings to where we had another nest. This one was right out
in an open field but was reached by a tunnel-like trench
which we had dug during many nights of hard labor. It—
the tunnel—was about three feet deep and nearly as wide,
and extended for more than one hundred feet out beyond
the corner of the last of the outlying buildings. In digging
it, we would first take off the sod and lay it aside, then ex-
cavate the earth to the desired depth, carrying all the dirt
back and hiding it in the building. Then we covered the top
with pieces of board from the wrecked building, put on a
little earth and replaced the sod. At the end, where we had
our "nest," was a good-sized chamber, big enough for the
two of us to stretch out comfortably, and with two holes,
one for the telescope and the other for the rifle. Small
bushes and clumps of grass immediately in front (which
were taken into account when planning it) effectively served
to screen it from enemy observation. We had finished it
more than a week before but had never used it; just waiting

to see whether Heinie had discovered it.   Apparently he had not, so we decided to make use of it now.   It was pretty muddy—everything in that part of the world was muddy in those days—but we managed to get in and set up our paraphernalia, ready for business.

We waited a long while, all the time carefully scanning the enemy line and the country behind it.   There's where I learned to chew tobacco.   We dared not smoke and I wanted something in the way of a stimulant.   The kid never would chew but I managed to do a fairly good job of it, only that I never could learn to spit like a real tobacco chewer.   Guess you have to learn that at an early age.

Finally, just as I was about to call it a day and pull out, the boy called my attention to a certain place in the German front line where we had been observing some kind of construction work going on for several days—building a new machine-gun emplacement, we surmised—and I noticed that there was movement of some kind going on behind the screen of muddy-colored cloth which they had erected at that point.   (On both sides there were many strips of this screen cloth, some of them concealing real operations but most of them merely decoys—camouflage.)   This one was the real thing as we soon discovered, as we caught occasional glimpses of men moving around the edges; so after watching them for some minutes, I decided to take a shot—just for luck.   Bou watched carefully through the 'scope and I put a shot right through the middle of the screen.   Then we saw them.   I got in two more shots as five or six men tried to climb over one another getting out of there.   Don't know whether or not any of them were hit, but Bou said he was pretty sure of one of them.   Under such conditions, it is virtually impossible to tell whether or not you have hit your man.

One day, just as I was about to start back to Sniper's Barn "to see what I could see," the Colonel came along,

accompanied by Capt. Cook, our Medical Officer. That
Colonel of ours was a wonder. Never a day passed, fair
weather or foul, heavy shelling or none, but he made the
rounds of his front lines in spite of "hell and high water."
He asked the usual questions about conditions and received
the customary answer, which was: "All right, sir." It seems
funny now, at the range of fourteen years, but that was the
conventional reply, even though we had just carried out
several killed and a lot more wounded. I well remember
one morning when Heinie had just "busted" one of his
"wooly bears" right over our trench and hit twelve men with
the one shell—about half of them killed and the others
horribly mangled by the razor-sharp pieces of shell—and the
Colonel came along and asked, as usual, "How is it with
you this morning?" And the answer came back, just the
same as if nothing had happened, "All right, sir."

Well, this morning, as I said, the Medico was with him,
and as their route back to Ridgewood, along the P. & O.
trench, was the same as mine, I accompanied them as far as
the place where we turned off to go to Sniper's Barn. Arriving there, I invited them to come along and have a look
at some Germans. The Colonel could not take the time
then (he did later), but Captain Cook came with me. I had
been watching and waiting until Fritz had finished his "daily
hate" and I had seen a dozen shells bursting in and around
the barn and so was satisfied there would be no more shelling there during the day. There's another funny thing.
Heinie was so thorough and methodical that we could tell
from day to day and hour to hour just what to expect. He
had a regular routine. Certain batteries would, at fixed
hours, shell certain localities. We even learned to know the
sound of the different guns and could, in many cases, tell
very close to where the shell was going and what kind and
size it was. He had one battery of 150 mm rifles which
always fired what we called "wooly bears," high explosive,

time-fuzed shells which burst overhead and scattered razor-sharp pieces of steel over a wide area. These were too fast to dodge. They arrived, like the whiz-bangs, right along with, or ahead of, the report of its coming. The howitzers, of any calibre, announced themselves long before their arrival—the sound taking a short cut, while the shells travelled a couple of miles up and then down. The sound of the report of the gun and the beginning of the theme song, if I may borrow a term from the movies, arrived at about the same time, the latter increasing in strength and volume for some time and then diminishing as the shell took to the higher altitude—then it would increase and then was when you had a right to worry. It was on its way down and coming closer all the time but—where the hell is it going to light? Just one of the little things that keep war from becoming monotonous.

Anyway, I felt sure that there would be no more shelling of Sniper's Barn that day unless someone foolishly exposed himself so the German observers could see him. So I had no compunctions about inviting the Captain and he was eager to go. We crawled along a shallow trench and behind the hedge and made our way into the little chamber which I had fixed up as a sniping nest. The telescope was already in place and we soon located several of the Fritzes, away behind their lines. They were too far away for effective rifle fire but I guess the Captain got a thrill out of just seeing them. Up to that time he had never had a chance to see one of the enemy—excepting prisoners. Our Medical Corps was pretty busy, those days, patching up the cripples and seldom had a chance to go sightseeing.

Under the ordinary conditions of trench warfare, where the opposing lines are but one hundred yards apart—and often less—the opportunities for accurate rifle shooting from the front line are few and far between, that is, unless special snipers "nests" have been built into the parapet. Several times, by doing a lot of night work, we managed to construct chambers in the embankments under our parapets, with concealed loop-holes, from whence we were able to do some real and accurate short-range sniping. Unless these emplacements were planned in advance and built during the initial construction of the trench, it was a matter of several nights of downright hard labor to fix one up, as it necessitated the digging out of a considerable section of the whole embankment, reinforcing the chamber with timbers and then replacing all the dirt and sand bags so as to give no indication that they had been disturbed. The hoop-hole must be screened with a frayed sand-bag and, to be reasonably safe, should be made with two of the steel plates which are commonly used at the peep-holes along the top of the parapet; one of them forming the top, or roof, of the loop-hole and the other set in below at such an angle that any shot striking it will be deflected downward, into the ground. If the hole is down near the bottom of the parapet it will be impossible for an enemy to put a bullet into it—even if he discovers the place. From one such position I was able to shoot straight into the loop-hole of a machine gun emplacement, diagonally across the way and at a distance of not over one hundred yards. I only did it once, however—that is, one day—for next day, when I tried it, it was just like shooting in one of those galleries where they have a hole for the bulls-eye and a hanging piece of steel behind it so that, when you get a bull, you "ring the bell." Heinie had simply put a steel plate in the hole and all I could do was to ring the bell, without doing any damage. I presume it was so fixed that they could swing it out of the way when they wanted to fire; but, as all the shooting they did with that gun was done at night, when, of course, I could not see to use the rifle, I had to give it up until, acting on my information, the F. O. O. (Forward Observing Officer) of the Lahore battery decided to have a try at it.

That was a wicked-shooting bunch—those Indians. Formerly a six-gun horse artillery battery, they had exchanged their thirteen-pounders for the regulation eighteen-pounders of the field artillery. For some reason or other, they never seemed to be restricted as to the amount of ammunition they could expend in any one day—as was the case with our other batteries at that time. They got on the target in record time and then proceeded to pour in the H. E. shells at a furious rate. They soon had the covering of earth and sand-bags entirely blown away, exposing a cubical concrete emplacement underneath. I knew it was there; in fact had been watching its construction for a month and had reported it, time and again but our own (Canadian) artillery officers evidently did not believe me. It had been so cleverly built into and under the old parapet that there was nothing to indicate its presence from our front line; but, from our elevated position back at Sniper's Barn, we could readily see the progress of the work.

Those eighteen-pounders could do nothing with it. Of course, a direct hit could chip off a few bits of concrete but the nut was too tough for the cracker, so they gave it up and turned the job over to the 9.2s. Those big boys finished it, and it happened that Bouchard and I were on the job at the time and managed to get some good shooting at the survivors as they scrambled out of the pill-box when one of the big shells uprooted it and turned it over on its side.

I spoke of the Lahore Battery as Indians. Lest I be misunderstood, I would explain that, while they came from the Indian city of Lahore, the personnel was composed entirely of white men—Englishmen, I should say; for, I am told, the native Indians are, for the most part, Aryans and therefore to be considered as members of the Caucasian family, despite their dusky complexion.

But, to get back to our loop-hole. It is never advisable to have it faced directly toward the front, but at an angle, up or down the line—preferably to the left for a right-handed shooter. Enemy observers, using periscopes, are prone to scan the ground in their immediate front, depending upon others, all along the line, to do the same; that is, to watch their own sectors. Thus, it is an easy matter to have the hole perfectly screened from the direct front, while giving a good field of fire along an adjacent portion of the line. This, of course, has always been the accepted method of constructing machine-gun emplacements and we always tried to have at least three guns in position to enfilade any (every) foot of ground in our front.

The use of the various skeleton mounts for rifles, by which the firer aims through a periscope and manipulates the rifle through a system of levers, never appealed to me. True, I sometimes used them, but never had much confidence as to my ability to hit anything. I sat and smoked my pipe (and laughed), one afternoon, while one of our best shots had the sight shot off his rifle—and the periscope, too, of course—while trying to get a crack at someone across the way. At that range—less than one hundred yards—he never had a chance. The other fellow was there first and was waiting for him all the time and, moreover, was probably well dug in in some such emplacement as has been above described—and using a telescope sight. Our man was persistent; I'll give him credit for that; but, after having the same thing happen three times, he was satisfied to go back to the rising ground behind our lines and try for them at a range of five or six hundred yards.

And right here I want to say that, at the short ranges—up to three hundred, possibly four hundred, yards—those German snipers could shoot. I do not think they were much good at long range; in fact I doubt whether they often attempted any of what we would call long-range shooting. I know we showed ourselves, with impunity, at anything beyond six or seven hundred yards. Sometimes they would snipe at us with a 77 m. m. whiz-bang, especially if there were more than two or three in the party, but, with the rifle, never. The greatest range at which I ever knew a German sniper to fire at any individual was about five hundred yards. This fellow did get Charlie Wendt; but, as he fired some fifteen or twenty shots at me while I was administering first aid to Charlie and trying to get him under cover, and never hit me; well, you'll have to admit that I have some grounds for belittling their ability as long-range shooters.

This was certainly not due to any inferiority in the range of their rifles. They had us beaten from the start, in that respect. I think it was due to the fact that, with character-istic German thoroughness, they had determined to their satisfaction that it was not a profitable business to fire single shots at men at the longer ranges. They were devilish cunning, however, with their "set rifles" or "fixed rifles." These were simply rifles bedded in an improvised machine-rest and aimed to cover some unprotected spot well back of our lines—sometimes at a range of as much as fifteen hun-dred yards—usually at road intersections or enfilading some trail which their airplane pictures told them was commonly used by our troops at night. By firing single shots at in-tervals during the night they nearly always knocked off a man or two; whereas, had they used a machine gun or ar-tillery, we would simply have detoured around the place. Single bullets were always floating around and it would take several such casualties before our men would get the idea that there was anything intentional about it.

We had devices of this character, some of them quite elaborate in that they were well constructed with steel frames and well anchored with sand-bags; some of them carrying as many as six rifles. Some man was detailed to make the rounds each night and pull the triggers at certain intervals. Later, after we had perfected our machine gun strafing, we abandoned this procedure and would fire just one or two shots at a time with the machine guns and I suppose we got about the same results.

Now, a friend who has read the foregoing and the following pages has voiced the complaint that there is not enough about actual rifle shooting.

Well, I'll tell you how it is. I did not make that war, so cannot be blamed if a lot of other things happened and that there were so many soldiers engaged in various other diversions, such as bombing, artillery firing, machine gunning and so on. The truth is that the poor rifleman sometimes had to go for days and weeks—yes, even months—without having a chance to shoot at anything. I have tried to describe, to the best of my limited ability, the actual happenings as they came along. Naturally, had I been arranging things, I would have limited the armament of all the contending forces to the rifle; but, as it was, we had to take it as we found it. Plenty of preachers went to war and never had a chance to do any preaching and the same applies to men of all the other vocations—riflemen included. A thoroughly trained soldier is probably the most versatile man in the world. He knows how to do everything—and has to do it.

So, if any of our dyed-in-the-wool riflemen are disappointed at finding that there is too little on their own favorite subject and too much about other things, I can only hope that they will be able to take consolation from the fact that a lot of us had to do the same thing—and under far more arduous conditions. Some of these departures we found quite diverting. Hunting in the dark, for instance, when the other side was hunting in the dark, also, and in the same territory, provided good entertainment for the riflemen on those evenings when the theater was a forgotten thing belonging to a past life. I shall touch upon this in the next chapter.

Chapter 7

Scouting and Patrolling

THE rifleman, being a hunter, naturally always has an eye, and an ear, for game. The great game movement along the front took place at night. That in the back-areas, of course, could only be deduced, from daytime observation, and at night became the business of the artillery and machine guns. But no-man's-land, in quiet times, was the scene of an almost purely nocturnal life. The sniper was lucky if, during the day, he spotted a couple of Germans; but if he really cared for hunting he might have a dozen pass within as many feet of him at night. He can well afford to abandon his rifle for this—if he can still find time to get the necessary sleep. There is nothing just like it for making one feel at home in the trench areas. To spend the night in a funky dugout or musty cellar, whether in the front line, supports or reserves, is like closing the tent-fly at nightfall as soon as you have made camp on the mountainside overlooking a pleasant—and unknown—valley. Much better to get outside and see what's happening.

And since scouting was a necessary and regular part of intelligence work, he could always tie up with our patrols and make himself useful in the general scheme, and at the same time further his first-hand knowledge and gratify his curiosity. Incidentally, he could get into a scrap about as often as he liked; and it was my contention that patrols

should do as much as possible of this—after their real
work was done. Of course, there were patrols whose real
work was fighting; but most of them had other duties, and
took up fighting only as a sideline—or of necessity. Their
regular business was to exercise control over the permanent
battlefield that was a feature of this war. Condition of the
wire, on both sides; enemy outposts and front-line positions;
establishing listening posts, and daytime observation posts
at times; checking on all enemy activity, patrols, etc., and
various special investigations—all were matters for patrols
and scouts. Generally, fighting was optional; but since this
is the particular business of the soldier, it is my notion
that he shouldn't miss an opportunity.

This scouting work developed haphazardly, like a good
many other things. Primarily intelligence work, it was
finally grouped along with Sniping and Observation, and
the organization became the S. O. S. of the British Army
in charge of a battalion intelligence officer under the intelligence officer of brigade. It was not definitely established
until after I left the front; so I got most of my experience
without it. Quite aside from the matter of information,
I think it had an important value in trench warfare, a value
which I didn't fully appreciate until during my last weeks,
when at various times and on various business, I had opportunities to observe. This was in the winter, at the beginning of 1917. For a spell I was attached to another
battalion. Then I was helping to train the Canadians for
the coming attack at Vimy Ridge. (At one time I even
led a pack-train for a spell, and at another I was sort of
directing traffic—this is the sort of work that a rifleman
may be called upon to do).

Well, anyway, I found time and occasion to look things
over and see what trench warfare was beginning to look
like. It is difficult for anyone who has not lived in a trench
and had no-man's-land as a front yard for weeks on end

to understand the conditions under which patrols worked.
It is not difficult to picture a shell-torn, wire-strewn stretch
of land, and one may well accept the word of numbers who
have done it that it was not much of a problem to move
about in this area in comparative safety. But this leaves
us with a fairly fixed picture that is not at all representative,
and the difficulties I am talking about are not of movement
only, but of moving effectively—of securing results. It is
necessary to remember that this area stretched from the
North Sea to Switzerland, across the level muddy fields of
northern Belgium, winding over the semi-circle of hills that
bound Ypres from Kemmel to Passchendaele, to low land
from Ploegsteert to Neuve Chappelle, rising a trifle around
La Bassee, thence to the higher land at Loos, from which
place it continued high and uneven. It ran through almost
every sort of terrain which western Europe had to offer
and included within its boundaries hills, valleys, hedges,
orchards, forests, rivers and canals. It wavered back and
forth (this is where the war was fought, you know) to cut
off and desolate at one time and place a solitary cabaret,
at another an isolated farmhouse, and at another an entire
village—and the village may be shelled to powder or standing up reasonably like a group of human habitations.

In this game, both sides, of course, attempted to hold
dominant positions; for trench "warfare" consisted largely
of dominating enemy territory without occupying it. This,
at its best, was to keep him in the mud where life was
miserable and strong defenses impossible while we occupied
high land from which we could see every move and reduce
to mud every effort at fortification. Struggles for such
advantage of position accounted for the bloody fighting,
sometimes back and forth for days, at such places as Passchendaele Ridge, St. Eloi, Vimy, Hill 60, Telegraph Hill,
and countless lesser mounds, woods, slag-heaps, strong
points, sugar-mills, etc. which seldom made the headlines.

Usually before the two lines could settle down to the stalemate of the trenches the positions were nearly equal so far as topography was concerned. Then, domination took the form of extending our knowledge of enemy territory and activities, less with a view to immediate action than to anticipating and defending his point of attack or to launching one of our own.

I risk this resume of the obvious because I find that it is frequently lost sight of, and also to emphasize the importance of patrols and observation from the ground.

This preparatory domination was primarily the business of the Intelligence System, of which spies and aerial observers were concerned largely with the back areas; with the plans of the High Command and with the movement, concentrations and positions of men, guns and supplies. Aeroplane photographs, of course, supplied an exact layout of the trench system and revealed changes from time to time; but they could not be relied upon to disclose many vital details, such as sniping, observation and machine-gun positions. For these, the map was supplemented by endless painstaking observation and study from the ground, in which work patrols played only a secondary part. The particular—and vital—concern of patrols was activity in no-man's-land. They, and the listening-posts established through them, were almost the only protection against saps, tunnels and mines. They were not—as they had been in the old open warfare—primarily interested in locating the enemy. We were always in contact with him, and it became the business of patrols to see that this contact was not disastrous. Disaster came from the direction of no-man's-land, and this, at night, belonged to patrols. Anything beyond this area was generally the concern of observers by daylight. In many cases patrols could learn how strongly the front trench was held; and they often located machine-gun positions there. This of itself is of vast importance.

It may be decisive; a single machine-gun advantageously placed and unsuspected until lines of infantry are abreast of it on either flank means disaster until it is dealt with; and confusion and loss, right at the outset, may result in total failure.   Such a gun, in an advanced position, escapes the destructive barrage, and is ready and undisturbed when the opportunity comes for it to get in its work.   But even in a good position close behind the trench, unless this position is exactly known, it may escape shell-fire; and one of the most pitiable spectacles in modern warfare is that of men caught in the wire by crossfire from such guns.

The idea is to remember that no-man's-land was the battleground. When it disappeared the war was over. You were always "in touch with the enemy."   There were no wide-ranging patrols, skirmishing parties and advanced guards trying to locate the opposing army and determine its movements; and no forced marches to intercept it and fall upon its rear or flank or cut it in two before it could get itself in shape on its chosen battleground.   There was none of this ranging all over central Europe, clashing in one place today, withdrawing during the night to come together again a week or month later at some point fifty miles away. What I am getting at is that the battle was joined from the outset of the war and remained joined until the end, and we would gain every day a little of the ultimate victory, not only by extending our knowledge of the enemy positions, but by claiming a toll of his men.

This trench warfare was the only sort I had known by actual experience. I had gone into it, as had everyone else, not knowing what it was to be like, but having my notions more or less colored by history, by what I had read and heard of the great battles and wars of the past.   Then this one began to take shape in my experience; I began to see what it was like; and I would find myself, every now and then, toying with the thought of what would happen if every man in our trenches should constantly stir himself and make it *his* business to get a German soldier.

I intend elsewhere to outline the usual method of carrying out trench raids, and to say something of the one or two in which I took part, and also of trench-raiding in general. I don't believe that I can sufficiently emphasize this sort of warfare. Its importance is not merely in getting prisoners for purposes of information; it is in thinning out the enemy's ranks and putting the fear of God into them; and this can often be nicely done by a patrol. At one time and another during the course of the war the wise ones told us what was wrong and how the conflict might be brought to a speedy and successful end. Sometimes particular wise ones changed their views, as is the way of a certain sort of them who are always ready with the answer reinforced by recent example. Others stuck to their own hobby through thick and thin, and were ominous or confident of victory according to the nature of the recent example and the use or neglect of their particular hobby. At one time it was guns; we were confidently told that when we had superiority of artillery fire at all times we would soon see the end of things. This camp arose in full chorus at the fall of Antwerp. And they were right; but only in so far as those who had insisted that artillery was noisy but harmless had been so absurdly wrong. Artillery wasn't the whole of success. After Verdun even the most prejudiced and partial of them were forced to a clearer recognition of the truth of the matter. They each saw their particular pet for the vital *part* it played—in strict cooperation with and with full support from all the others. But the significant thing that emerged from this coordinated effort, the concrete and definite and lasting result of this achievement, was the ghastly casualty list of the other side. The one indispensible adjunct to the war machine is men. I imagine that the most outspoken advocate of this or that

arm of defense or attack would have conceded at any time
during the war, that once the Germans did not have enough
men to stretch across the continent of Europe, in the various
lines of defense and to serve the drawn-out and diverging
lines of communication and supply, they would have to
give in.

If the two or three or half-dozen taken in a raid, or the
"missing" enemy patrol, seem ridiculously negligible in proportion to the vast army from which they come, it should
be remembered that this resulted from an operation involv-
ing only a hundred yards or so of front. Put this in terms
of the hundreds of miles of the Western Front and multiply
this again by the days and days of a long, inactive winter
and you have a casualty list which, though it may not dwarf
that of a major battle, is significant beyond its mere numbers.

The numbers are only half of the effect. Of the other
half, one part consists likewise in weakening the enemy;
the other is in strengthening our own position, not only
relatively but absolutely. As to the first, a thousand
casualties inflicted in this way are worse than twice that
number in a battle lasting one day. The patrol that never
comes back (with often no sound to give any inkling as to
its fate), the raiding party that went amiss, the wiring party
that was wiped out with machine guns after being quietly
spotted by a couple of scouts, are missed, with no excitement to divert the men from realizing that they are missed.
In a battle they are not so much thought of; there is excitement, and a natural expectation of paying the price, and
the satisfaction of knowing that something was being done
to the other side. This is not true in the trenches. The
life is abominable anyway and the untidy mess left by a
grenade in a sleepy dugout doesn't help it. Despondency
follows easily upon misery and discomfort, and with a man
disappearing here and there night after night and others
falling to snipers' fire by day, the darkness of no-man's-land

soon comes to hold something a good deal worse than the sword of Damocles, and men begin to wonder if God is really on their side after all.

For the other half of this effect which doesn't appear in the casualty-list we look to our own side. The best way to keep a machine in perfect running condition is, with proper care, to run it often. When this machine is composed of men, this is the *only* way. Even the stoutest and gruffest old drill-sergeant—who is sometimes accused of knowing but one thing—knows this. It is generally the accepted method in the billeting areas and training camps. It is even more important in the trenches. Not only does the machine get out of fix; but its individual parts become sluggish, dull and apathetic, and the entire battalion is worth about as much as a wide-awake company. The blanket terms are *morale* and *esprit de corps,* and when these are up to scratch, troops are invincible; when they are down, they are well-nigh worthless.

And along with this moral effect you get almost the only actual and practical training it is possible to get as preparation for the big battles. Men get into the spirit of the game, gain confidence in themselves and see what they can do. It is a part of that strange process through which men unconsciously go which enables them to kill men without being murderers. When this reaches its perfection, soldiers become men of the chase. They take delight in battle and kill without hatred. This primitive man didn't have much of a chance to emerge from his civilized veneer under the terrific shell-fire of the hotly contested sectors where both sides clung to the strongly entrenched positions and were shelled out, back and forth, night and day, for a week or more, generally in the rain, with men disemboweled and torn to bits while the others could do nothing but cower in the mud and wait their turn. This was simply inhuman, and certainly not any less appalling to the primitive man than to the civilized one. But when they got together and really had a chance to fight, there was remarkably little of hatred or revengefulness. Hatred is a slow, calculating, cold-blooded business. There was no time for it in battle. You often hear of it, to explain the soldier's feeling; I have used it myself. But it disappears in battle.

I have elsewhere explained how I came to do my first real sniping after I had watched the Germans shoot down our stretcher-bearers, and Charlie Wendt and others. I had nothing to do but think about it; but even then I didn't hate them as much as I liked to think I did. My hatred had been measured by the intensity of a lot of other emotions which had been aroused by this inhuman murder. But I assure you that when I was behind the rifle, the principal feeling was one of keen satisfaction and excitement of the same kind that the hunter always knows. That's the spirit. That's what makes good riflemen and good soldiers.

And that's the spirit that work in no-man's-land fostered. (By work, I don't mean hard labor, such as digging to push the front line out over the brow of an inconvenient hill; I mean the business of carrying on the war. As for this other stuff, I think it's about time that some bright boy got busy and invented a portable, non-collapsible, always-disinfected, water-tight trench-system.)

Even the men who were disposed to let well enough alone and let somebody else do the running around liked scouting, patrols and trench-raiding, once they had tried them. And I know that during my last weeks in France I was a little disappointed because I couldn't always be up in front of the front where there was first-hand contact with the other of the two sides necessary to make a war. I managed to get up once or twice on each new stretch of front and see exactly how matters stood. And matters always stood best when I got up there just before stand-to in the morning and found everybody wide-awake and I knew that there was some sort of excitement somewhere, though I may have heard nothing and seen only a few Very lights since leaving my dug-out. The sentries had forgot that they were damn tired of standing there looking at nothing, and glad to be relieved of the temptation to go to sleep.

Wherever it was, trench warfare was best when it was *warfare*. I always felt better—and I believe that everybody else did—when there was excitement somewhere in the air. Many men were glad to go on patrols. It was not that they were foolhardy or reckless, but simply that they preferred action to acute and unrelenting discomfort. Patrols were, of course, the specific duty of the Intelligence Section and when the particular business of the patrol was to supplement the work of observation, it was necessary to use men from this Section. At other times it was advisable—often necessary—to use men from the platoon. These men needed to know, at first hand, the land before them, and it was the best sort of training to fit them for raids. The wise intelligence officer knew the men in the front line and checked with the platoon commander on the men who proved most useful and apt on duties of any sort in no-man's-land. Then he was able, at the last moment, to turn his own little information-seeking party into one that went out looking for the unexpected and rather hoping that it would happen. And he could feel confident thereafter in leaving the unexpected in the hands of the platoon sergeant during those hours when no-man's-land was not covered by his own regular scouts.

I think some such arrangement as this was responsible for a good deal of that "Silent Death" business for which the Canadians had something of a reputation. There is no reason in the world why a patrol that is out to look over the wire or to protect against a surprise raid shouldn't surprise an enemy patrol, if it could be done neatly.

This is the sort of stuff that the sentry in the front line welcomed. When a raid was on, everybody, of course, was alert; but regular raids were few, and scouting parties went and came frequently without his knowing it, further than that he was warned that there was one out. It may be gone for hours and he dismissed it from his mind, except to remember to look twice and listen for the pass-word before shooting up that little disturbance in the wire. This is monotonous business when nothing ever happens; and there is a constant temptation to rest grimy eyelids. But when a certain spirit has taken possession of the platoon; the right sergeant has returned from leave; Smith, who was out with a crippled foot last time, is back on the job, and the old combination is working; things may be expected to pick up, and the madman's land before him is worth looking at. It is the more exciting because it is often just on the borderland of exceeding authority. A patrol that is charged with the particular duty of reporting on the movement of a previously observed enemy party, to see if it is a nightly routine, might just as well return one night to report an unavoidable encounter—for which it was quite well prepared, even to selecting the battleground.

I was interested in this sort of work from the start, but we quite often had our hands full without it, then. It became really necessary (the fighting part of it) during the next winter, when the war had definitely settled down to the dull business of the trenches. I was back of the lines most of the time, but I got up as often as possible— sometimes on business—and I began to appreciate the tonic properties in a little excitement at night. The only mornings worth remembering are those on which something was happening, or had happened. It was a treat to go into a trench where there was excitement in the air—to sense, in the first sentry I came to, a sort of question mark in the dark, as I did one morning. He wanted to know what all the noise was about, and anyone passing along at that hour was a possible source of information. (The soldier always looks to the rear to know what is happening, anyway, and is better informed in billets than in the trenches.) Usually, two sentries work together, taking turns at the parapet. The free one dozes on the firing step or shifts miserably about in the bay in an effort to keep circulation up. He welcomes almost anything that moves, or which can be seen or heard. Listening for something which never comes and looking when it is so dark you can't see, become tiresome. So the sound of a rat scurrying along the duckboards is likely to be followed with interest. But a pistolshot in no-man's-land, or the crash of a grenade, or a muffled confusion of thumpings, oaths and exclamations, like the sound of a pleasant brawl in an alley, brings him to the parapet beside his fellow. They have a ringside seat from which they cannot see. They can only speculate; and it is significant of the attitude of our troops that these speculations were always agreeable; they never doubted the outcome or feared for the safety of our patrols. After a minute or two, quiet is restored and they can only wait to know the outcome—perhaps at stand-to in the morning.

It was at this stage that I came along, turning from the communication trench to encounter a man at the corner of the first traverse.

"Can you tell us what all the noise is about, sir?"

I couldn't. I had noticed nothing in particular since leaving the quarters of a gun crew just back of the support trench, where I had stopped for fifteen minutes or so.

"Well, I guess we'll know in a minute, sir, if they come back the same way. They went out right there along that little gully under the wire. I can't imagine what they did. First, there was a Mills or two, close together; then something that sounded about like a crump, but it wasn't a shell. We haven't heard anything since the big explosion, though it wasn't more than a hundred and twenty-five yards away."

We moved up into the bay, near the sentry. I asked if their intelligence officer was out, and was told that he wasn't. It was the platoon sergeant and three men.

"Hush," said the man at the parapet, largely to himself. The other man got quickly to the firing-step, keeping his eyes low in an effort to make near objects stand out against what there was of skylight. The usual ground-fog blurred everything. A man making no sound and keeping flat could have come within fifteen feet of us. I thought that I heard a faint creak of wire and slight rustle or two, but could not have sworn to it thirty seconds afterward. But two minutes later we heard the sounds of movement. Rifles were quietly brought to bear in that direction, and in a voice that was firm enough, but no louder than was thought necessary to reach them, the sentry demanded assurances. I was interested in observing again what I had often noticed in this business of challenging in the front line, where danger is the probability and not mere fiction as it generally is out of the active area. First, there is a reluctance to resort to the formality of challenge and pass-word. Second, there is a tendency on the part of the sentry to wait until he can see well enough to do something about it in case the answer is unsatisfactory. A man doesn't like to give himself away or look foolish by challenging a noise. He wants to challenge something which he can shoot the next instant. In the present case, the challenge should have come from a sentry on our right. The disturbance was nearer there, though bearing in our direction. I can imagine the man at that point waiting until he could see a lump into which he could put a bullet. This is fine, for quick and definite results; but it is not the way to warn all hands in time and to keep enemy grenades—and a raiding party—out of the trench. A Very light will show things up; but their use is bad policy—Heinie's policy—particularly when you know one of your own patrols is out. It may bring a burst of machine-gun fire.

The answer to our challenge was: "Aw, dry up, Robinson; I've got a souvenir for you." And there were moving blurs in the darkness as four men hurried toward the trench. The first one dropped something into the bay as he slid over the parapet.

"There you are," he said.

Now, I have forgotten whether the man's name was Robinson or not. What I do remember is that the second sentry picked up the object, and we examined—largely by feeling of it—a new version of the old mace, which I hadn't thought about in this war of hidden enemies and long-range rifles. It looked like a deadly sort of thing for close-up work, but it was not to my liking. I understand they were first found in possession of certain Austrian troops (though these were Germans before us), and that they became fairly numerous later.

The last man to enter the trench reached for the curiosity.

"Let's see that damned thing a minute," he said.

He was the sergeant. I noticed on the lower part of his sleeve the small chevrons which indicated that he had been out from the first. He hefted the mace judicially, then handed it back. As I took it, he looked up at me, doubt-less guessing, from the sleeve of my trenchcoat, that I was an officer.

"What do you think of it, sir?"

"Pretty crude," I said.

"Too damned slow and uncertain in the dark, sir? I'll keep my Colt; and if I'm too close for that, the knife's the thing." Then, turning to the others, he said, "Well, fight it out, fellows; but don't keep so much noise the sentry can't hear. Don't forget your business, Robinson." He disappeared into the communication trench along which I had come. (He returned presently, accompanied by the platoon commander, rum ration and the order to stand to.)

The others meanwhile, had been producing other spoils of battle, including several Lugers. Then they remembered there had been a fight. The sentry wanted an explanation of that peculiar explosion; and this added another novel touch, not less interesting than the mace.

"What the hell were you fellows doing out there?" the sentry asked. "I didn't know you took any artillery out with you?"

"Wasn't that a hell of a noise?" one of them said. "Did you ever hear of potato-mashers going off in a bunch?" he continued addressing any and all of us, seriously. "I don't know what happened, but it sounded like a whole case of 'em exploded at once. We threw four Mills and the whole damned place blew up."

"They must have heard the click of our firing-pins," said another, who had been excitedly relating disjointed fragments of the battle for some time: "We weren't twenty feet apart. They walked right under our nose. They didn't even know what happened."

I gathered that he was a comparatively new man. He had been on patrols before, but this was the first time that he had had the experience of fighting in the dark. It was easy to see that trench warfare had suddenly developed a new and very decided interest for him. He was still over-charged with excitement.

"I don't know about that," said the first speaker. "It may be that they saw us and were holding theirs a bit, so we couldn't throw 'em back. But I didn't think they saw us. Anyway, they never threw 'em. And they'll never be able to tell you now; the place was a wreck."

"Aw, dammit," Robinson said, "what happened—if anything?"

This is, substantially, the manner in which the story was related. Before we go back and get the first of it, we might

as well say a word about the plausibility of the theory
accounting for the explosion. If you have never seen a
potato-masher grenade, I can tell you they are quite a bit
like a potato-masher—in general appearance. The whole
thing is about sixteen inches long. The business end is a
metal shell of thin stuff, about four inches long, filled with
T. N. T. A Mills grenade, landing directly on a pile of
them and exploding, might well set off the lot. A party
such as this German one turned out to be might, naturally
enough, place several grenades together while they rested—
unaware of any danger—in a shell-hole. A man well loaded
with them could, quite possibly, find some of them uncomfortable when he sat down or reclined against the side of a
shell-hole, because they are carried hooked to the belt, swinging about the hips like the tails of fur-bearing animals
affected by certain savages in their more formal dress. If
some were detached, placed together in a clear spot free
of wire and water, ready to be picked up again in the dark,
we have a mine all fixed. That is about the situation that
appeared as the story came out, between one and another
of the men, substantially as follows:

"Well, they sat down in a shell-hole right under our
noses for a pow-wow. We couldn't move; so we had to
bomb 'em out if we wanted to get back home by sunrise.
I don't know whether they were waiting for the rest of
the army, or just framing a yarn about running into enemy
patrols which prevented them from doing their dirty work."

"How did you come to let 'em hold a pow-wow under
the end of your nose?"

"That's what we were there for—to get information," the
wit of the party said. But Robinson was not to be out-
done: "I suppose you sent 'em an invitation to come out
and talk things over."

"Aw, we had been along inside their wire, inspected their
sentries and so on, and had come out and were waiting to

see what we could see when this troop of squareheads come
along. We were in a shell-hole right beside that long gully.
They got into this and come along a piece until they were
right off against us. Then they stopped and put their heads
together. We could see the potato-mashers hanging to
their belts. They didn't seem to know what it was all about.
They had come from towards our lines, up on the right,
and they couldn't make up their minds about something.
In a minute, the caretaker over the way woke up and sent
up a flare, and we could see they needed a shave. When
it burned out, they all got into a shell-hole, the one right
next to ours. We waited a while. It looked like there
was plenty of time. There were eight of 'em. We counted
'em when they were standing up. We had their range
exactly. We held our grenades until they were ready to
go off in our hands. Then we tossed them over and this mine
blew up and we went in and got their pistols. We never
would have found them if Heinie hadn't got busy and sent
up that bunch of flares. You needn't worry about any
wounded."

That, to my notion, is a fine way for a patrol to perform.

Before we go too far along with this patrolling, and get
too busy with the real fighting, I suppose I better tell you
about that flag business I was mixed up in; although there
was, really, not very much to it at the time. Anyhow,
I'll go back a bit with my story and tell how it happened.

Opposite our line (near the right end of our sector, and
just to the left of the Voormezeele Road) the Germans had
planted some sort of a flag. Its history dated back to the
early days of the war; seems like they had taken it from
someone else, who, in turn had stolen it from the other
fellow in the first place. It was a sort of mix-up, just
where the thing *did* originate, but the idea was—"Here
it is, come and get it if you can." It was a dark blue
affair with some sort of diamond-shaped device in the center,

and had already resulted in two or three bitter daytime
fights. From our Sniper's Barn position we could see it
very plainly, and I had often idly conjectured whether it
was worth going after.

One night, it was the ninth of November, 1915, I had
made up my mind to go over by myself and try to locate a
new machine-gun emplacement which we were sure Heinie
was building right opposite our right flank. From our observations, we were satisfied that he was building something
of the kind as we had seen men carrying timbers and other
material to that point. It was a dark, dismal, rainy night,
like the one when George Paudash stuck his head into the
dug-out and announced, "War's postponed, account of rain."

I was not drinking at that time, or, rather I had not been,
but I felt the need of a little "Dutch courage," so, to fortify
my nerves a little, I persuaded Sergeant Harvey to give
me a couple of good hookers of rum—now maybe it was
three—and then slipped over the parapet. It was only about
seventy yards across at this point to where I wanted to go.
Getting through our wire was easy enough, as we had
certain little alleyways left for that purpose, so I soon got
through there and then crawled along the side of an old
road where a shallow ditch gave quite a bit of concealment.
At one point in this ditch there was lying the body of a
soldier, and in trying to roll it out of the way, I twisted
off one of the feet—that extra shot of rum was very much
appreciated right then and there.

I crawled around that dead man after that and slowly
worked my way over to the German wire, but it took a
long time and much crawling up and down the wire before
I could find a gap through which I could wriggle. Finally
got through though and up to the parapet. Everything was
quiet; apparently the Germans were also satisfied to post-
pone the war until we had better weather. I finally managed to locate their new machine-gun emplacement and in

order to mark it clearly, used a page from the old *Arms and the Man,* our old shooting paper which later became *The American Rifleman.* They had been sending me this magazine right along and I had a copy folded up in my tunic. So after pinning this sheet of paper directly below the loophole where it would be in plain sight from our lines, I started to work my way back.

It was only then that I thought of that flag. It was about a hundred yards down the German trench from where I then was. "So long as I am inside their wire," I said to myself, "why not go get the damn thing and take it back?" Our Machine Gun Officer, Lieutenant White, and the Scout Officer had just discussed, in my presence, the matter of going over and getting that flag and whatever compunctions I may have had about spoiling their fun were effectively dispelled by the action of those slugs of rum. So in the end I decided it would be right and proper to slip down there and get it.

It was simply a matter of moving quietly and cautiously down the outside of the German embankment. There were a lot of tin cans and rubbish to be avoided but in a short time I came up to their flag; it was planted right in the midst of an area of what we called "trip wire;" that is, wire strung on stakes which were driven in almost to the ground, the wire (barbed, of course) sticking up about ankle high. Nasty stuff to get through all right. The flagstaff was firmly embedded in the ground and was further braced by several guy-wires which were anchored in the ground. I managed to unfasten these guy-wires and then pulled the staff out of the ground. Guess I must have overlooked something—some wire connected with an alarm in their trench, or possibly a "set" rifle or two. At any rate, a couple of rifle shots rang out and the bullets came uncomfortably close. I think one of them hit the stick on which the flag was fastened, and I had two pretty severe cuts in my hand which were suspiciously like bullet marks. Some one in the German trench sent up a flare and a machine gun chattered for a while, but I lay still, and, in a few minutes the excitement died down and I started for home. Up to that time I had not really noticed the rum which I had taken before starting out; but, about then, it began to get in its work. "Hell," says I to myself, "what's the use fooling around; why not just get up and walk back?" Which I proceeded to do. Believe it or not, as Ripley says, I walked back to our wire as casually as one would walk down the street today. Arriving at the wire, however, I found that I had missed the alley through which I had gone out, so proceeded to bawl out everybody in general for having locked me out. (That rum sure had authority). It was but a few moments until someone slipped over our parapet and showed me the way home. I think it was Lieutenant Bowerbank. I made a perfect ass of myself; I know that; but they were very lenient with me and I went down to where Lieutenant White had his dug-out and gave him the flag with the request that he turn it over to the Colonel. That is the whole story. They even gave me a medal for it later on.

The paper which I had affixed just below the port-hole of the machine gun emplacement enabled us to definitely locate it on the map, and, a few days later, our artillery put it out of business.

Next morning, when Fritz discovered that his flag was gone, he proceeded to give us a shelling. We then thought it severe as we had a few men killed and several wounded. A few months later, we would have called it a mild shelling.

That evening, as I was standing in the bay directly behind my dugout, with several others, including Sam Comigoe, they sent over a lot of rifle grenades. Did you ever hear one of those birds in flight? They make a noise just like a little dog that has received a swift kick. I cannot translate it into words, but if you have ever heard a little tyke, running down the street and yelping at every step—well, that's it. This applies, of course, only to the old form of grenade, with its ramrod tail. The later forms have entirely different voices. In daylight it was no trouble to dodge the yelpers; they announced themselves well in advance and were plainly visible, but at night you had to take your chances. By ill luck, one of them dropped right into our bay. Now, those devilish things shoot from the ground up; that is, they burst on impact and, as that is usually on the ground level, the splinters that do the damage are always ranging upward. Sam was at the right end of the bay and that was where the missile fell. Some of the others received inconsequential scratches on the legs (those wrap puttees are a great protection), but Sam was evidently hard hit. He grasped his belly—he was a big, fat fellow—and grunted: "guess they got me;" sat down on an ammunition box and died almost instantly. Just one of the small fragments had entered his abdomen and ranged upward to the heart. He and his brother and another pair of brothers, the Paudashes, in our Battalion, were of the Chippewa Tribe—full-blooded Indians—and among the best soldiers in the outfit. He was buried in our little cemetery at Ridgewood—right alongside Lieutenant Wilgress, the first of our officers to make the supreme sacrifice.

At the time I felt pretty badly about the matter. I knew that all this strafing was due to the flag-stealing, but then what would you? War is War. Many times I have been unmercifully cursed by the infantry for using a machine gun on a likely-looking target. "No; no," they would shout; "don't do that. They will retaliate." That was the word: "they will retaliate." Well; hells-bells; let 'em. What the devil are we here for? A summer picnic? While I do not think that I had a personal enemy in the battalion—in fact I was glad and proud to call them all my friends—

still, there is no getting around the fact they all, individually and collectively, did hate me at those times when I thought it worth while to hand Fritz a dose of poison. If I had been allowed my way, Heinie would have been kept "retaliating" along every foot of the Front.

To me it was a game; the greatest game in the world. Whenever they came back with their retaliation I was just as much pleased as a school-boy who has received the highest possible grade. It was proof positive that I had stung them. I well remember one night. Just before dark we had seen, from our Sniper's Barn position, a German battery pulling into position at a place called Hiele Farm—not more than eight hundred yards back of the enemy front line. They always kept a whiz-bang battery there and were, evidently, changing over; that is, a new battery was coming in to relieve the one that had been there for some time. We knew all about that battery—we machine gunners—and so did our artillery; but there seemed to be some sort of "gentleman's agreement" between the artillery on both sides; to leave one another alone and see how much fun they could have with the infantry. However, as Emma Gees, we were not bound by any such covenant.

So, when I saw that bunch moving in, I immediately got word to our reserve guns in the redoubts in the Bois Carré and gave them the target number. (We had every inch of "Germany" within range, plotted and all I had to do was to give them the number and when to commence firing.) I figured that, as soon as it commenced to get dark, all hands would be out in the open, carrying on with the work of getting the one lot of guns out and the others into the pits. Just after dusk, we opened on them with four guns. The orders were to fire a full belt and then, after letting the guns cool down a bit, to keep up an intermittent fire, all through the night.

Having attended to all this and remaining until the first

belt was started, I went down to the front line where we had other guns in good emplacements, for defensive purposes. I had a notion that we would stir up something and waited to see that the boys up there were ready for business. I made the rounds and explained matters to them and was standing at the left end of our line, where the last gun was located; talking to Major Jones when, all of a sudden; here came the shells. Now, Heinie was not much given to night shooting—in fact seldom did it unless as the preliminary to an attack—and when the shells commenced to come in, all hands were called to stand to.

They crowded into the bays, ready to hop up onto the firing step whenever the barrage lifted. The shells ripped the top of the parapet and burst all round. The Major and I were standing in an open space and some distance behind the parapet when a H. E. whiz-bang shell zipped between our heads—we were not more than two feet apart—and burst in a cook's dugout, which was, fortunately, unoccupied at the time. Oh—sure; we moved.

Of course I knew what it was all about and was very well pleased with myself and those accurate-shooting boys behind the guns; but the others; the infantry, knowing nothing about the strafing we had given those batteries, were in blissful ignorance. All they knew was that, when the enemy put on a show like that at night, it usually meant *business.* So far as I could learn, we did not have a man hurt that night and I always figured that it was well worth while. We surely did some damage to the Germans and the matter of being called to the alert was good training for our troops.

Thus the early winter months passed. I was sniping most of the time but made the rounds of the guns every day, just to see how things were going. There was the usual shelling and we were losing men every day from that and the various forms of trench-mortar projectiles and rifle grenades. Rifle and machine gun fire accounted for a man now and then, especially among the signallers who had to go out and repair breaks in the line. Our situation in the salient was such that it was possible for long range bullets to get us in flank, and even from the rear, and more than one man was hit in that manner.

In constructing our trenches we had to take into account this enfilading fire and build overhead traverses at frequent intervals. These were planned on the theoretical trajectory of the German bullets at the ranges from which we might expect to be fired upon. They did not take into consideration the fact that a bullet might come from some two miles away—which they occasionally did. I was standing right under one of these arch-like traverses, talking with Corporal Johnson, one day, apparently in just about the safest position one could find, when a bullet struck him in the cheek and went on through his neck. It must have scraped the juglar vein (or the carotid artery), but he soon recovered. The enemy had the same kind of protective traverses and I often wished that I had some low velocity, short-range ammunition—something like our guard cartridges or the reduced loads used for gallery firing—so I could drop a few shots down into his trench. In fact, I made an effort to have our armourer load up some of that kind of stuff but never got any action on it. I also made the suggestion that we be given a few shotguns—sawed-off—and buckshot loads, but the proposal was rejected with horror by the British higher-ups. It was not sporting, or something to that effect. Can you imagine that—against an enemy who had violated all the rules of civilized warfare, both on land and sea?

I was not made a sergeant until along about Christmas-time, but, for some reason or another, was allowed all the latitude I wanted—to go where I pleased and do as I liked. All I particularly wanted to do at that time was to stay on top long enough to clean up on about a hundred Germans.

The only time I was away from the line, (that is, outside the zone of active shelling), was on November 25, 1915, when I took a flying trip to Bailleul, to visit Charlie Wendt's grave and then I left just before daybreak and was back in the front line soon after dark the same day. While in Bailleul I had the first meal I had eaten in a house for several months. At the Hotel Faucon, I had a good dinner, and, happening to remember that it was the last Thursday in November, and therefore Thanksgiving-day at home, I made the best of it by persuading the Chef (bribed with a bottle of their best wine) to procure and cook for me the best *poulet* available in the market. Turkey was out of the question but I made that old hen serve as a substitute— and not at all bad, at that. A couple of boys from the Fifth Battalion came along just then and helped me out with it—otherwise I might not have been able to get "home" that night.

Mud: *mud:* MUD. That is the one thing, above all others, that I shall remember always--the memory of that mud in Flanders. We wallowed in it in daytime and slept in it at night. There was one period of forty-two days during which I never had my clothes off. I could have done so on one of the irregular occasions when the outfit was permitted to go back to billets, but it came at a time when I was more interested in sniping than a bath, so I chose to remain up there where I could keep up on my rifle practice.

Chapter 8

Trench Raiding

PATROLS were a natural prelude to trench raiding. They provided much of the necessary information, and they afforded the best sort of training for this work. Combat patrols, in fact, were, essentially, raiding parties which confined their activities to no-man's-land. It only remained to scale the parapet, raise hell, take a couple of prisoners and come back. I do not intend to be drawn into any argument regarding this subject. Perhaps I am wrong, but, from the best information at hand, I think that the systematic raiding of the enemy trenches was first conceived and carried out by Canadian troops at Ploegsteert. My recollection is that it was members of the Fifth Battalion, of the First Canadian Division, who pulled off the first 'show'. These affairs were always referred to as "shows".

The technique is quite simple. Just wait until the enemy is quiet, slip over, bomb 'em a little, hop into their trench, grab off a few prisoners and any machine guns you happen to see and beat it back home. Sounds easy enough and, strange to say, it is easy—provided no unexpected thing happens to disrupt the scheduled performance.

Many raids were made just as easy as I am now writing about them. The sheer audacity of the thing was what carried them through. The slow, methodical Teutonic mind could not at once grasp the idea that some dozen or so of men would ever dare to invade the sacred precincts of their

123

trenches. As one result of which, we had considerable numbers of very efficient workers on our roads, behind the lines.

During the time, from 1915, when the first stunt of this kind was demonstrated, up to early in 1917, when the writer left the front, these raids grew from merely small, local (I almost said *personal*) affairs, to operations of such magnitude that, at the latter date, whole brigades were taking part in them.

Now, that is literally true. The first enterprise of this character, in my experience, was my little solo affair, related in the last chapter, which netted no prisoners nor information, but a flag; and the last was when the entire Fourth Brigade staged a show opposite Bully-Grenay and brought back 101 German prisoners. The first episode was in November, 1915, and the last January 17, 1917.

The purpose of these raids is, ostensibly, to secure information—that is, to grab off a few prisoners, so as to know just what troops are opposite that particular position. As a matter of fact, from our view-point, it was to "put the fear of God" into those poor sons of something or other and make them behave.

During our initial experiments in this line we had varied luck. I remember the first time our outfit made an attempt to go over and get a prisoner. I had no share in it other than to mount a machine gun up on top of the parapet and maintain a continuous fire along the top of the enemy parapet (which was less than one hundred yards away) just to make them keep their heads down until our raiding party got through their wire. That one was not much of a success. Our party never succeeded in getting through the German wire. They did get close enough to throw a few bombs into the enemy trenches and fondly hoped that they had done some damage. Anyway, they came back—all of them—mad as hornets and resolved that the next time they would do better.

And they did. The next venture was away down at the other end of our line, where the opposing trenches were nearly two hundred yards apart. As previously, I am simply an observer, operating a machine gun from the top of the parapet and sort of acting as protection for the raiding party by running a burst here and there along the top of the enemy parapet. As I had been over to the enemy parapet several times previously, in search of machine gun emplacements and sniper holes, I had been able to assist a little in the preliminary work but the officer in charge of the raiding party, Lieutenant Miller, a cool and resourceful officer, had taken the precaution to send out parties several nights in advance to cut paths through the German wire. This show was well staged and undoubtedly the enemy suffered severe damage. Our party did not bring back any live prisoners, as they were forced to retire because of the unexpected arrival of large numbers of German reinforcements; but every man of our contingent came back, a few slightly wounded, but nothing serious, while it was evident that, with their well-placed bombs, they had inflicted considerable damage to the enemy.

The next time was still better—in fact, a complete success. After a carefully planned scheme of operations, we staged what might be called a twin bill. Two parties went out, one merely as a feint and the other the real raiding party. The first one followed the same tactics as the two previous ones; that is, the machine guns swept the enemy parapet and the raiders made their way through the previously cut wire and proceeded to heave bombs into the enemy trench. This resulted in quite a little battle between the bombers on both sides and, as we had hoped and expected, in bringing all the German reserves down to the point of attack. But, in the meantime, our real raiding party, of whom I was fortunate enough to be a member (although I was supposed to be back there directing the machine guns) had quietly slipped through and were ready to hop over. When we were satisfied from the sounds that the time was ripe, this party rushed up and over the parapet and dropped down upon the few and unsuspecting sentries and very quickly escorted them back over the top and to our own lines. There were some very good, hand-to-hand fights and one German had to be shot before he would give up. The others, taken altogether by surprise, offered no resistance. Our party got home with several live prisoners and with no serious casualties. The other crowd, who had staged the feint, had several slightly wounded from bomb splinters but none killed. A pretty good night's work, we thought.

The success or failure of any trench raid depends to a great extent upon the thoroughness of the preparation for it. To be sure, the officer in command of the venture must be competent, but really most of his work will be in planning the operation, instructing his men and supervising the preliminary preparation. When it comes to the actual invasion of the enemy lines, he is just one man and can do no more, individually, than any other.

The first requisite is to be thoroughly familiar with all the physical characteristics of the section of line to be invaded. This information must be compiled from reports of observers and snipers, from airplane maps and, finally, by the work of patrols, which establish first-hand practical knowledge of conditions as they will be encountered—in the dark—even to visiting the enemy parapet and making a study of the actual battlefield.

Next comes the selection of the men—and that is the hardest part of all. These *shows* are usually taken over in turn by all the young and enterprising subalterns in the outfit and each will have to make his own selection from the available men at his command. He would hate to go outside his own platoon for help as these things are matters of pride to all the members of whatever unit is engaged. If he has plenty of seasoned soldiers his task will be easy but if, as is often the case, he is overstocked with new replacements, he will have to do a lot of guessing—and trust the Lord. One false move, on the part of a single man, may ruin the whole enterprise.

Having selected his objective and organized his party, he gets them together and goes over the whole program with them, sketching the lay-out of the enemy line and the ground to be covered in reaching that point. For the usual, small, raid, for the purpose of bringing in a prisoner, he may have anywhere from twelve to sixteen men, or sometimes as few as eight, depending on local conditions.

Each will be assigned to certain specific duties which will be explained later. When practicable, especially if he has a number of new men, he will personally take them out in front on little scouting and patrolling expeditions for several nights so as to accustom them to the difficult task of moving about in the open without being detected. During this process, he will probably have to weed out some and replace them with others who are better fitted for this kind of work.

All that now remains is to await favorable weather. The best of all conditions is a cold, driving rain. However, he may have to make the attempt regardless of weather, especially if his tour of duty is drawing to a close and he is under instructions to do the job before leaving the lines. In any case, the date is set and he gets his gang together about dark for final instructions and inspection. He carefully goes over the uniform and equipment of each man. No bit of metal must show that would give out a flash of light under the glare of a star shell. Faces and hands are to be blackened or rubbed with mud. (At one time we were issued masks for this work). Supposing he has twelve men, two of them have been selected as wire cutters and they go out about an hour ahead of the others to cut a lane through the enemy wire at the designated spot, and to remain there throughout the whole maneuver to direct the others when they return. Sometimes they will hang a strip of white tape along the side of a lane, but this is seldom done excepting in the case of large raids.

The remaining ten men have been divided into two groups of three each and one of four. All hands are armed with hand grenades, bayonets and, when available, with pistols. Each group has a designated leader—N. C. O. or private.

Someone suddenly discovers that there are thirteen in the party, and the Lieutenant, with a sigh of resignation, turns to the nearest soldier in the trench and directs him to accompany them to the outside of our wire and to remain there until the party returns. This important matter attended to, he looks at his watch and decides that the wire cutters have had time to do their work, then leads the group over the parapet and out through the previously prepared lanes in our own wire.

The officer leading, they move slowly across the narrow bit of no-man's-land which lies between the opposing strips of barbed-wire entanglements. A star-shell (Very light) goes up and all hands stop and remain like statues until the light dies. A sudden sound, off to the left, and again they stop; then obeying the signal of the leader, drop quietly to the ground. The lieutenant thinks fast, "what was it?" Ah! another flare is fired, away up the line and against the lighted background he can see the figures of several men— Germans of course—a patrol. "Now the question is, which way are they going? If they come this way, they are liable to run into us. Also, they are pretty apt to see the gap in their wire. Well, all we can do is lie doggo and find out. If they want a scrap, we can surely lick them but would probably lose a man or two and we don't want that tonight."

After an interval which must have seemed ages to the new men, but which was probably not more than two or three minutes, sounds were heard indicating the approach of the patrol. The officer quietly drew his pistol and all the others held grenades, ready to pull the pins and throw when ordered. Slowly and cautiously the enemy party approached, their movements only betrayed by an occasional rasping sound, as one encountered a bit of old wire or other debris, or the suck of a boot being pulled out of the mud. Lord, will they never get here? The suspense of awaiting such an encounter soon wears men's nerves to a frazzle—even old heads at the game, too. One's heart pounds away so loudly that it seems that they will surely hear it.

This contingency had been anticipated and every man knew just what to do. Time after time, in a secluded spot behind their own parapet, they had gone over every movement. Signals were passed by a mere touch of the hand or a wiggle of the foot and anxiously they awaited some sign from the leader.

The whispering noises came nearer and nearer. "Are they going to bump right into us, or will they pass?" The matter was soon settled (even if it *did* seem like hours). The sounds gradually diminished and were now coming from the right. They had passed, probably within fifteen feet and gone on their way—which, as we knew from former observation, would take them to a point a safe distance further along the line.

After a short wait, the raiding party agáin moved forward and soon came to the point where the wire cutters had been instructed to go through. At first the officer thought that there had been a mistake and his heart sank; but he was quickly reassured by the whispered voice of Collins, one of the wire cutters. "We heard that patrol, so we only cut the lower wires on the outside, so we could crawl under," he said. "Everything is clear inside". "Good head", complimented the officer. "Now you can cut the rest so as to give us a clear getaway. You and Jackson keep your ears open. That damn patrol *may* come back before we are ready for it". With which he proceeded along through the narrow lane and soon encountered Jackson, at the inside edge of the barrier and within a few feet of the foot of the parapet.

With no other greeting than a squeeze of the hand, he quietly slipped through and directed the others as they followed. The groups of three moved off, one to the right and the other to the left. They would each proceed a distance of about fifty yards, then wait a full minute, as nearly as the leaders could estimate it by counting, then each man would hurl a grenade over and during the noise and confusion of the bursts they would move in toward the center, stopping at a point about twenty yards from the actual point of attack—which was exactly opposite the gap in the wire. The group of four, accompanied by the officer, inched their way up the sloping side of the parapet, disposed as follows: the officer in the center, with an old-time sergeant on his right and another old timer on his left. The flanks were occupied by two experienced soldiers whose duty it was to each have a grenade ready, with the pin out, and at the first explosion of a bomb from either of the outside parties they would throw *their* grenade so as to drop into the bays next to the right and left of the one selected for the attack.

The officer and the two old soldiers with him would be the only ones to actually go over into the trench—unless they met with unexpected resistance. In that case, the other two would follow, while the flanking groups smothered the trench on both sides with bombs.

"KER-OOMP" went the first grenade and, before the flash had faded, the raiders were over. The two soldiers immediately jumped to the ends of the bay and threw their grenades around the corners of the traverses. The officer, in the center, had expected to land right on top of a German but, lo and behold, the bay was unoccupied so he ran after the sergeant, who had entered the next bay and was feeling around for what he might find. Numerous flares were now being sent up, and by their light the officer discovered the entrance to a dugout. Telling the sergeant to protect his flank, he jerked away the burlap curtain and called for whoever was inside to come out or he would blow them out. Whether or not the occupants understood the words, they certainly got the intent, for three men came scrambling up the steps in a hurry.

"I got 'em", he shouted. "Come on boys, let's get to hell out of here", at the same time herding the prisoners into the next bay and driving them over the parapet where they were received by Jackson and the other two men and started, at a rapid pace, toward our lines. The sergeant and the other man were right at his heels and they amused themselves by hurling grenades to the right and left, inside the German trench, until the flanking groups arrived.

The officer checked them up, found all present and started them for home, while he brought up the rear. No attempt was made at concealment. Less than three minutes had elapsed since the explosion of the first bomb and the enemy had not had time to figure out what was going on. A few scattered grenades were coming over his parapet and a machine gun began to stutter but it was just blind firing and no one was hurt.

That was a remarkable performance—getting three unharmed prisoners with no loss beyond a few minor scratches which two of our men received from small fragments of the potato-masher grenades. It was not always that way. Usually there was more or less hand to hand scrapping before we got away with a prisoner and, all too frequently, we went home empty handed. But that was the method of procedure, as practiced by our crowd, and whenever it was carefully followed success was almost assured and casualties negligible. In fact, the possibility of casualties was about

the last consideration. The men hardly gave it a thought.
Their principal concern was how to inflict the most damage—and the most amusing and daring damage—in the
limited time.

This raiding was a fine incentive to inventive genius, and
there were always a few in each platoon who were busy
devising neat methods of handing out "misery" to the Dutchman. This work was sometimes inspired simply by a desire
to repay Heinie for what we had suffered from such nui-
sances as *minnenwerfers* and pineapples—to repay him with
interest, to give him something bigger and better, as the
movie directors would say. But this was only an occasional
motive; I think the real and lasting motive was a genuine
interest in the game and a desire to score as often as possible, rather than wait about in the mud for something to
happen. Once the inventive and ingenious ones had a taste
of what might be done in this matter of trench-raiding, warfare developed a new and personal interest. They came to
view all the resources and implements of war with an eye
mainly to their use in raids; and trench-mortar pits,
engineers' dumps and supply depots of all sorts yielded surprising treasurers. Dud shells were eyed with regret that
all that "dynamite" and steel was going to waste, with no
way to fix the thing with a short fuse to explode it in the
depths of a German dugout. The Stokes gun did yield
something along this line, though it was not a dud, but a
live shell taken from an ammunition dump. I never knew
just how they fixed it so that it could be lugged across no-
man's-land and trusted to explode when it had reached the
bottom of a dugout. As I remember, it was a Yankee (there
were many of them in the Canadian Corps) who received
credit for adapting the first one. And I don't know how
often they were used; but any man who intimated that he
could fix one was told to do his stuff at once, and there was
always a ready volunteer to steal or borrow a shell from the

nearest Stokes gun crew. If the officer in charge of the
next raid was a good scout he was in on the business and
welcomed the contribution; if not, it was a simple matter
to manage it secretly, content in the knowledge that the
results would approve the method.

As a matter of fact, there could be no sound objection;
but close cooperation was the watchword in these raids, and
individual exploits might easily cause failure or disaster.
Within the limitations of the tactical necessities, however, individual initiative and daring was valuable, and the ideal
raiding party was the one that utilized them to the full,
drawing upon the entire platoon or company for ideas and
devices. Thus everybody became a participant in the raid,
and the chosen dozen men were charged with carrying out—
in twenty or thirty minutes of action—the work of the entire
platoon or company; and even the man who never went over,
but who, on the way into the trenches, espied an odd case
of dynamite about an engineers' dump and made a stick or
two of it available, was as much interested in the raid as
the man who took it over. Or, back on a ration party at
night, he might encounter a detachment of engineers and
remember that raid scheduled to come off to-morrow night:
"Say, Jack; got a dump about here? How about a 'buckshee' stick of dynamite?"

Buckshee is one of those useful words such as come into
use in any army. The British Army had many of them,
drawn from all quarters of the globe, and so readily borrowed and adapted that only a trace—and sometimes none
at all—of original meaning survived. This one had come
home with troops who had served in India, where it was
spelled, I believe, *backsheek*. With us it meant, something
that could be spared, or which could be used in a manner
not foreseen by the issuing authorities, or something left
over after the regular distribution was made, or an odd
article that came in too small quantities to be issued and

thus, not being expected, found its way, ordinarily into the haversacks of the quartermaster's staff.

As a rule, the engineer was willing to contribute. He might have to be content with intimating where the stuff could be picked up; but if he was not under direct supervision at the moment, he might make it his business to see what could be found in the way of fuses, detonaters, etc., even to locating some of the match-fuses, such as were used early in the war in the manufacture of grenades from jam-tins. Such helpfulness might result in the acquisition of a veritable store of munitions, which was quietly put aside until a raid was ordered. When the men were selected and it was learned how they were to be officially armed, it only remained to pick a couple of men who could be trusted to do the work properly and load them with as much stuff as they could carry *unofficially*. A Stokes shell per man was enough, or two sticks of dynamite suitably lashed and capped.

If you think these were harmless pranks, you have only to imagine yourself in an underground chamber six feet or so wide, at the bottom of a narrow twelve-foot flight of steps. Now sit quiet while a Stokes shell goes off in your midst. The more I think about it, the more thoroughly convinced I am that trench-raiding was a vital and important part of trench-warfare. I know that it worked out with very satisfying results on our side. It provides the best sort of training in the important matter of working together, seizing the moment when it arrives, doing not only all that was expected of you, but all that you would like to expect of yourself, and yet being able to retire neatly and in order with the party, conscious of a job well done.

As the war went on, the idea finally percolated into Heinie's head that this trench raiding stuff might be all right, after all. With characteristic German thoroughness, he had to try it out, this way and that. While I am not and never was in the confidence of the German Higher Command, I feel quite sure that I can interpret their deductions. They found out, right at the start, that they had no chance whatever of slipping over and surprising us. Our scouting system and our sentries were too good for that. So they conceived the idea that they would isolate a certain area by a box-barrage and then send over an overwhelming force against the holders of the isolated bit of trench. They tried it on us several times but without success, as we guessed their intention quickly enough to take effective preventive measures. After a month or two of observation, it is nearly always possible to figure out just about what is meant by any artillery demonstration. Our raids were, generally, carried out without any artillery preparation. Stealth and quietness were the main requisites for success. Grenades and firearms were habitually carried but used only when the necessity for stealth had passed. The bayonet, well sharpened and carried in the hand—not on the rifle—was the most effective weapon. I have seen, somewhere, the statement that it was contrary to the recognized rules of war to sharpen the bayonet. Well, now, that is just too bad. The last thing we did before leaving England was to take all our bayonets to the armourer and have them ground to a keen edge and, afterward, there were always files available to keep them in that condition. Personally, if I have to be stabbed with a bayonet, I think I should prefer it to be a sharp, rather than a blunt one, but, of course, other people may have different ideas about it.

Whether they were not properly instructed by the French or due to the well-known cock-sureness and conceit of the American soldier, when the first United States troops went into the line, at Bathlemont, November 3, 1917, they were caught in this old box-barrage game and lost quite a bunch of prisoners, several wounded and three killed—Gresham, Hay and Enright, of the 16th U. S., (regular) Infantry. Eager but over-confident, they allowed themselves to be caught in a trap that would never have bothered older, seasoned troops. No intelligent enemy is going to waste several thousand perfectly good shells. When any kind of bombardment starts, it means something and it is incumbent on whoever is in charge to be able to read the signs and interpret the message. After a month or two, one gets to recognize the symptoms and can nearly always figure out what is contemplated and take whatever precautions are possible to frustrate the attempted raid.

In the Canadian Corps we generally did one of two things when a bombardment started which indicated a raid would be made on that particular section of the trenches. If possible, we promptly pulled out of the first lines and drew back into the supporting trenches and got in readiness to blow hell out of that raiding party as soon as they came over and into our abandoned trenches. Sometimes we drew off into the adjoining trenches to the sides and from there helped to hand it back as soon as the German barrage lifted and their raiding party came over our parapet. There isn't much doubt but what any individuals caught in such a barrage and forced to remain in dugouts until the raiding party gets into their trench are strictly S O L. The thing to do is to be somewhere else and up on your feet, ready to hand things back as soon as the barrage lifts and they come over.

There were times when those caught in such a box barrage went right on out in the open no-man's-land in front of their parapet, and met the raiding party before they really got started and broke up their game then and there. It all depended upon conditions and circumstances, but experienced troops soon learned not to be right where Heinie expected them to be—which always busted up the Dutchman's plan badly.

There was one rather startling, but also amusing, feature in the big raid of January, 1917. Our men had been trained for a week or more—working on dummy trenches which

were constructed behind our lines, exact replicas of the
enemy trenches which were to be raided. During the early
hours of the night, the wire cutting details had gone over
and opened lanes through the enemy defenses, and just before dawn the raiding party, which comprised a full battalion, slipped over. Everything went like clock-work, but,
where they had expected to encounter only the usual thin
line of men in the enemy front line trench, they piled in
right on top of several hundred Germans who were just
being brought up for a raid on *our* trench, which was
scheduled for exactly fifteen minutes later. That's how we
got the 101 prisoners. Ordinarily the bag would not have
been more than fifteen or twenty. Taken utterly by surprise,
the enemy lost heavily but our total casualties were some
six or seven wounded.

It got so that it was considered a point of honor for each
battalion to put on a show and get a prisoner or two during
every tour of duty in the front line. Usually these were
small affairs—perhaps a platoon doing the work—and many
a young subaltern earned his Military Cross by leading such
a venture.

This is what made trench warfare really war—in between
the bigger scraps. I could better appreciate the worth of
it during my last few weeks, when I was back a bit with
my special duties, and could sort of look on things from the
outside. I recall another incident in this same sector that
happened just before the big raid which netted the 101
prisoners for the Fourth Brigade. This sector was just to
the left of that front and the raid was a small one, such as
I have described elsewhere and, though every raid was different and had interesting features of its own, I don't suppose I should go on relating them indefinitely just because
they happened to interest me. So I will only mention this
one to record the appearance of another gadget of Heinie's.
This was a small pencil-flashlight to be attached to the rifle

barrel, evidently designed to enable Fritz to get his man in the dark. He tried it on one of our raiding party, but like many innovations, had not gotten thoroughly acquainted with it and was too slow with the trigger. Our man simply sat down in the bottom of the trench, and from that position used his Colt—and brought back the flashlighted rifle to show us.

There was not much the German could do to protect himself against our raids. We got the upper hand and kept it. In war, as in most other things, nothing succeeds like success. Our fellows were confident while the Germans just got into the habit of expecting to be taken, which made taking them a comparatively easy matter.

And it didn't get Heinie anything when he attempted to take the offensive in the matter. Along with his box-barrage affairs he tried some of our methods, amongst which was that one of silent raids, where no advance shooting is indulged in, but the raiding party merely crawls over stealthily until against the parapet, heaves over his grenades and then tries to follow up in the confusion; bombing the dugouts and grabbing off what sentries and men he can. I never knew anyone to fall a victim to these raids; but one of them took place with the battalion I was working with just before leaving the front. There then happened a most interesting occurrence, so I suppose you will have to suffer the old man's wandering about on a new topic until I tell all about this incident.

This German raiding party comprised but eight Heinies and they got almost through our wire before being discovered by the sentry. That is the main defense against trench raids of this sort, just have sentries which keep awake and on their feet, doing what they should be doing—watching. This sentry immediately spread the alarm. Other sentries looked about sharp and promptly vacated the bays where the potato-mashers started falling. Some of them mounted the parapet just as soon as the Germans got into the trench, and went running along toward what seemed to be the center of the excitement. This center was a deep dugout, the exact position of which the Germans probably knew quite well, since it had been built some months before.

The men in that main dugout heard the alarm and were already on their way out by the time those Germans got into that bay. It happened that the company sergeant-major (first sergeant) was in that dugout at the time, having come up to see the platoon sergeant about something, and he was the first man out and into the main trench, where he ran head-on into three Heinies coming along pulling the strings and heaving their potato-mashers.

Now, often since the war, I have been with folks who were examining one of those Very pistols and invariably somebody in the crowd commences to wonder what the result would be if you shot a man with one of those hand cannons. Well, I can tell them, because I saw a German who was shot with one and it happened during this very incident I am now describing. The sergeant-major had a Very pistol stuck in his belt when the alarm was sounded, so he drew it as he came out of the dugout and promptly shot the first Heinie in the face with it at a range of about three feet. The slug, or canister, or whatever *is* in one of those shells, caught this first man in the temple, knocked him off his feet, and then from the bottom of the trench provided a fine light which made good shooting for the men up on top the parapet. They promptly shot down both the other two Germans, killing one and wounding the other. The remaining five of the raiding party never got out of the bay they landed in, three being killed there and the other two captured. That Dutchman who caught the Very shell had the entire side of his head taken off.

And such was about the usual outcome of the affair when Heinie tried to emulate our tactics in this trench raiding business. The best defense against such small raids is to keep alert, give the alarm promptly and then everyone get out of the dugouts and front trench and go for the raiders. The open is really the safest place of any, because the enemy will not be able to shoot up the exact spot being raided for fear of killing his own men. So much for defense against such trench raids.

Chapter 9

Sighting Shots

T HAT winter of 1915-1916 was a wet one. It rained almost every day and seldom got cold enough to freeze, although the nights were always cool enough to cause keen discomfort. We had thin ice a few times and a couple of light snowstorms. The water and liquid mud in our trenches was anywhere from ankle deep to waist deep. We lived like muskrats. Looking at it from this range, I don't see how any human beings could have survived it, but the amazing fact is that we not only did survive but that there was very little illness of any character and, so far as my personal knowledge goes, not a single case of either rheumatism or pneumonia.

How did the others take it? Well, I suppose about the same as I did. They were intensely patriotic: those Canadians. Much more so than the average man I found in the United States Army later on. The Americans did not seem to have the feeling that they were fighting, literally, for the homeland. It was more of a gesture of recognition of the assistance given us in the Revolutionary War by the French, and, with the volunteer soldiers, was taken more as a lark and in the spirit of adventure than as a patriotic duty. But WE, the Canadians (I emphasize that *we,* because, as long as I was in the Canadian service, I was, heart and soul, a Canadian, myself) realized that it was for Britain we were fighting—the Motherland. We took the

141

game seriously, realizing, generally, that mud was a part of it, and not chargeable to red tape or the Brass Hats, who had done about the best they could by providing suitable clothing. Further, we felt that they were actually concerned as to our welfare.

All this time, we were learning more about war and were rapidly becoming what might be called "real soldiers". You know, it takes a long time to learn that game. Of course, a great many of those best qualified, physically and mentally, never do learn it. As things go in modern warfare, many a man is killed before he ever gets within miles of the enemy. What with shells ranging over all the country for ten miles or so behind the lines, especially on the roads, a lot of them never get into it at all—just like the ambulance and transport drivers and the artillery and some of the staff officers. They get bumped off and, I suppose they are entitled to all the honor we can render them, but it does seem a pity that they never even had a chance to see what it is all about. That is something that can only be learned at the front. Now, I know, a lot of mighty good men and good soldiers will rear up on their hind legs and take exception to that remark. They, as well as the artillery, will claim that *they* were "at the front". Well; all I got to say is, "there is only one actual *front* in war and that is when there is not another damn man between you and the enemy." The F. O. Os (forward observing officers) of the artillery and their accompanying signallers see it from time to time and it has been recorded that some staff officers have, during quiet times, made the rounds of the front lines but, for the most part, their duties keep them farther back. Right here, I want to mention one staff officer who appeared to take delight in coming up and he is no other than H. R. H. The Prince of Wales—or Captain Windsor, as he was then known. That boy sure wanted to see it all.

Now, this will probably sound like a fool statement but

I am willing to abide the consequences. "No soldier is really fit to go into a battle until after he has been through one." Figure it out for yourself.

During peace times soldiers can be trained *for war*. To the layman and, even the inexperienced soldier himself, this may be considered all that is necessary to fit him for *battle*. But, I hope to show you, such is not the case at all. The training for war; which is the training which all soldiers receive, is to instruct them in personal hygiene, (so that they may keep in good physical condition) ; close and open order drills; the use of and care for the weapons with which they are armed, and *discipline*, which, in its broadest sense, covers all the other requirements.

All these things they can learn in any training camp. But the experience necessary to make them fit for *battle* is of a much more serious nature. As can readily be realized, this can come only in battle itself. It is out of the question to take men through a barrage of artillery and machine gun fire (which is sure to kill and wound some of them) in any instruction camp. The writer, fresh from nearly two years of actual combat and while in command of a Battalion of Machine Gunners of the Thirty-eighth Division, at Camp Shelby, Mississippi, suggested this thing to the General in command of the Division, in 1917, and was, thereafter called crazy. "Well," says I "a lot of them are due to get theirs anyway, the minute they get into action, so why not let the rest learn something about the game before they get in so deep that the stretcher-bearers won't find them for two or three days."

But as I said, the idea was promptly vetoed, so all I could do was to try and tell the thousand or so men under me that they could expect such and so and let it go at that.

The training for battle might be called a post graduate course and no man can claim a diploma in this course until he has actually participated, as a combatant, in at least one

major engagement. Nothing that can be written or spoken—
no words—can express or bring a realization of the actual
experience. The usual training for war is but the foundation—the real game must be learned by playing it.

A man may know all the text-books by heart and be able
to repeat them forward and backward, may be an expert
rifleman and all that, but it is only in actual combat that
he can really *find* himself. In the old days, when men
marched into battle shoulder to shoulder and won or lost
by virtue of mass formations, this was not so essential, but
in this Year of our Lord, after the show starts, it is pretty
much an individual and personal matter, with each soldier
working out his own salvation as best he can, for the good
of the cause and the preservation of his own hide.

The rifleman finds a very different state of affairs than
that to which he was accustomed on the range. Tramping,
creeping or crawling over the hellish desolation which is a
modern battlefield, amid the crash of bursting shells and the
wild screams of the ricochetting fragments, the crack and
whistle of bullets, amid smoke and dust—yes, it is different.
Here he must learn to take advantage of all available cover
while, at the same time, keeping up with the advance; he
must learn to seek out individual targets and deliberately fire
at them and not just shoot in the general direction of the
enemy. The machine guns and automatic rifles will be doing
plenty of that. If the rifleman is to be retained, at all, in
the composition of the armies of the future, it will be only
by virtue of the fact that he can and will, conscientiously
and ably deliver an accurate and *effective* fire upon single,
individual targets.

It is too much to expect that any human being, when first
exposed to such an ordeal, can properly control himself and
settle down to anything approaching clear-headed, logical
thinking. When a man has to crawl over the top of a parapet where the bullets are ripping the tops of the sandbags

and the whiz-bang shells are zipping past his head and
bursting all around, he is apt to forget a lot of things he
learned in the training camp. His only thought is that he is
bound to get his the minute he sticks his head over the top.
After a few such performances, if he survives, he knows
quite well that there is quite a lot of space between the
bullets and shells and he has at least an even chance to miss
them.

When that time comes, he is eligible to the designation of
a "trained" soldier—a Veteran. (It is my humble contention that no soldier deserves the honorable title of Veteran
unless he has, personally, gone through at least one real
fight as an actual combatant.)

The day before Christmas 1915, just after noon, I was
lounging in our gun position at S-P-7 (Strong Point No.
7). It was one of the redoubts of our support line. Only
about four hundred yards behind our front line and less
than five hundred from the enemy line, it was established
on a small eminence under cover of the trees at the edge of
the Bois Carré. From there, screened by the overhanging
branches of the trees, I could see, not only a large portion
of our own line, but a lot of the enemy territory. Directly
in front of my position was a road which ran from Ypres to
Wyschaette. At the point where this road crossed our front
line, we had a machine gun station which now—we being in
support—was occupied by the Twentieth Battalion M. G.
Section. To my right front was a field of chicory, through
which one of our communication trenches ran. In this
field, about one hundred yards behind our line, one of our
trench-mortar batteries had just completed a pit in which
they had established one of their mortars. Evidently the
enemy had located this emplacement, for they were now engaged in dropping howitzer shells of about five-inch calibre
all around it and I was idly watching and wondering when
they would make a direct hit. There were no men there as

they only used the weapon at night.   Now, the path of these shells took them right over the machine gun emplacement in the front line and the gun crew there were just having their noon meal when one of the shells fell short and dropped among them, killing and wounding several when it burst.

One of the wounded was in such a serious state that it was imperative that he be taken back to a dressing station at once if his life were to be saved.   Chicory trench was impassable, being nearly filled with mud.   An officer called for volunteers to carry the wounded man out, down the road, which would expose them to the plain view of the enemy. We had had several men killed on that road and knew that there was a good sniper hidden in the woods over yonder but the officer reasoned that, as it was Christmas eve, it was hardly likely that any person would fire upon unarmed stretcher-bearers.   But he reckoned without understanding the cold-blooded and utterly inhuman instincts of that German.   When they came down the road, two men carrying the stretcher and the officer accompanying them (he would not ask men to take a chance he was not willing to share with them), I watched them carefully, dreading the very thing that actually happened.   They had no sooner entered the exposed stretch of road when a bullet struck one of the bearers and, before the others could take cover, the second one was down.   A third shot struck the officer, who was trying to assist the wounded man.

From my position, I could see each bullet strike in the water alongside the road and thus get a very accurate line on the position of the sniper.   From the sharp angle of fall— the bullets striking within fifty feet of the men, after passing through their bodies, it was a certainty that the sniper was up in one of the trees just behind the enemy front line.   I had been trying for a month, to locate that fellow, and, by tracing back the line from the strike of some of his bullets, had him spotted within a very limited area.   Now I was sure of it. A certain thickly limbed tree, the top of which had been severed by a shell and, in falling, had lodged in such a manner as to form a dense mass of tangled branches some twenty-five or thirty feet up. That was the place, without a doubt.

Now this S-P-7 redoubt was a secret place. Concealed, as it was, by the trees, it had never been discovered by the enemy—or, at least, we had reason to think so, as it had never been shelled. In addition to the machine-gun crew, a platoon of infantry and a signallers' station were located there, all comfortably housed in real dugouts in the reverse side of the hill. Very strict orders had been issued that there was to be no firing whatever from that position excepting in case of an attack. Of course I knew all about that—but that wasn't the first time I had disobeyed orders, nor the last, for that matter.

Without hesitation, I swung the gun around and commenced to pepper that tree-top, at the same time sending one of my men to call our battery (the 16th) to get busy. Down at the front line, the Emma Gees of the Twentieth seemed to get the idea, for they promptly opened up with all their guns and when, within a very few minutes, the artillery joined in, well, it sounded like a real battle—a one sided one, however, as there was no return fire. One of our men, watching with glasses, said he saw a man fall from the tree. I cannot vouch for that but I do know that, from that day on, we had no further trouble with that particular sniper and I have always fondly cherished the hope that we did actually *get* him.

That night I accepted the invitation of the Forward Observing Officer of one of our batteries to have Christmas Dinner with him back at the Cafe de Dickebusch Etang. There were a few places, close behind our lines and well within the shelling area where native civilians still held on and catered to the appetites of the soldiers. One such was this place—on the shore of Dickebusch lake. It had evidently been a prominent as well as exclusive road-house before the war. Now, it was literally surrounded by artillery emplacements, probably half-a-dozen batteries having taken advantage of the concealment offered by Ridgewood immediately in front, to establish their guns there and many of the artillery officers were quartered in the cafe itself.

We slipped out of the front line soon after dark and, within an hour, were at the rendezvous. His battery, it seemed, had arranged for a big feed. Beside myself, there were several other guests, officers of the different units along that immediate front. I was the only enlisted man (a sergeant) but the captains and majors treated me like an equal —and the lieutenants had, perforce, to do the same. That is one thing about front line work, rank don't mean a thing —if you play the game and show a little initiative.

They had real turkey and, in addition to all the usual trimmings, plum pudding, of course. And drinks? Certainly. Anything you wanted was right there, waiting for you. We all got comfortably exhilarated, as a matter of course, but I do not think that anyone became incapacitated. We all had our work to do and we knew it—and I guess we did it. But for two or three hours, we forgot the war. Songs were in order and how those old rafters did ring. They sang all the conventional Yule-tide songs and carols and then commenced on others. I happened to know a few distinctively American songs which I contributed to the best of my ability. Fortunately, everybody was feeling so good that almost any noise sounded like music, so I got away with it. They all took to "The Old Gray Mare" (sung without expurgations) and, for a long time thereafter, I heard that song, hummed or sung, by officers and men of many British regiments, all along the line.

But that was just a little respite. The next day—Christmas—by mutual consent, there was no firing whatever. It was so quiet as to be disturbing—unnatural it seemed. Men of both sides showed themselves with impunity, even going out into no-man's-land to hunt for souvenirs but there was none of the close fraternizing such as we had heard was carried on the previous year.

Christmas day, 1914, it seems that the troops came right out of their lines and played around in no-man's-land. I think it was in Ian Hay's story of the *First Hundred Thousand* that I first read about that. At any rate, I often heard of it, by word of mouth, from others who were there. Why, in one place, the Germans even carried out a piano and held a regular concert.

On this next Christmas, however, although either by mutual consent or by some pre-arrangement through the underground channels, it was well known on both sides that there would be no actual firing; still we fought a bit shy of them. They had literally and actually murdered some of our unarmed stretcher-bearers on the afternoon of the previous day and I, for one, could not forget it; so, while the rest of the boys were wandering around out there in between the lines, with the Germans likewise prowling around in plain sight, I spent my time right behind the breech of a machine gun—fearing—or maybe it was hoping—that they would start something.

Now, I have and have always had, numerous close friends, either German born or of German parentage but I am willing to go on record as saying that I will *never,* so long as I live, ever trust to the honor or the humanity of any German war organization. It simply is not within the limits of their creed or code—or whatever you want to call it—to observe anything bordering upon humanity when they are at war.

A few days after Christmas the Germans opened up on that cafe at Dickebusch and got a major and two or three others who had been in our party. Of course we knew that some one of the habitües of the place had relayed the message over the lines but never found out which one it was. At any rate, none of the civilians were present when the shelling took place. That was one of the tough things about that war in Flanders. Too large a proportion of the natives were in favor of Germany and they had plenty of ways of getting information across.

So the winter dragged along. We had ample opportunities to observe and study the various kinds of shells and trench-mortar projectiles and rifle grenades. In the latter class, about this time the Germans brought out the "pineapple." It was about as big as a man's fist and shaped somewhat like the fruit which gave it its name, and to complete the resemblance it was scored, fore and aft and crosswise, with deep grooves, giving it a checkered appearance. Upon bursting, each of the small segments became a deadly missile, just like the Mills hand grenades—only these were somewhat larger. They were fired from the regular service rifle and with the ordinary ball cartridge, there being a hole through the center for the bullet, while the grenade, itself, was propelled by the gasses from the discharge. The rear end was equipped with three small vanes which acted as rudders to keep the thing head on, as they burst only on impact and, unless the nose struck directly against some solid object, they did not explode.

The Germans followed the practice, when they were about to launch these things, of firing several rifle shots, as a sort of mask and, right in the midst of these, to send over the grenade, but we quickly learned to notice the difference in the sound of the report when the grenade was fired—it was muffled in a peculiar way and was easily identified. So, when we heard that, we simply took shelter and watched to see where it would land. During just one afternoon, more than fifty of these jokers were dropped in the immediate vicinity of one of our machine guns, without doing a particle of damage. Several, which failed to explode, were picked up, so we had ample opportunity to examine them. A day or so later, however, they did get one man—"Paddy" Logan. He heard it coming and crowded up against the wall of the parapet but, unfortunately, the grenade struck fairly on the top of the parados immediately back of him and exploded, pieces striking him in the head, from the effect of which he died within a short time.

From that time on we seldom saw any of the older forms of rifle grenade—I mean the ramrod type. This newer kind could be and were fired from the service rifle, with the service cartridge while the others had to be fired with a blank cartridge and, in some instances, with a special rifle. Someone, about that time, had discovered the fact that the expanding gasses coming out of the muzzle of a rifle, were really and truly efficient propellants and that just this gas, itself, without the aid of any ramrod or other projection stuck down in the bore of the gun, would exert a force sufficient to throw one of the small grenades several hundred yards.

As to hand grenades: well, at first they were just exactly that. Made by hand and thrown by hand. If anyone cares to make one of the first type we used, I can easily tell him how to do it.

First, get a little jam tin. Well, being an American, you might not know exactly what I mean by that but, looking over at the kitchen cupboard, I see some little cans of Borden's milk. That is it, exactly. Get yourself a can of that size and, in opening it, do not use a regular can-opener. If you have no bayonet handy, get a good big butcher-knife or a hatchet and cut it cross-wise on top and turn the corners back—just as you would open any can out in camp somewhere, where you had no regular can-opener. Then take a stick of either 40 or 60 per-cent dynamite and cut off about an inch. Next, take a detonator and about an inch of ordinary blasting fuse. Stick the fuse into the detonator and crimp it. (If you are really *tough* you will do this with your teeth.) Poke a hole in the dynamite and stick the detonator into it—pinching it in carefully, so it won't slip out on you. Put the powder in the can and fill up all around it with any little, loose but hard things you can find. Gravel will do fine if there are no loose nuts and bolts handy. Then all you have to do is to press the corners of the opened can back in and she is ready for business. To make sure that it will light easily and quickly, you should slit the end of the fuse where it sticks out and smear in a pinch of dynamite. Some people are so conservative that they do not like to do this so they just break off the head of a match and stick it in the slitted fuse.

Well, there you are. All you got to do when you want to use it is to light 'er up and throw it. I have said an inch of fuse because I am afraid some enterprising youngster may take this thing seriously and I want to give him a break. As a matter of fact, many such grenades, lighted and thrown from one line, have been picked up and returned before exploding.

Many other types of grenades were developed during the war. The German potato-masher type was rather clumsy to look at but really very handy to use. They had a playful habit of fitting some of these things with *instantaneous* fuses and then leaving them lying around out in no-man's-land where one of our men might pick them up. If the poor devil tried to use the thing, he was blown apart the minute he pulled the string.

In my opinion, the Mills grenade was the best developed during the war. It was compact and easily carried and reliable in action. There may be better ones by this time. I don't know.

A great many people, including some who actually served in the armies, speak and write of fragments of shells or grenades as *"shrapnel."* It always grates on my nerves when I hear or see in print that phrase, a *piece* of shrapnel. Any person who knows anything at all about it, knows that there are no such things as *pieces* of shrapnel—unless each separate bullet be called a *piece.* One may be hit by the fuse-cap, which I have known to happen, or he may be struck by the shrapnel case, as I have good reason to know from painful recollection. But the shrapnel, itself, the bullets which constitute the real, effective component of this particular class of shell, are entirely different from the fragments from the ordinary, high-explosive shell. Invented by a Colonel Shrapnel, of the British Army, toward the latter part of the Eighteenth Century, the shell which bears his name is nothing more nor less than a travelling shot-gun—a hollow shell case, filled with iron balls and with a bursting charge in the base. The fuse can be set to burst this charge at any desired range, whereupon the balls are discharged and sweep a considerable area of ground. Shrapnel is particularly effective out in the open but is of little or no use against entrenched positions. The High Explosive shell (H. E. for short) is the only thing that will penetrate or knock down a parapet.

Along about this time we also made the acquaintance of the new armor-piercing bullets which the Germans brought out. I was standing, one morning, with several others, in a bay where we had an emergency machine-gun emplacement. The loop-hole was protected with one of the ordinary steel plates which were commonly used at the peep-holes from whence we observed the ground out in front. I do not now remember the exact thickness of these plates, but they were impervious to ordinary rifle bullets. The Germans had the same kind and it was an ordinary practice for one and the other to shoot at the things now and then—for sighting-in purposes or just for the fun of ringing the bell.

So, when a bullet pinged against the plate, no one paid

any attention. Soon another one came and still another. By this time we were beginning to wonder just what it was all about. Suddenly, someone let out a shout and pointed to the plate. Say; that fellow could certainly shoot, and it is too bad he never saw that group. There were three holes through the plate and all would have been covered by a three-inch circle. Just by luck—nothing else—none of us was right in line and the bullets had gone on and over the parados, which was very low at that point. We quickly piled up some sandbags in the rear to catch the next one, but that was all for the day. Some of the men did get one or two of the bullets later on and I salvaged one from the loop-hole of another gun emplacement. This was one of the very few real souvenirs I brought back. It was very ably described by Captain Crossman in an article in the Scientific American. It consisted of a solid core of very hard steel, about twenty-five calibre, wrapped in a sheet of soft lead and the whole thing encased in what appeared to be the ordinary cupro-nickle jacket of the service bullet. The jacket of the one I saved was so badly broken up that I cannot be sure about this point and, although I saw one or two others that were recovered, intact, from the sand-bags, I have no distinct recollection of them. Of course, we immediately banked up plenty of sand-bags behind all those plates and that was that.

Upon reporting this business, our people started in to find some way of getting even. They perfected their own armor-piercing bullets, but I personally, never saw one or used them. Later on, when the tanks became common, they found considerable need for them, but it just happened that my Section never had any available while I was with the outfit.

But I did see a lot of "elephant rifles" brought up and issued to be used on Heinie's loop-holes. And while I had plenty of chances to try out these heavy, double-barreled guns, for some reason or other—strange as it seems, even to myself now—I did not care enough about it at the time to even look them over carefully. Guess I was so completely immersed in my own machine-gun and sniping work that I had no room in my single-track mind for anything else at that time. Whether or not those big, double guns did any effective work, I don't know. It was just one of the many little side-issues, like bringing dogs in to kill off the rats.

Yes, they actually did that very thing—brought in dogs to kill off the trench rats—because I was right on the spot when the first dog happened to be brought into our sector and I saw the tragic ending to what started off to be a bit of harmless excitement and fun. Might as well ramble around a bit and tell about it right here, because this story I am telling you has rambled around from beginning to end anyhow.

About three hundred yards behind our front line position was a small creek or "beek" as it is called in Flemish. This one happened to be the Ballartbeek. It was narrow, perhaps twenty feet wide, but deep, and was lined on both sides with a fringe of small bushes and the inevitable willows which are found everywhere in that part of the world, especially along the hedge-rows and water-courses—usually "polled," that is, with the tops cut off, so they never get very high but are thick with branches down toward the base, thus offering the very best of concealment.

Now, we had picked out a well hidden spot amongst these thick willow trees and had established a little, private, ammunition dump or cache there. At the time, we had accumulated some sixty or seventy thousand rounds of "honest-to-God" machine gun ammunition, and we kept a pretty close eye on it, too.

I have to run off the track every now and then to explain these things because of the fact that a lot of the people who will read this have not had the opportunity to learn, at first hand, many of the things *we* had to learn in the school of experience and, often, under the most adverse conditions. While we seldom encountered a serious shortage of ammunition, that is, cartridges supposed to be manufactured for the guns we were using, we soon found that very few of the brands made under the press of war demands were worth a "tinkers damn" for use in machine guns. To enable the guns to function perfectly, it is absolutely imperative that the cartridges be *right*. By that I mean they must be of such uniform construction and loading that they will all seat properly in the chamber, be of sufficiently close fit that the case will not break under the strain of firing; the primers must be seated alike; the cases not too hard or too soft and the bullets must be of uniform calibre and seated in the cases at just the right depth.

This is just to mention a few of the things that make the difference between good ammunition and the other kind. There were several brands made by the old, established companies and some of the Government Arsenals that were really up to standard and could be depended upon to function properly at all times and when we came upon any of these particular brands, we made it a point to hide out all we could for use in emergency, shooting the other stuff at odd times when we had plenty of time to clear out jams and replace broken extractors and such things.

This particular dump, or as we Canadians called it, "cache," was filled with all the good machine gun ammunition we had been able to "accumulate" during the past two months. In previous years I had often "accumulated" ammunition at Camp Perry so the practice came in good stead in those days, and I generally thought of the cases I had lugged off back there in Ohio. (Where all firing stopped at six o'clock. Here it kept up all during the night, however.) One of our communication trenches ran right close to our cache and when we could grab off a case of good ammunition we would slip right over and hide it away with the rest. The communication trench had been constructed so that the crossing of the creek was under cover. It was merely a bridge of "duck-boards" with a support or "bent" in the middle, but sufficiently strong to carry a single line of men.

Four of our men (from the Machine Gun Section) were at the ammunition cache, putting in a couple of cases which we had acquired that day. We got it when and where we could and if some of the infantry companies in the immediate vicinity found themselves short of their allotment, well —never mind—we usually managed to replace what we took with an equal amount of the other stuff, which would work all right in the rifles, and they never knew the difference.

About this time there happened to be a party of new-comers walk down the communication trench, and the odd thing about it was that one of the crowd, an officer, was carrying a dog in his arms. He was a pretty little dog and everyone stopped to look at him and wonder "how come" because we knew it must have taken especial permission to bring him in, dogs being strictly "taboo" in our lines. I have learned all about the "war-dogs" during the years since the war—just as I have learned about the phenomenal pistol shooting of my former associates on the plains—through the medium of the movies. It makes me ashamed of myself, who had ranged the West, from Mexico to Canada during the last forty years or so, that I never learned how to "fan" a gun or to shoot a man in any particular spot on the short notice that was generally given when any shooting was necessary. Well, that's the way it goes—live and learn.

Just as the officer carrying the dog came to the bridge, a big rat scampered out from under his feet and took a nose-dive into the creek. Those rats seemed to be a cross between ordinary rats and muskrats. They were as much at home in the water as on land. (Aside: we had to be the same way, so they may have learned it by the same method

we did—by force of circumstances.)   Anyway, just as the
officer (I never did know his name or rank) had turned to
pass the word to his men to keep low and string out a little
while crossing, the dog saw the rat and, being the kind of
dog he was, immediately started after it.   Jumping from his
master's arms, he landed on the bridge and bounced from
there into the water, after the rat which was making good
time up stream toward the place where our men were hiding
the ammunition.

I was just coming down to see how the boys were getting
along and was in time to witness the "tragical farce," if you
understand what I mean.   With never a thought for anything else, the officer and the men at the head of the column,
started after that rat.   Up along the shore they raced, right
out into the open, where all Germany could see them, trying
to spear that rat with bayonets.   Thomas (he was in charge
of our detail) shouted, "down! down you blighters!"—and
more expressive names—"down! Oh, for the love of Christ,
have ye no sense?   You'll have those Dutchmen shellin' us
in a minute."   He and the others of our crowd tried to
stop the rush and seeing me, as I just then arrived on the
scene, ran over to me.   I, too, knew what it meant and took
them back into the comparative shelter of the trench, then
went out and tried to hammer some sense, by word of
mouth, into the excited rat hunters.   But it was no use;
they had the hunting fever and were determined to get that
rat.   A few weeks later they would have been accustomed
to having the vermin crawling all over them in the dugouts, at night, but they were new to the war game and did
not know that.

In less than a minute, here came the whiz-bangs, bursting
with terrible accuracy over the whole area.   Heinie knew all
about that place, so used nothing but shrapnel.   Men went
sprawling into the creek and beside it, while the long line
in the trench took shelter as best they could.   It lasted only

a few minutes but at least a dozen men were dead and as many more wounded. The officer having disappeared, I managed by dint of hard swearing to get the head of the column straightened out and started along up the trench. Thomas and the others of our outfit did what they could for the wounded until the stretcher bearers got there. Of the officer we could find no trace—nor of the dog. I learned afterward that he was what they call an Otter Hound and had been brought in to see if that kind of a dog would be of any use in ridding the trenches of rats. From what I saw of the actions of this one, I would unhesitatingly, vote YES.

A while back, we were talking about armor-piercing bullets I believe. Well, while on or around that subject I might as well tell you my experience with "explosive" bullets. We heard a lot about these explosive bullets—just as you will, now and then, run across a soldier who will tell you he was hit with one of them. While not pretending to be an authority on such things, I do not believe and never did believe that the Germans ever used anything of this kind, at least not on men in the trenches.

Of course I know that explosive bullets have been made. I have a great volume, printed by the U. S. Government, which is the report of our officers who went over and acted as the official observers during the Crimean War in which several types of such bullets are very accurately described. Also another official report of the commission headed by General Sheridan which observed the operations during the Franco-Prussian war. Moreover, I have actually seen the things used, in .45 and .50 calibre cartridges made for and used in our American rifles. All I have tried to indicate here is my opinion that no such bullets were used during the late war. Aside from the difficulty and expense of manufacturing them for the modern, high-power rifle, there was no reason for it. The effect of the bullet as it is is sufficiently "explosive."

The effect of any bullets fired from the German Mauser was very similar to that of the 150-grain bullet fired from the Springfield. At short ranges, due to the high velocity, it does have an explosive effect and, not only that effect but, when it strikes, it sounds like an explosion. Bullets may be cracking viciously all around you when, all of a sudden, you hear a "whop" and the man alongside goes down. If it is in daylight and you are looking that way, you may see a little tuft of cloth sticking out from his clothes. Wherever the bullet comes out, it carries a little of the clothing—just a bit of fuzz—but it is unmistakable, just as the sound of a bullet hitting a man can never be mistaken for anything else. At the short ranges, as I have said, it is a loud and distinct "pop" or, as I gave it before, "whop." (If any of the readers can remember the sound of a Champagne cork when turned loose, they will get the approximate sound.) And the effect of the bullet, at short range, also suggests the idea of an explosion, especially if a large bone be struck. I remember one instance when one of our men was struck in the knee (it was a man named T. M. Flanagan and he was hit January 2, 1916) and the bullet almost amputated the leg. He died before he could be taken to a dressing station. I mention these details so that any person of enquiring mind can check up on me in case he should doubt any of my statements.

At the longer ranges, the bullet *slips in,* if I may use the term. Unless it strikes the head, there is but little sound. I can recall one instance, where a man was struck by a bullet, which lodged in his leg, and never knew it at the time. He was just leaving a latrine, some thousand yards or so behind the front line, and became entangled in some old barbed wire at the entrance. One of the barbs caught in the leg of his trousers above the knee and stung him severely. After a bit of swearing, he disengaged himself and went on his way. That night he was still complaining about the hurt and a brother told him he better go back to the dressing station and have them dope the scratch with iodine. He did so and the surgeon pulled a German bullet out of the "scratch." Just one of the casual, long-range floaters that were dropping in now and then, but it had struck him just at the time he encountered the wire. This man's name was Williams—brother of one of our machine-gun sergeants.

My friends back home have often asked me about the experiences we had with poison gas. I suppose the best way to explain about this is to state the fact that after the initial, devastating attack with chlorine gas, in April, 1915, we had very little serious difficulty from that source up to the time I left—in February, 1917.

When my Division went in, in September, 1915, we were equipped with what were called "respirators"—hoods or helmets made of cloth which had been impregnated with certain chemicals which served to neutralize the effect of the chlorine. The only time in my experience when we needed them was on the night of December 19th, when the enemy again tried to smother our line and come over. Troops to our left and in our rear got the most of it but we got some. However, few if any of our Battalion were incapacitated. The attack was a fizzle, as it was promptly stopped by rifle fire.

About that time the Germans commenced to use shell gas of various kinds—mostly the lachrymatory or tear gas—and we were issued special goggles with sponge-rubber padding which proved to be a satisfactory defense against this gas. They had just begun to make use of the phosgene and other really deadly gasses and the mustard gas did not come into use until long after I had left the front, so I can say nothing about it.

We got a few of the new type gas masks about the first of January, 1916. They were called Tower Helmets—Lord knows why—and one was issued to each machine-gun crew,

together with one of the new steel hats, the idea being, I
suppose, that at least one member of the crew might survive
and carry on even if the rest were all killed off. No one
particularly wanted to be saddled with this extra weight so
they were usually shunted off onto the newest recruit. We
all had our respirators and figured that they were sufficient
protection.

We soon learned to tell the difference between *real* shells
and gas shells, both by the sound in flight and by the burst.
Sound cannot well be put into words but the gas shells had
a sort of bubbling or gurgling sound in addition to the regular "whish." The burst was very light—just enough to open
the container and release the gas, and was unmistakable if
one were close enough to notice it at all.

In the course of time enough supplies had come forward
to equip all hands with both the new-style gas mask and the
tin hats, but a lot of us put off the wearing of the latter until
actually compelled, by personal orders, to do so. I get a
grin out of it, whenever I remember the first time I really
wore mine. Prior to that time I had carried it slung over
my arm. Having received a very pointed and emphatic
"bawling out," I donned it and started up the line to look
over a machine gun that was working up that way. I had
not gone ten yards until a big "wooly bear" burst right
overhead and a chunk of steel hit right on top of that "lid"
with sufficient force to knock me down and make a very
noticeable dent in the hat.

As I have just stated, the poison gas did not cause us
any great amount of trouble while I was with the Canadian
Corps. It was the artillery which caused us the most of our
grief. "Now, tell me: why was that?" (The girl asked that
question.) I'll tell you. Just because the doughboys depended on their own feet and their own guts—and these
things were not much defense against shells.

Artillery worked from various ranges: the three-inch of

the American Army, the 75 m/m of the French, the British 18-pounders: all had about the same range; and the German 77s come in the same class.

What a lot of us infantrymen and machine gunners could never understand was why the artillerymen did not shoot at one another. They knew exactly where the opposing batteries were located. What the hell were their observation planes for?

Every action in warfare is for the purpose of taking certain areas of land from the enemy. Either that, or to so completely whip his personnel that they will just lie down and be "good doggies." Well; the men of the Northern races do not take their licking in that way. We took many a blasting from shell-fire—but, to the eternal credit of the Canadian Army, as a whole—did we ever take a licking? I'll tell the world—NEVER.

Now, personally, I am not crying about this. I went to war expecting it to be plenty tough. It was. So I hope you will understand that I am not belly-achen' about what happened to us or the many better men who are not here to tell you about it.

The guns above mentioned were all "rifles"—that is, guns that fired high-velocity shells with a correspondingly low or flat trajectory. There was little chance to dodge a shell from any of that type or of the other, larger calibre rifles— mostly of the type used in the navy. Some of these latter, used by the Germans, ran up to about eleven inches. The French and British both had howitzers of twelve- and fifteen-inch calibre. Of course everybody knows about the original "Big Berthas" used by the Germans. Curiously enough, they were not German guns, at all, having been manufactured at the Austrian Skoda works. They had been used to reduce the Belgian forts and we saw plenty of the great craters formed by the bursts of these 42-centimeter shells in and around Ypres but, to the best of my knowledge, they were not much used after the winter campaign of 1914-15.

There were plenty of others, however, of smaller calibre, to make life miserable for us. One in particular—also Austrian—threw a shell of about eleven inches in diameter. All those big shells had the fuzes in the base and not on the nose-cap and it was a frequent occurrence for the whole base of the shell, which was the size of a large dinner plate and screwed into the shell proper, to blow out backward and go hurtling through the air for a mile or more.

For use against any entrenched or fortified positions the howitzers are much more effective than the rifles, due to the fact that they throw their shells up at a sharp angle and they drop at a correspondingly sharp angle. The rifle shells have more of a grazing effect and often, after striking on hard ground, will ricochet for miles beyond the target.

Aside from the light field guns—commonly designated as "whiz-bangs"—the most generally used both by the Germans and the allied armies was of approximately six inch calibre and the shells from these were called "crumps." The British had both "four-point-sevens" and "nine-point-twos," this latter being an exceptionally efficient device for rooting out the concrete machine-gun emplacements—called Pill Boxes.

Then, of course, there were the innumerable types of trench mortars; throwing everything from the size of a small pineapple up to monstrous cargoes of high explosive weighing, in some cases, as much as two hundred pounds.

Yes, the artillery caused us plenty of grief but, now here is something for the ordinary tax-payer to consider; they also cost several times as much as the infantry or machine gunners. It was a common jest with us that, when one of the fifteen inch howitzers sent a shell over our heads, someone would remark: "there goes another hundred pounds." No, he did not mean the weight of the shell, but that it cost about one hundred pounds, Sterling (approximately

$500) for each and every one of those shots. Oh, yes, of course, they did a lot of execution—mostly in some vacant lot or field; but my opinion is, based on close observation during the war and careful thought since that time, that, excepting for the purpose of breaking down the strongest fortifications and for the use of heavily armoured battle-ships, it is a woeful and unwarranted waste of the tax-payer's money to construct and operate these large-calibred guns. I mean, so far as actual *destruction* is con-cerned. There is, of course, the other angle—the *moral* effect on our own men. I readily admit that it was a great comfort to me the first time our people brought up some of those big fellows of twelve and fifteen-inch calibre. The Royal Marine Artillery handled them in firing but we of the infantry did most of the work of getting the huge and unwieldy monsters into place. The Railway Corps, of course, did their part but it was usually working parties from the infantry, during their periods back at the REST camps, who put in the long hours of night work necessary to lay the tracks and get the guns under cover and then obliterate all traces of the work before Heinie came over with his photographing planes in the morning.

What we had to do was to build literally miles of rail-way, first removing all the sod and, when they had brought the gun up to the appointed place, to replace everything that might give an indication of what had happened. Usually these big guns were ensconced in buildings, and it was necessary to remove a large part of the roof and one side and replace these parts with the especially-prepared camouflage. Also, in most instances, it was necessary to tear out a lot of the inside walls of the house. Taken all in all, it was a tough job, as it all had to be done during the hours of darkness—in one night. The real Railway Guns were, of course, different. They remained on their mounts and were fired from the curved tracks which the

Railway Corps had prepared for them. The 14-inch naval guns used by the U. S. army at the close of the war were of that type, but there were plenty of them in use a long time before that.

Now, I may be "all wet" about this but I still believe and insist that the actual results of heavy calibred and long range gun-fire is not worth what it costs in actual dollars and cents.

The fire of the lighter "rifles"—say up to about six inches—is not only more accurate but the guns themselves are so much more mobile that they can readily be moved from point to point quickly enough to keep the other fellow guessing. The French 75s and the German 77s, in my opinion, killed off more men than all the heavier guns used during the war.

What good did it do the Germans to shoot shells into Paris from a range of sixty or seventy miles. Just exactly the same as dropping Zeppelin bombs on England. What it did was to make both those people resolve to fight harder. The material damage, I venture to say, never in any case was equal to the cost of the effort and as to the *personal* damage, well, it was so small as compared to an hour or so of real battle, that it is not worth considering at all. It is possible, as I have before remarked, that such a policy of frightfulness might be effective against Germans. They, I believe, called it *"schrecklichkeit."* Now, anyone who can think up a name like that is liable to have some funny emotions—I don't know—but I *do* know that all of their bombing in England never scared anyone. It just made them madder. And I presume the effect on the French of that willfully murderous shelling of the non-combatants of Paris was probably about the same. It certainly had no *military* significance.

Chapter 10

The Pistol in War

SO FAR, our fighting had not amounted to much. There we were—the Germans all the time trying to find a weak spot to break through and we trying to hand back some of the misery we were enduring. We staged a few raids, sometimes with the idea of catching a prisoner or two but more often just to harass the enemy and break the monotony of the game.

By this time, many of the machine gunners had equipped themselves with pistols and discarded their rifles. I can't say that I blamed them in the least. There was only one method by which the rifle could be carried—slung diagonally across the back—as both hands were occupied and the man loaded down with ammunition boxes, tools, the gun or its tripod. Slung in this manner, the rifle proved to be much of a hindrance and annoyance, and on top of all this it could not be gotten into action very speedily. Hence, it soon became common for the machine gunners to "lose" their rifles. Some of us, however, tried to always have a rifle handy, although aside from the sniping which I was doing from behind the line, there had so far been but little chance for any real rifle shooting.

Right here, lets have another shift of subject and talk about pistols for a change. One-hand guns were, undoubtedly, designed for the use of mounted men so that they could deliver fire at the enemy while, at the same time,

167

they had the other hand free for the management of their horses. They only fired the one shot and were then useless until reloaded, so they made them big and cumbersome in order that they could be used effectively as a club until a time came when they could again be loaded—a slow process in that day. They were, really and truly, "horse pistols," being so big and cumbersome that no gentleman could have carried one on his person while afoot. When and where they were first invented is probably known to some of our specialists in antique weapons—I don't know and it is really of no consequence here as this is not supposed to be a treatise on the evolution of firearms anyway.

But I am afraid that I shall, now and then, refer to some of the old timers. You see, I'm just as big a "nut" as the next one, and anything pertaining to firearms—yes anything pertaining to killing, whether it be with a stone axe or a blow gun, excites my interest and I want to know about it. As the son of an ex-cavalryman, born soon after the end of the Civil War, I had a good initiation into the pistol question. Everything from Starr and Colt revolvers back to Tower flintlocks were available for my education. Pepper-boxes, derringers—I tried them all and just naturally grew up with the idea that it was a part of the education of every American citizen to know how to shoot a pistol well enough to disable your enemy before he gets you. I never, then or since, have made any effort to become a prize-winning shot on the range. I am not and never have been a threat to the pistol shooters in the National Matches, but have always tried to keep in practice sufficiently to give myself the feeling of assurance that in a pinch I can get my gun out and shoot as fast and as straight as the other fellow.

Well, that's the way it was when the war started in 1914, and I went up to Canada to see what it was all about. The regulation equipment for officers in the Canadian Army, or at least in the Second Division, included the Colt .45 Automatic, an exact duplicate of our Model 1911. Naturally I was quite familiar with this gun and it was my privilege, as Musketry Instructor, to be present when these arms were received by the officers of the Twenty-first Battalion.

The officers first tried out these .45s on our improvised indoor rifle range, in the armouries at Kingston, and their experience was exactly the same as I had seen, numberless times, in the United States Army. The range was fifty feet, and the targets of the usual short-range type used by the infantry for indoor instruction firing with reduced ammunition. At the first attempts, many of the shots struck on the concrete floor, anywhere from fifteen to forty feet in front of the firer. You can probably imagine the effect this had upon that crowd. It required a lot of argument to persuade some of those officers that the gun was "worth a damn." But that was only temporary. After a little instruction, emphasized by practical demonstration with those same guns, they soon learned the game and could hold and squeeze as well as the next fellow.

I have said that this pistol was the authorized "regulation." Well, that is true in the sense that they were authorized for use, and quantities had been purchased so that the officers could procure them, but it was not obligatory. Those who so desired were at liberty to use the Webley or the .45 Colt or Smith and Wesson revolver. One, whom I well remember, had two Colts which took the .455 Webley cartridge—and did good work with them too. The Webley pistol never appealed to me, probably because of its cumbersome appearance. The thing would *shoot* however, and it made a dandy club with which to bean an obstreperous prisoner.

As I was quite familiar with the new Colt Automatic I was able to be of some assistance during the preliminary work of breaking them in and it was not long until the officers were accustomed to the peculiarities of the gun and could make it behave to their satisfaction. Those who had had experience with the revolver entertained the almost universal prejudice against the automatic: 's funny, isn't it —how we hate to discard our old loves and take up with new ones (in this shooting game I mean, it appears to be easy enough regarding some other things). But even the most conservative of the old timers soon recognized the real advantages of the later type weapon. I staged several realistic demonstrations; including fast reloading in the dark and such stunts, and that converted most of them. As to reliability—dependability in an emergency—there was little choice between the revolver and the automatic. Both types would function properly with the same degree of care. It is possible that there were instances of an automatic "jamming" now and then, but personally I never had it happen to me during the war, nor did I see or hear of any instance of it happening.

All these arguments as to the relative merits of the revolver and the automatic pistol will probably continue for another generation. Most of the old timers who learned to shoot with the revolver have a deep seated prejudice against the automatic—but when you come down to the root of their argument, it all seems to base upon the "hang" of the two guns, the newer automatic does not point right with the same old habitual kink in the wrist. I have used the .45 Automatic ever since 1911, but for twenty years prior to that time had used the revolver. Even now, I find myself having a sneaking sort of preference for the revolver and feel confident that I can make a better score on the target with it, either slow or rapid fire. But in spite of all this, I unhesitatingly choose the automatic for actual use in war. To my mind, the great advantage of the automatic lies in the ease and rapidity with which it can be reloaded—especially in the dark. Any one who doubts this can easily satisfy himself by trying to hurridly reload a revolver *in the dark,* with a crowd of roughnecks milling all around and trying to hit some one with clubs, knives and fists. Or, if this seems too rough, just get some friend to jostle you about or run into you while trying it. There is really no comparison between slipping a fresh magazine into the butt of the pistol, and fumbling with six small cartridges in trying to get them into six *different* revolver chambers.

There is just one little trick the user of the automatic should train himself to keep in mind—and do—reload while there is still a cartridge in the chamber; do not shoot until the gun is entirely empty. Even though you have fired but four or five shots, better drop out that old magazine and slip in a full one.

Now, all this time and for a year or so afterwards, machine gunners were supposed to carry rifles. Some of us always tried to have one handy, even after we had accumulated pistols. I was the first to sport a hand-gun and others of the section followed suit as fast as they could have the guns bought for them and sent on. None of the others secured any, however, until after we had been in England for some time, but as fast as they came I would take their fortunate possessors up to the chalk pit on Tolsford Hill and give them a work-out, and they all soon became sufficiently proficient for our purpose. This was just another case of where the King's Regulations were modified to suit the Colonial—just as in the case of the moustache. Now, those King's Regulations, which are the Bible of all British soldiers, specifically ordain that each and every officer and soldier must shave regularly but must *not* shave the upper lip. Well, most of us Canadians shaved clean—and got away with it. A lot of others, who lacked the nerve to go the whole way, left a little trace of hair on the upper lip; that's probably where all these little dinky ingrown moustaches originated.

The pistol is particularly adapted to the needs of the machine gunner, and in my humble opinion every member of the crew should be armed with one and trained in its use. I will admit that a machine gunner seldom has a chance to use either rifle or pistol, unless it is during a long stretch of trench warfare where he may have the opportunity, as I did, to kill time (and a few of the enemy) by doing sniping and scouting work. In anything like open warfare, or during an assault or attack by the enemy, he will be plenty busy taking care of his machine guns. With adequate flank protection (riflemen) he will never be called upon to meet the direct assault of enemy infantrymen. Artillery, trench mortars and tanks will make life plenty miserable for him without that.

But "nevertheless and notwithstanding" he should be armed with a good pistol and know how to use it. Those flank-protecting riflemen may not be on hand when most needed, and pistols are especially suited to repelling a sudden rush upon the gun by an enemy coming in from the flanks —the only way they can get in on a working machine gun and its crew. The men lying about operating a machine gun are invariably in such positions that a rifle cannot be picked up or swung into action within the necessarily short notice given; but a pistol can be drawn from its holster when in any position and once out, any number of men rushing in should be stopped before they can get close enough to use the bayonet.

The entire case of the pistol may be summed up in "I don't want this thing often, but when I do I want it damn bad." A historical instance in point, is the plight of those men who worked the two "sacrifice guns" at Sanctuary Wood during the Third Battle of Ypres on June 2, 1916. The Germans had launched a sudden and intense drive against the Princess Pats at Hooge and a large forest nearby called Sanctuary Wood. In this latter forest were two guns, placed to cover an exposed approach, with orders to stay there and fight to a finish. And they did—they worked those two guns until the last man was killed *by German bayonets*. This was one of the exceedingly rare instances of where the bayonet was actually used in the war. Those gunners had no arms at all excepting the two eighteen-pounders, yet every one of them was bayoneted at the guns, after having shot down many times their own number of the enemy. BUT—had those gunners all been equipped with pistols, there is no doubt in the world that most of them would have been able to make their getaway, after the guns had been silenced, or would have taken an additional number of the enemy with them to the happy hunting grounds.

Those of us in the Machine Gun Section who were fortunate enough to have pistols thoroughly appreciated the advantages of such weapons and we were much envied by the others who were not so armed. No pistol was ever permitted to be taken to the rear on a dead or wounded man; someone always grabbed for it as soon as the owner was picked up.

I am also of the opinion that every man in an army who is not armed with a rifle should carry a pistol. By this, I mean all those men who are in any manner liable to come into actual contact with the enemy—"rub bellies with them" as old Colonel Evans used to say. In war, a pistol is liable to be needed at what may seem a most inopportune time and without a second's notice. Maybe I better describe an incident in which I consider a lucky pistol shot to have saved my entire machine gun crew.

Early one afternoon, during the fighting of the St. Eloi scrap, a crew of six men and myself were working a gun forward over some ground which had been changing hands quite a bit during the preceding days. We had a Colt gun and its tripod, together with the usual loads of filled belts

in boxes. Some few of the crowd had rifles slung across
their backs and all hands were loaded down to the limit.
We crawled and worked our way ahead slowly, finally
rushing over into a bit of trench and dropped right on top
of a few Germans who were hidden in there unknown to
any of us. With the exception of one Heinie, who was
sitting on a fire step, the rest of this crowd bolted down a
side trench and got away easily, but we jumped on the one
sitting down and soon knocked him out. What really happened was that the man carrying the Colt gun actually
threw it on this German and then fell on top himself.
We others dropped our loads and ran on after the German
party, but only went a few yards and then returned, leaving a man down at the end of the trench to watch in case
any of them came back.

Our Dutchman was not hurt much and he soon got to
his feet and seemingly made the best of the deal. He was a
big, surly looking chap and did not seem to be any too
well pleased with the mauling he had just received—what
else he could have expected I do not know. I was in a
hurry to get along and have the machine gun set up so we
could handle the counter attack we all felt would soon be
pulled off, so I motioned to this Heinie to jump on out
of the trench and take himself back to the rear, where some
of our fellows would see to it that he was sent on further
back with other prisoners. This was our usual method of
handling prisoners taken by an advanced or small unit.
Often such a detachment could not spare a man to escort
them back, so we just took their arms away and then made
them run back across the open ground with their hands
held up in the air. Neither our men nor the Germans
were likely to shoot at prisoners going to the rear in this
manner, but in case they did, it was just too bad, that's all.

Those Germans who ran out on us had evidently been a
combat group or outpost of some sort, for they left two

rifles and plenty of ammunition behind them, and also a sizable stack of "potato-masher" grenades piled up in a corner of the trench. I had the prisoner climbing out, and we all picked up our loads and started on when that Heinie slid back into the trench and reached for those grenades. Very fortunately, the last man in our party was one who carried a pistol—he dropped his load, made one of the quickest draws I have ever seen, fired twice, and shot that smart Dutchman through the knee joint, almost smashing his leg apart. All this was done and over with in much less time than it has taken me to tell you about it—and none of our party could possibly have unslung a rifle, or fired it in time to have stopped that German—had he managed to pick up three or four of those grenades and gotten around the corner with them we would simply have been S. O. L.

To make matters worse, we got up to where I had left the man on watch and found it impossible to get any further ahead. So we had to stick in that bit of trench until night and listen to the "goings on" of that shot-up German. By that time, I for one, was sorry our man was not a better pistol shot.

So much for the occasional "emergency" use of a pistol. However, there comes a time when any fighting man may find that his very existence depends upon a pistol hanging from his side. Now, every new war starts where the last one left off. Of course, the instigator of it will probably have an ace or two up his sleeve in the nature of new inventions, but generally speaking, it will be just the same old game with a new dealer. Innovations will develop, probably more rapidly than in the past. What with the daily-increasing knowledge of the effect of "rays" (for want of a better designation) it is well within the bounds of reason to expect that, when the next great war between modern powers comes along, far more effective measures will have been perfected to separate the soldier from his grocery and rent bills and to transport him to Paradise.

Think I am trying to get away from our subject? Nay, nay my friend. Just trying to bring this matter back to where it "has been, is now, and ever shall be." Wars are fought by men, against other men. New weapons, new schemes and devices will be conceived, but when it comes right down to the finish there will be nothing on earth but man opposed to man. If one man has a club and the other has none, the man with the club will undoubtedly win. If one has a sword or bayonet and the other a pistol, the man with the pistol will surely be the survivor. For every aircraft, for every tank or any other as yet unknown mechanical device, there must needs be, not only men to direct and control them but many more men to build, rebuild, repair and service them. Historically, wars are won by nations. Literally and practically, they are won by *men*— individuals working in concert and following certain well-conceived plans. The last living man able to stand on his feet and fight may decide the issue between victory and defeat.

Until something better is invented, I believe that the pistol is the best weapon for this last stand. Personally, I have had but three chances to prove it, but I know of many others who have had more than that. If a man really knows how to handle his pistol, he can whip—yes, kill—five men within the last ten yards of any assault. He may be killed, often is, by a shot from the side or from someone behind his immediate adversaries, but he can, with the utmost confidence, undertake to handle at least three enemy bayonet men.

It must be understood that the pistol is not, habitually, used for sniping—that is, for picking off individual targets by aimed fire at any range from, say, twenty yards up. It is especially adapted for use at any range within that limit, but is seldom actually used beyond fifteen or twenty *feet*. Most of the men killed with the one-hand gun, including all the more-or-less bad men in the early days of the West have "got their needin's" at these shorter distances—mostly shorter than that. The average old time bar-rooms were pretty small, and what shooting was done was generally between men spaced the width of a poker table apart. The outside shooting—and I have this from no less authorities than Bat Masterson, Jim Lee and Schwin Box—was not so very effective. They have told me innumerable tales of how this one and that one had emptied their guns, reloaded and emptied them again at adversaries who were doing the same thing, within less than one hundred feet and with scant damage on either side.

Bat and Lee were both in the famous "Battle of the Barrels" at Abilene, I think it was (possibly Dodge; they were active at both places) and Jim got two .45 bullets right through his chest; "one on either side of my wish-bone," as he described it one day we were both stripped and in bathing. I often thought of these old incidents when we were in France, because the experiences we were then having just about agreed in most respects with the tales these old timers had told to me in my earlier days in New Mexico. Personally I did not have very much experience when it came to using my own automatic, but what little I did have seemed highly essential at the time and if I had not had that pistol along I would not be telling this now. Maybe I better tell about one of those times right here and now.

During the course of the war, those of us who were equipped with pistols were sometimes called upon to do a little scouting, and if not called, occasionally did it anyway, just to break the monotony. If it were a regularly organized and authorized patrol, probably the only one in the detachment who carried a pistol would be the officer in charge, the others carrying bombs (Mills hand grenades) and rifles. Some of us however, among my machine gun crews, were prone to slip out at night, just to "see what we could see" or to try and locate some new machine-gun emplacement which we had 'reason to believe that Heinie had built, and we *always* "packed a gun". On these ventures we soon learned that the only logical place to carry your pistol was in a holster slung right square in the middle of your back. You simply can't carry it anywhere else. I carried mine on the waist belt and saw to it that it didn't slide about too much. I know of other chaps who slung their pistol between their shoulder blades and reached up over their shoulder to get the gun out. In an argument with one of these lads he told me he could get under the wire better with the pistol holster fastened up there, and could reach up and unfasten it much easier if it *did* get caught. If you attempt to crawl about with the holster strapped to your side it immediately slides around to the front and punches you in the belly—and gets in the mud, which is worse—and if you try tying the bottom of the holster to your leg, it still hobbles you—and still gets in the mud. Often we had to crawl through mud and slime several inches deep, and the back was the only place where it was possible to keep anything reasonably clean and dry—and ready for use. Even our gas masks, after we were equipped with them, were either carried in the same manner, or (as was usually the case) left at home.

As these patrols, or scouts, were primarily for the purpose of getting information and not to fight, we did not as a rule, go out looking for trouble. Quite frequently we would pass enemy patrols, within easy bombing distance, without either party "starting things". Just like a couple of strange dogs which will pass, one on either side of the street, both very watchful and with hair bristling, watching for the first hostile move on the part of the other. But there were times, perhaps just because we were feeling pretty low and ornery, or maybe because the rum ration was late in arriving, that some of us would go out "with blood in our eyes". Then we went looking for trouble—and nearly always found it.

On the first expedition of this kind in which I participated, we all carried bombs—no rifles. I happened to have a French bayonet which I had picked up that day and Norton-Taylor also had one of them. I think that he was the first and I the second to grasp the fact that these silent but terribly effective weapons were perfectly adapted to this stealthy night work. I believe that this was the origin of the "trench knives" which were later introduced. Of course, the Gurkhas, with their curious knives were ahead of us; it is the white troops that I refer to.

Well, this night I am telling about, we slipped over the parapet and through the wire and took up a position where we had reason to believe the regular German patrol would pass. It was understood by all hands that we were out to "clean up", get a live prisoner if possible, but to kill them all if necessary.

It was tedious waiting. No man who has not gone through it can imagine the terrific strain under which a person lives during such a time. There we were, spread out along the edge of an old crater, trying to look as much like the surrounding, shell-torn ground as we could. Every time a flare went up, from our side or the other, we simply "froze". Any movement at that time would surely expose us to the watchful eyes of the enemy, across the way. It was only about a hundred and fifty yards between our trenches at that place and there was no more than one hundred feet between our outside wire and that of the "Allemand". There were only four of us and we knew that the regular German patrol, at that time and place, consisted of from six to eight men. We had agreed that we would wait until they were directly opposite our position and then each one of us was to throw a bomb, duck until after the explosion, and then wade into them and try to pick up a live prisoner. We knew, from previous observations, just about where they would pass. That is, we thought we knew but, in this case as in many others, the unexpected happened. Whether they had a new and more enterprising leader or whether they had simply lost their way, we never will know, but that patrol came upon us from the rear.

We all heard them and saw them. They were scouting right along our wire and between us and our own line. Well, that was fine and dandy, if we had had any previous understanding as to what we would do in such a case—but we had never even thought of any thing like that. They would probably have passed our position without seeing us had it not been for one of our crowd who shall be nameless. This individual squirmed around and threw a bomb at the head of the German procession. It so happened that he was at the very left of our line. I was the right-hand man, and Taylor was next to me. We all had grenades—six apiece—but Hugh and I had agreed that we would see what we could do with the French bayonets as persuaders, and our pistols if it came to a show-down.

Well, then things commenced to happen. The kid who threw the bomb used his head to the extent that he held it a bit, after pulling the pin and releasing the lever, so that it burst at the instant it hit the ground. It probably got a German but it also got himself (the thrower) and the man next him. That left Taylor and me with six or seven Heinies to look after.

Those Dutchmen were well trained. I remember taking one long jump, over into another big crater and felt Hughie landing on top of me when there came the terrific blasts of the bombs that the other fellows had hurled at us. I think we each threw back at least one—possibly two and then, finding that we were not hurt, started out to "get" someone. It was pretty much an individual matter from that time on. I hunted around at my back until I found my pistol—just in time to use it on a big hulk of a German who was trying to find the way home. I think I fired three shots—at ranges all the way up to four or five feet. Hughie, with more presence of mind than I possessed, had stuck to the bayonet (used as a short sword) and had a cripple to show for it. We got home some way but, on the whole, the venture was more or less of a fizzle.

From that time on, my scouting was mostly an individual affair. Sometimes I would go out with another man—after the orders were issued that no man was to go out alone— but that was merely a way of evading the spirit of the order while, at the same time, observing the letter. One man can do pretty much as he pleases—that is, if he is not hit by one of the chance bullets or shells which are always floating around—but if there are two or more in the party, not one single individual dare make a move without, possibly, interrupting the game of some other. I learned that it was no serious matter to crawl out, locate a gap in the enemy wire, squirm up alongside their parapet—and take a short course in German. But my chief object was to try and locate their machine gun emplacements. That was something that vitally interested us—me, especially, as a machine gunner. Time after time, I had spent hours, trying to locate a new one. One night Bouchard and I went over and checked up on one which we had been observing from our Snipers Barn look-out. As we lay there, under the lee of the enemy parapet and right alongside the loop-hole of the newly constructed "pill-box", I was listening to the talk from within while the kid, who understood and spoke good French but knew not a word of German, suddenly grabbed me by the arm and whispered, "let's get-a-hell out a this" and dragged me down the embankment. Almost instantly came the sound of a terrific explosion in the M. G. emplacement. The little rascal had pulled the pin and slipped a Mills grenade right through the loop-hole. That was a favorite stunt of his and we repeated it several times.

Well, now, it looks as if we were again getting off the track. This chapter is supposed to be about pistols and here we are, yarning about bombs, machine guns and what-not. But that's all right. It is all about "close-up" work and that is the only place that the pistol figures in warfare. Now I am going to tell you the honest truth about something. During my war experience, which extended from September, 1915 to February, 1917 and included innumerable little "contacts" with the enemy and several major battles, I fired exactly seven shots at an enemy with my pistol. *Seven*—count 'em. I used up quite a lot of ammunition, shoting at rats, rabbits and tin cans but as to shooting Germans, well, I've told you, seven was all and the longest range at which I fired at these individuals was never more than ten feet. But brother, those were seven badly needed shots. There may be a moral in this: I don't know. If so, figure it out for yourself.

But there is no doubt in my mind that the mere possession of a reliable pistol—and the knowledge how to use it— is a tower of strength for the soldier who goes up against any enemy. He may never use it, may never have a chance to use it, but it sure does give you a lot of confidence to know that you have the old "gat" right there and handy, in case you do happen to bump into some wild-eyed individual coming at you with a bayonet.

War automatically declares an "open season" on men. You shoot or stab or club them and think no more of it than you do of breaking a clay pigeon thrown from a trap. There's nothing very personal about it but you know that if you don't get the other fellow, he will probably get you— and you do your best.

As to the various kinds of pistols used, both by the Allies and the Germans, after all these years during which to think it over, I still believe that the Colt, .45 Automatic is King of Them All. This new .38 Super-Colt appears to be a still better bet if one is looking for high velocity and all that but I do not believe that it has any point of superiority, as a military arm, over the .45 caliber. I have no authority for the statement, but it is my belief that it is brought out simply to show that we can produce a high-velocity, medium caliber pistol that not only equals but excels the German Lugers and Mausers in both range and power. Candidly, I do not know what it is good for—unless some of our sportsmen are contemplating going in for big game shooting with the pistol. No telling what some of our new crop of cranks will do. They shoot 'em with bow and arrow and I expect, any day, to read in the headlines of where some brave nimrod has slain one of our pet Park bears with a stone hammer.

I had used both the Luger and Mauser pistols before the war, and often during the war I would pick up one and give it a tryout; but, without attempting to enumerate any specific merits or faults of either, they just did not appeal to me. Now, this is not because of any prejudice against the German, because no such feeling exists. A lot of the best friends I have in the world are either German bred or of German extraction and about the greatest pleasures I have enjoyed have been connected with steins of good German beer and the accompanying good-fellowship—the songs and camaraderie of good fellows when they get together.

No, it was just that, like the Webley, they always appeared to be clumsy—cumbersome. Shoot? Hell yes, they shot all right for the three Ps—Punch, Penetration and Power—they were about in a class by themselves for these, but to go on down the alphabet, when you come to W, just stop and consider the Colt .45 and it's Wallop. You better

also go back to the beginning of the alphabet and add
Accuracy. That old .45 slug has more authority than any
of the others, not excepting the 9 m/m Luger, and as for
accuracy, there never was a Luger or Mauser made to even
come within hailing distance of our Service Colt.

Say—wait a minute though. I do happen to remember
one instance in which the German Luger had wallop enough
to do the job right, and maybe I had better tell about it
right here. The incident occurred down on the Somme,
where I was working along with the advance, commanding
a scratch crew of machine gunners. There was a lull in
the fighting and we were waiting on something or other at
the time, the Germans having all pulled out of their trenches
and moved back a bit to the rear. So I decided to look
about the German trenches and dugouts and see if we could
locate some loaded belts of their machine gun ammunition,
as we had just found two perfectly good Maxim heavies
that might as well have been put back to work.

Calling upon a couple of the gun crew to come along with
me, the three of us crawled over into the main German
trenches and commenced searching around for some loaded
belts. One of the chaps who accompanied me was evidently
a new replacement, at any rate he still had the souvenir bug
in his head, and tried to pick up everything lying in that
trench. I soon put a stop to this, and made him throw
away most of the junk he was carrying, but he held on to
a Luger pistol which was in a holster slung onto a black
leather waist belt—this find I decided to overlook. Those
trenches were the usual deep and well made German affair,
showing the result of months of hard pick and shovel work,
but they had been pretty badly battered by our guns and
the bottom was mostly covered with a layer of loose dirt,
upon which we made no noise as we crawled around the
traverses and bays.

The souvenir hound kept sticking a bit in front of us, I

suppose he wanted another pistol or two, but at any rate he kept ahead, swinging that Luger from the buckled belt held in his right hand. In this manner we stepped around the end of a deep traverse and our "point" almost fell over a big Heinie who was down on his knees going through the pockets of a dead British officer—the Dutchman was so busy he never even knew we were around. It was all over in a second—the kid just swung the belt and that holstered Luger made a circle and came down on top of the German's head with a "womp"—and we went on, leaving both dead men lying there. And that is about the only time I can remember a "slug" from a Luger having sufficient wallop to do a "bang up" job of things.

But the main thing in considering any military pistol is the matter of *dependability*. Will it work in all kinds of weather? In mud—in sand—in water? Well, we all know what tests were applied during the two or three years before our Ordnance officers finally approved the Colt. Two solid years of real, practical use, in service in the Islands and then the tests for what you might call "durability" in which all others (there were only two, which shall not be named by me) fell by the wayside while the old Colt, refusing to quit, finally wore out the time and patience of the members of the Board and had to leave it with an unfinished run of some ten thousand rounds without a stoppage or malfunction. I was present at that last test, and that may have had something to do with my attitude toward the ugly brute.

Still, I can say that my experience in France, as well as that of others of my acquaintance, only tended towards verifying the findings and opinion of our ordnance board. Those of us who were fortunate enough to be armed with the .45 Colt Automatic found it to be a sufficient and *dependable* arm in every respect. Let me repeat that I have never had a failure to function properly while in action nor did I ever hear or know of any such failure occuring with any of my associates or acquaintances. After I came back from the battlefield I commenced to hear of a great many instances in which the gun supposedly gave trouble, but these were invariably told by persons not in the army or whose line of duty was such as to preclude their ever having actually participated in real fighting, or even front-line service for that matter.

Furthermore, I did not consider the automatic pistol to need any special care or attention to keep it in serviceable condition. We had trouble enough with *all* our firearms for that matter, and any rifle, machine gun, revolver or pistol had to be looked to daily to keep the mud and dirt out of its action and bore. If anything, our one-hand guns were a bit easier to keep in proper shape than the others, because they remained in a holster or inside pocket of a tunic and were not laid down on the ground or exposed to the elements very often. Any military firearm requires daily attention and care to keep it in proper readiness for instant use and neither pistol nor revolver is any exception to this standing rule.

For extremely accurate target shooting and for what I may call *comfortable,* peace-time pistol practice, there are many revolvers and single-shot target pistols—not forgetting the little .22 caliber automatics—which are more desirable than the .45 Automatic. But when you go to war, you want a regular "he-man" gun with a WALLOP.

Chapter 11

The Battle of St. Eloi

ALONG in February, 1916 business began to pick up a bit and we soon entered upon what turned out to be a continuous engagement—running along until June. The Battle of the Bluff, which started the latter part of February, carried on into March. Then began the St. Eloi scrap which, considering the small bit of line involved, was one of the nastiest and most hard-fought "minor" actions on record. From the 27th of March until late in May, it was a continuous dog fight for possession of what was known as "The Mound", a dominating height at the extreme southern end of the Ypres salient, in what had been the village of St. Eloi. I remember that, in writing home to my father, himself a veteran of the Civil War, I quoted Kit Carson's famous remark, "lovely fighting all along the line, go in anywhere". That described it, exactly. Plenty of action for all. Artillery, machine guns, rifles and grenades—all had their innings, every day and night.

The ruckus started when our engineers blew a series of six great mines under the Mound—which was, at that time, occupied by the enemy—and the Northumbrian Division, consisting of the Northumberland Fusiliers, the Royal Fusiliers and the Yorkshire Regiment, swarmed over and occupied the craters and some of the ground beyond and tried to consolidate it. They were soon relieved by a Scottish Division, consisting of Royal Scots and Gordons.

The Argyll and Sutherlands were also in there for a short time but the job was finally wished onto the Second Canadian Division (that was *us*), and we stuck around there until the finish. When the action started we were stationed adjoining and to the right of the Northumbrian Division, so all we had to do was to "side step" over to the left a little way to be right in it. We of the machine guns, however, had been in the fight from the start, but our infantry did not take over for a week or so after it commenced.

As this was our first real *battle,* the recollection of many of the things that happened there are much more vivid and distinct than those of many other, greater battles that came later. These latter were "just a little more of the same", that was all; but it is a true saying that first impressions are the strongest, so I will probably have a good deal more to say about that St. Eloi affair than its real significance in the war may seem to warrant.

It was the evening of March 26, 1916. Two hundred Yorkshire men were coming down the communication trench. They were replacements for the Northumbrian Division, on the left, due to go over the top in an attack in the morning. I was standing at the mouth of the trench where they would enter the front line. The whiz-bangs were coming over from Germany and bursting all around, but we were so used to these that I paid no attention until I happened to notice that there appeared to be an unusual concentration of fire on that particular communication trench. It was only about four hundred yards long and, from my slightly elevated position, all in plain sight. It was just about dark—dusk, we call it—and the bursts of the shells were plainly visible. By this time the "fireflies" were so thick and continuous that I could not help noticing them, and mildly wondered what was going on. We had men whose duty it was to count and report the number of shells that fell on any area and it is a matter of record that more than one thousand shells burst in and over that short bit of trench in less than thirty minutes. The enemy evidently knew about that detachment coming in and tried to clean up on them. Pretty soon the head of the line came into the front line trench, lead by an old, grizzled, sergeant-major who waved them off to the left and, himself, stepped up beside me and dug up an old pipe which he proceeded to fill with shag. After getting the thing going, he straightened up and I ventured to remark: "pretty hot down there, wasn't it?" He took a few puffs, to keep the pipe going and answered: "Aye: pretty good: gives the younguns an idea what they may expect on the morrow."

That night we saw the Yorkshiremen sewing squares of white cloth on the backs of their tunics. It was the first time we had seen any such thing as "battle-colors." Thereafter, they were universally used—but sewn on the sleeve, at the shoulder. The same practice was followed by the U. S. troops, when they came in—that is, the divisional insignia. With the Canadians, the system was such that you could tell, at a glance, not only the division, but the battalion to which the soldier belonged.

It seems a pity that the expression: "Over the Top" has been so cheapened—yes, desecrated—by thoughtless or ignorant civilians. To the soldier it is an event of the most tremendous meaning: the very apotheosis of war. To endure the tense hour of waiting the "zero" and then, in the gray dawn and amid the thunderbolts of steel and the sleet of bullets, to climb up and advance—well, it requires something more than the willingness to buy a Liberty bond or subscribe to a Community Chest fund.

The battle opened with the exploding of the six great mines simultaneously. It was a magnificent spectacle for those of us who were in position to view it. To the enemy it must have been something beyond any descriptive effort, as the mines were laid in a line that cut off a large corner or salient of their line and took in their first and second lines for a distance of some six hundred yards. Whatever force they had in those trenches was simply annihiliated.

The Fusiliers and Yorks promptly advanced to a point beyond the craters and started vigorously to work to consolidate the position by reversing parts of the German third line trench and connecting it up with our original front line. They made a brave effort but were unable to complete the work under the overwhelming concentration of artillery. All during that day and for many succeeding days, attacks and counter-attacks followed one another, continuously.

Any attempt to relate, chronologically, the progress of the battle, would be futile. It was the same thing, over and over with first one side and then the other holding the dominating positions.

I was in charge of a number of machine guns which had been brought up to support the advance. Our job was to lay a barrage which would harrass and impede the progress of reinforcements which the enemy would send up, and in order to do this effectively it was necessary to mount the guns on the parapet with little or no protection, as all our regular, permanent, gun emplacements were designed for defense only, and commanded nothing beyond the no-man's-land between the opposing front line trenches. It was all indirect fire, of course, but I had worked out the firing data the previous night, and we, later, had the testimony of prisoners to the effect that the machine gun barrage was decidedly efficient—far worse, they said, than that of our artillery.

This is not difficult to understand—that is, if one has a general knowledge of the methods of artillery fire. When a barrage starts, if it does not get you right then, you can nearly always tell just what sort of an operation they are intending. All artillery work, just the same as other tactical operations, has been very carefully figured out beforehand.

A certain area of enemy territory is to be swept by each
battery. The rate of fire has been calculated, so as to insure
an adequate ammunition supply. They, necessarily, work on
a very rigid schedule and the first few moves of the game
give the enemy at least an inkling as to the particular "gam-
bit" they are working on.

The very thoroughness and perfection of an artillery
barrage often defeats itself. That was one thing in which
the Germans were exceptionally good. They were so
methodical that we could, and often did, take large bodies
of men through their barrages with small loss. In a way,
it supports the theory, long ago propounded by one of our,
(U. S.), military experts, that it is better to have a force
of more or less inexpert shooters than to have them all
"Expert Riflemen". The idea, of course, being that there
would be such a wide dispersion of fire that a certain number
of the enemy would be hit by the *wide* shots.

A machine gun barrage is different, in a way. While the
field and rate of fire is just as carefully calculated, the guns
fire so rapidly and, if properly coordinated, so continuously,
on every yard of enemy line that there is no chance to
"jump through a hole," as we used to say.

Many additional trench mortars had been brought up,
ranging all the way from Stokes guns to one that fired a
"drumstick" affair with a sixty-pound round shell on its
business end. The firing of the mines was our signal to
open up; also for our artillery, and for several minutes all
the noise was either on or *from* our side. But only for a
few minutes. The rapidity with which the enemy got into
action indicated that he was expecting something to happen
and the devilish accuracy of his fire was a distinct revelation
to us. His shells swept the tops of our parapets like a
broom. Two guns were dismounted almost at the first
fire. Men were killed all about us. I made a short trip of
some fifty yards or so, to get a spare barrel, and was

knocked down, time after time, and partially buried by shells
that just did miss me. This lasted for about an hour, by
which time the enemy had found out just where the main
attack was directed and concentrated most of their fire on
that area, so we had a chance to get reorganized. Of course,
we were still subjected to a continuous shelling, but not so
severe as at first. We lost guns and men every day from
that time on, but managed to keep up a pretty effective fire
at that.

Soon after daylight, while standing beside one of my
guns which was temporarily out of action, I saw a column
of enemy infantry hurrying across an open space behind
their lines, and, taking a rifle, opened up on them. They
were less than two hundred yards away but the noise was
so deafening that they never did discover where the bullets
were coming from. For a long time, possibly thirty minutes,
I had the pleasure of directing deliberate, aimed fire at those
fellows. I used several rifles—men in the trench loading
and passing them up to me. Many times during the next
few weeks, I had chances to get in a few shots in the same
manner and others of our crowd had the same experience.
They were all keen riflemen and never overlooked such
opportunities.

Days and nights merged, one into another. All track of
time was lost. For fourteen days I was never out of that
inferno, but I never knew how long it was until I got out
and checked up on the calendar. In the meantime, the
Northumbrian Division had been relieved by a Scottish Division. Well do I remember when they came in.

It was "hell to tell the Captain," that morning. For many
days we had endured such a hurricane of shells as should,
theoretically, have annihilated any force. Our parapets were
blown down and dead and wounded were lying all around.
The Border Regiment and the Durham Light Infantry, who
were on our right and not subjected to the heavy shelling,

had sent in many volunteer stretcher-bearers and they worked heroically, but the casualties mounted so fast that, even with their help, it was impossible to evacuate all the wounded.   As to the dead, it was out of the question to even think of moving them, so we did the best we could— laid them up, out of the way, on firing step or parados— anywhere so we did not have to step on them. *Hell?* Yes, Ma'am : it was all that and then some.

The Fusiliers and the Yorks had taken their dose and were whittled down to a point where lieutenants were commanding battalions and sergeants commanding companies. To relieve them these Scots were sent in.   They were Gordons and Royal Scots, mostly new, replacement men who had never before been under fire and here they sent them into one of the nastiest and bitterest fights ever waged on the Western Front.   They were "braw laddies," lank and lean but tall and strong; fresh from the heather of their native land, uncertain but willing, they were going to meet death half-way—and they knew it.

We had been in the fight so long that it was no longer a novelty, but to those youngsters, it must have seemed like something worse than Dante ever dreamed about. But, they came in; and, wonder of wonders, their pipers came with them.   That was the first time I ever heard the bagpipes in battle.   We had a pipe-band in our battalion and a good one, too, but, during the time we were simply holding the line, the pipers and all the other bandsmen served as stretcher-bearers and first-aid men—getting the wounded out and back to the dressing stations which were anywhere from a mile to three miles in the rear. But now we learned (we saw the same thing several times thereafter), that when the Scots go into battle, or over the top, in an offensive, their pipers go along, or, at least the Pipe Major and perhaps, another one or two, to "play them in."

Man! Man! if you have never seen it, you can never

get the thrill. Marching along as though on parade, never missing a note or a step, skirling those wild, heartrending airs that date back to the time of Bonnie Prince Charlie, they march into battle as though no such things as bullets or shells existed.

Well, here they came, Gordons ahead—a few old timers with ribbons that dated back to Kandahar—and the youngsters following. They had come through a tough barrage and lost quite a lot of men and the recruits were looking pretty white. I happened to be at the mouth of the communication trench when they arrived, and stood by to watch them. Six generations have passed since my ancestors came from Scotland but I take no shame in telling you that, as I watched those boys walk into that fight, scared though they were, with their chins up and their rifles ready—and the pipers playing "The Cock o' the North," which was our own Regimental air, I cried like a baby; aye, cried; while, all the time I was calling out to them, "Go to it, lads, it's a good fight; go in and do your best." The old timers gave me a wave of the hand and the younkers seemed to perk up a bit. I followed along, as we had some half-dozen machine guns up where they were going and I was due there, anyway. The pipers changed to "The March of Gordon's Own" but it was all the same to me. I was ready and eager, right then, to march to hell and beyond, behind that music. (?) Is it *music,* or just a noise? You will never prove it by me, but I do know that whenever I hear it I want to go out and kill somebody.

They did not last long, those Scots. No one lasted very long in that inferno, excepting a few ornery Emma Gees who were too tough to die just yet. But they performed gloriously during the time they were there. I saw a company of them one day engage in hand-to-hand combat with a greatly superior (numerically) force of Germans. It was a bayonet fight, pure and simple, and when it was ended, there was not a living German on the field, and no prisoners were taken.   Strong, agile, long-legged—the slower, calculating Boche had no chance against them.   As I watched, from my vantage point on the parapet, unable to fire because of the way they were mixed up in the melee, I could not but think of the stories I had read of Bannockburn, Culloden and many other bloody battles that figure largely in Scottish history.   I imagined the claymore in place of the modern bayonet; and, though I could hear nothing amid the continuous crash of shells, I fancied that they were shouting the old Gaelic battle cries.

But the shells got them eventually, as they got everybody who stayed too long in one place.   They melted away.   That six-hundred-yard bit of ground claimed more than ten thousand lives during that week, but, as the French were wont to say: *"Que voulez vou? c'est le guerre."*

After the Scots had had their innings, the debatable ground was turned over to the Second Canadian Division and from that time on we had our own private war.   Alternating by brigades, we took and re-took the various craters and lost them.   We could get in all right, but could not stay there long enough to consolidate the positions effectively against the heavy enemy artillery fire.   Soon the whole terrain where the front lines had been and for nearly a half-mile behind them became a desolate waste.   No trenches, no roads, no trees—nothing but a barren stretch of muddy ground, so thickly pock-marked with shell-holes that they were interlocked over the whole area.   Our "line" was merely an irregular series of detached posts, established in shell holes.   From these points, every night some detachments would advance and gain a foothold in or near some one of the craters.   Determined bombing attacks more than once secured possession of all of them but the ensuing artillery fire could not be withstood by flesh and blood and eventually we were forced to rebuild our front line in approximately the same location it had occupied before the commencement of the fight.

Just to try and give you an idea of the game as we played it during that time, I'll tell you a little story. It might be entitled "All in the day's Work," for that was what it was.

Six of us, sitting in a shell-hole one night waiting for something to happen. Heinie was plastering us, pretty regularly, with crumps and whiz-bangs, so we dug in as deep as the water would permit and hoped he would not drop one right on top of us. The mud was so deep that even a five-point-nine H. E. could burst within twenty feet without doing any more damage than to add a little more to our coating of the nasty, stinking soil of Flanders.

It was the usual machine-gun crew, with the difference that, instead of being commanded by a "lance-jack," as was customary, we had a sergeant with us. Either due to the importance of the position or, perhaps, just because he wanted a little action, the sergeant had come along. As we had lost one man earlier in the day, and had had no chance to get a replacement, the unit remained at its normal strength. All hands had been through considerable fighting and had settled down to the game with the fatalistic assurance of veterans.

No one was saying much, but pretty soon the sergeant sat up and listened, then said, "you fellows notice anything?" Then, without waiting for an answer, he continued, "a little while ago all those shells were dropping right around here and now they are going back to about where our front line used to be. You know what that means. Better dig yourselves out of that muck and get ready for business. If Fritz don't pay us a call right soon, I'll buy the beer for the crowd—if we ever get where there is any beer."

All hands knew exactly what to expect, so no more words were necessary. We quickly pulled the protecting sand-bags and rubber sheet off the gun and the Kid gave her a couple of flips, just to make sure she was working all right, and Dan got up where he could see over the edge of the hole. He hadn't been there long when he saw something moving, out in front, so he pulled the sergeant up and pointed. He (the sergeant) just took one look, then: "Holy Moses, here comes the whole German Army. Get that damn gun up here, where we can do something." And then he grabbed the gun and yanked it up onto a level spot, the others helping by steadying the legs of the tripod and the ammunition box. By that time, we could see a lot of men coming out over the parapet of the crater, not more than fifty yards away. They were outlined against the sky and were in some sort of column formation—probably to get through a gap in the tangled wire. It was a sure thing they did not know we were there, as we had come out since dark. It was impossible to see the sights of the gun, but the sergeant just leveled her up, loosened the traversing gear and cut loose with a burst of fifteen or twenty shots and then kept up a steady gait, burst—pause—burst—pause—swinging back and forth all the time, so as not to slight anyone.

For a spell, maybe half a minute nothing happened. Then a few hand grenades burst just in front—too short to reach us. "Get in on this, you fellows", shouted the sergeant, "hand 'em back a few of Mr. Mills' specials." So, we heaved over one or two apiece and that held 'em. Just then, some-one on our side sent up a flare which sailed over our heads and dropped smack in the crater. That was sure a sign of bad luck for the Dutchmen as it showed us every foot of their parapet, like a silhouette cut out of black paper. "Now, your rifles, boys and see if you can pick 'em off as they try to go home," sang out the sergeant, all the time searching out the dark shadows at the foot of the em-bankment with M. G. bullets.

Well, we got most of them, one way and another. Of course, you can't see to do much aiming at night but, if a man is thoroughly familiar with the feel of his rifle, as we were, it is possible to do considerable execution, even in the dark. Some of them may have got back, but most of them stayed—for keeps. Then there was nothing for us to do but wait for the next move.

We did not have very long to wait, at that. First thing we knew, here came the whiz-bangs, popping and flashing all around us, like a bunch of fire-crackers. Simpson and Black Dan both got splinters that made them swear and I guess we all had a few scratches.

What to do? What to do? That was what all hands were wondering, but it was the sergeant, as usual and proper, who took charge and decided the matter. "Come on, boys," he says and, taking the gun off the tripod, started straight toward Germany; and we all followed, carrying and dragging the rest of the paraphernalia.

We walked, crawled and stumbled, right up under the lee of the parapet of the crater. A lot of Germans were scattered around there, some dead and some wounded. One of the latter let out a yell and started to crawl up the bank but someone jumped up and cracked him over the head with a gun barrel and he rolled back again. None of the others appeared to be able to do any damage, so we left them alone for the time.

Well, there were we, safe enough for the moment, but the sergeant was doing some heavy thinking. It was something like this; "If we just stay here and wait, it won't be long until Fritz brings up a bunch of supports and bombs hell out of us. On the other hand, the chances are that those fellows in the crater are pretty much demoralized right now and it ought to be easy to stampede them clean out of the place. Yep, that's the dope." Turning to the bunch and getting their heads close enough so that his words could be understood above the din of the bombardment, he shouted, "It's up to us to get into that crater.

How many grenades you fellows got left in your pockets?"
A canvass revealed six, in all. "Hum, not enough, better
get a few off those Dutchmen." So we searched around
and found quite a lot of the potato-mashers. We all knew
how they worked, having used them on previous occasions.
We got about a dozen of them, altogether. By this time
Simpson was pretty groggy from a bad cut on the head
(that was before we had tin hats) and Dan McGuire was
having a lot of trouble, stopping the bleeding from a nasty,
slashing cut in his side, made by a splinter of shell. Otherwise we were unhurt and those two said they could carry
on for a while longer.

When we were all fixed up with the grenades, the sergeant
got us together again. "Have you all got your rifles?" he
asked. All had, excepting the Kid. "Oh-ho," says the
sergeant, "threw it away again, did you? An' I know damn
well why you did it, laddie. Want to use that pistol, do
you? All right, get it out and see does the slide work nice
and easy, for this night you are sure going to have a chance
to try it." It was a standing joke among us about that
pistol which had been sent from Canada by the Kid's
mother—engraved with his initials and everything. It was
a regulation Colt .45 automatic, but he had had no chance
to do any practicing with it as it had been received since
we came into the line. He kept it, oiled and carefully
wrapped up in a cloth and stowed inside his tunic. "Ah-
hum," continued the sergeant, "well, here's where you find
out how good you are. Get all your extra magazines in your
left-hand pocket. Remember to throw out and reload after
every seventh shot—Oh, hell, no, nobody ever remembered
that much in a fight. Well, guess that's about all there is
to it. All set? Now, when I give the word, heave over
all the grenades and then follow me. When we go over
the bank you all start shooting and keep it up as long as
there is a German left on his feet.———Let's go."

Working fast, it took but a few seconds to throw all the grenades and but a few more seconds for all of them to explode. Curiously enough, none of us noticed, at the time, that there was no return from the crater. Up and over the top we jumped, firing as we went. Once inside, we realized that the place was practically unoccupied. A few dead and wounded men were there and that was all. Evidently the enemy had not been holding the crater in force but had only used it as a convenient jumping off place for the attempted attack which we had stopped. Whether or not they would at once attempt to re-occupy it was the question that most interested us. These craters (there were six of them) had been debatable ground for weeks, passing back and forth, sometimes twice during the same night. Both sides had made many ineffectual attempts to consolidate and fortify them and, at one time, we had a line of trench that completely surrounded them; but, in that case, as in others, the superiority of the German artillery had driven us out. Bombing attacks by our side would enable us to recapture any one of the places but we had never been able to construct adequate defense against the inevitable hail of shells which followed.

For the benefit of the layman, perhaps a short talk on the subject of mines, craters, saps, etc. may be in order.

In any kind of "siege warfare"—and trench war is just a form of siege operation—each side attempts to take and hold certain dominating points, positions which enable them to *command* or overlook the ground occupied by the enemy forces.

From such positions they can inflict much damage without incurring an equal measure of casualties. Naturally, then, these places become the focal points of much desperate fighting. Whenever one of the combatants has succeeded in so firmly entrenching himself in such a position that he cannot be dislodged by any of the usual methods of attack, then the job is turned over to the Engineers and they proceed to the work of sapping.

Now, there are saps and saps—the kind you see around you every day and the other kind, and it is to this other kind I refer. A sap, in military parlance, is merely a tunnel. A miner would call it a "drift." Starting from a point well behind our lines, it extends across the no-man's-land and under the enemy trench, where, if the operation has been successfully carried out, a chamber is dug and the space filled with powder or other explosive. The chamber is then sealed up and the tunnel filled in. Wires connected with the electric primers—detonators, they are called—which have been placed in the explosive charge, are carried back into our lines where they can be connected with a battery and the charge exploded.

If the work has been carried out without the knowledge of the enemy, the result of such an explosion is pretty awful. Earth, buildings and men go up in a veritable geyser and there remains a "crater" or pit, depending in size and depth upon the amount of explosive used. The inside will be in the shape of an inverted cone and all around the edge will be a wall of earth. Before the mine is fired, arrangements will have been made to have a force of men ready to rush forward and occupy the crater and then, for some time, it becomes a cock-pit in which the opposing forces contend for possession.

However, with the delicate instruments now available, it is nearly always possible to detect and follow the progress of any such sapping, with the result that the enemy will resort to one of two means to defeat the operation. He may elect to try what is known as "counter-sapping." In this case he endeavors to drive his own sap so as to reach a point directly beneath that of the enemy, from which point he will explode a charge of powder which will destroy the upper work.

Or, if he has reason to believe that the sap is near the surface, he will direct the fire of several heavy guns on the place in the effort to cave in and destroy the tunnel. During the entire period in which we occupied any part of the line up there around Ypres, such operations were going on. We knew, and the enemy knew, that any of us were liable to be blown up most any time. Which is just another of the things that help to keep war from becoming too monotonous.

I notice that I have been using the word "saps" rather loosely. I should have brought in the "Tunnelers." A sap, strictly speaking, is more of a trench than a tunnel but, in the old days, this whole branch of the Corps of Engineers was embraced under the title, "Miners and Sappers." Nowadays they have the regular "Tunneling Companies." However, the two lines of work are so closely associated and so often merged into a single operation that I do not expect to be severely criticized on this point, so we will let it go at that.

Now, these particular craters were the results of many months of work and were among the largest I have ever seen, one of them being at least two hundred feet across and three of the others were almost as large. The walls of earth, on the lips of the craters were raised up some ten feet or more above the surrounding ground and the pits inside were anywhere from ten to twenty feet deeper. At the time of which I write, the central part of all the craters was filled with water, only a few feet around the edge being available for standing room. The water was filled with things not pleasant to think about. Many men had died there and the bodies of these, together with the twisted metal, broken timbers and other debris from the blown-up trenches made a horrible mess, but, "believe it or not," we had become so accustomed to that sort of thing that we could and did move about, eat and sleep there without the slightest compunction.

After considerable groping around in the dark, assisted now and then by the light of a flare from one side or the other, we found the end of the trench which communicated with "Germany." Moving cautiously down this some fifty or sixty feet, we left one man there to watch. Returning to the crater we looked over the wounded men and found that only two of them still lived. One of these had a shattered leg and the other was suffering from a head wound and was delirious. We did what we could for them and then went outside and got three more whom we brought in. One of these was shot through the body and died before morning, while another had received two bullets through the legs and was unable to stand. The third, who proved to be the one who had been knocked out with the gun barrel, was but slightly injured, having been stunned by a grenade and cut in a few places by fragments. Fortunately, this one could talk English and we got a lot of information from him. Among other things, he said that he had been in this crater before and that they had orders that, if they were overwhelmed, to throw the machine guns into the water in the middle of the crater. Acting on this tip, we spent some time in fishing around and we really did find one tripod and several belts of ammunition.

Paul—that was this German's name—when he found that we did not intend to kill him—loosened up and told us all he knew. He was a Saxon and had lived in New York for several years, but, being in Germany on a visit when the war broke out, had been immediately drafted into the army. Owing to the fact that he happened to be sight-seeing in Munich at the time, as near as I could make out, he was put in with the Bavarian troops and had become a machine gunner. It was apparent that he had but little love for the Bavarians, especially the officers, and I rather think he was very well satisfied to be taken prisoner. I met more than one like that.

Along toward morning—just as it was beginning to get light in the east—the man who was on guard in the trench came hurrying in and said that he could hear someone coming our way. Without a moment's hesitation, the sergeant ran for the trench, calling for two men to follow. They ran down until they were concealed by a traverse, quickly hiding themselves under an overhanging roof—probably an ammunition bay. In a few moments men could be heard coming along the trench. Acting on the instructions of the sergeant, we all crouched close to the wall in silence. One after another, eight men passed us, the first six carrying a machine gun, with mount and many boxes of ammunition. The last two carried large cooking pots and sacks of something. When the last had passed, we slipped out behind them and followed until, just as they were rounding the corner leading into the crater, the sergeant called for them to halt. We all had our rifles and when those fellows turned around to see what it was all about, they simply gave a few grunts of astonishment, dropped their loads and put up their hands.

It was the easiest capture I ever saw. We made them carry all the stuff inside, and then, after disarming them, took them around to the other side of the hole and left them, with one man to watch. They were coming up to relieve the gun crew who were supposed to be in the crater and had two days cooked rations with them, in addition to the regular haversack ration. Pretty soft for us. In the sacks were several little loaves of *schwartzbrod,* cheese and some kind of *wurst* while one of the cans contained a mess of stew, the principal ingredient of which appeared to be onions. There were some other vegetables in it and, of meat there was, as a chemist or assayer might say "a trace." However, it was not at all hard to take at that time and we soon disposed of the lot, sharing, of course, with the prisoners. The other can held nothing but water but that, too, was very welcome.

About this time I noticed one of the prisoners taking his little round water bottle off his belt and slipping it into his inside coat pocket. Acting on a hunch, I went over and asked one of them to give me a drink. He pretended not to understand, so I took possession of his "canteen" and helped myself. My hunch was a good one, for the bottle was filled with brandy. We quickly possessed ourselves of the others and found that they all contained the same liquor. Oh, man: that was a godsend. We let each of the prisoners take a good drink and gave the wounded men a little extra and then put the rest where it would do the most good for the cause of "democracy." We then started a search of all the other bottles on the dead Germans lying around but found them to contain nothing but water. Paul did a little talking with the new bunch and learned that they had found a case of brandy which was intended for some officer's mess and had appropriated all they could carry.

By then it was broad daylight and high time to consider the future. The wounded men must be cared for very soon or it would be too late. In that place, where the earth, water and even the air, were polluted with the rotten flesh of long-dead men and all the other nasty things which your imagination can supply, it was imperative that wounds be thoroughly cleansed and disinfected without delay or death would probably result. After considerable cogitation the sergeant decided upon a course which might have been thought foolish but which, as events proved, was the correct one. It was obviously impossible to get back to our lines in daylight as the ground over that way was under direct observation from Germany and not even a snake could have covered it without being detected. So he called Paul and told him he was going to send two of the last batch of prisoners out with the wounded Germans—back to their own lines—as we did not wish to be encumbered with them and he emphasized the fact that it was their only chance for life. These men

were to take the wounded, one at a time, to the nearest
dressing station and leave them there. The carriers were
to be told that all the other prisoners were to be kept in the
crater—as hostages. He figured that this would serve to
prevent any shelling or other attempt at hostilities, during
the day.

By utilizing pieces of board from the wrecked dug-outs,
bits of chicken wire which had probably been used as revet-
ting material and strips of cloth torn from uniforms, a serviceable stretcher was made and the first man carried out.
The same procedure was carried out with the rest, only that
the carriers, when they came back from the first trip, had
brought a regular litter. As soon as they had departed with
the last of the wounded men, we went to work and built up
a substantial barricade across the trench, well outside the
crater—and then settled down for a rest. Imagine our surprise when the two stretcher-bearers came back and, without
a word, climbed over the barricade and went over and rejoined their comrades in the crater. We asked Paul "How
come?" but he just laughed and said they were sick of the
war and would rather be prisoners. Now, I cannot conceive of any Canadian, or other Britisher, for that matter,
doing a thing like that but you never can tell about a German. They do and think things that are beyond our comprehension.

We took turns sleeping and the only disturbance during
the day was when our own artillery put about a dozen shells
into and around the crater—evidently thinking it was occupied by the enemy. No one was hurt, and, as soon as it
was dark, Dan and Simpson were sent back to our lines with
the prisoners—all but Paul, whom we kept in case we might
have further use for an interpreter. He did not like it at
all as he wanted as he expressed it, to "get to hell out of
here."

Dan carried a message to be delivered to the first officer

he met, explaining the situation and requesting that a force be sent over to relieve us. We were not disturbed by the enemy and, shortly after midnight, a platoon of infantry and a machine gun crew came in and we returned to our lines— very well pleased with ourselves. And, as events turned out, we were *very* lucky. Just before daylight, the enemy turned loose with his artillery and killed nearly half of the members of the garrison of the crater: compelling the re- tirement of the survivors.

That was the way it went. There was one time, however, when one of our machine gun crews, under Sergeant Nor- ton-Taylor, occupied one of those craters for five days, sub- sisting on the food and water they took from dead Germans and they not only *held* the crater all this time but actually took prisoners, including one full crew of enemy machine gunners. During that time, such was the confusion, due to the craters changing hands so often, that we had given them up for lost. They were finally relieved by a patrol from the Nineteenth Battalion, on our left.

Telling you the incident about the prisoner, Paul, a few pages back reminds me of another extremely odd happening which occurred to me several weeks before this time. Dur- ing my more or less "checkered" career, I have had many practical demonstrations of the fact that "truth is stranger than fiction." One such comes to mind now.

About ten o'clock one night they commenced to give us an awful shelling. This was so unusual that we felt certain that Fritz was up to some devilment so, of course, all hands were wide awake and on the alert. I had been standing beside Major Gray when a couple of shells ripped through the top of our parapet, one on each side of us and not more than five or six feet distant, both going on and exploding in the ditch behind the trench without doing any damage. Hun- dreds of others were bursting all along the line and, despite all efforts to take cover, many casualties resulted.

This Major Gray, by the way, was the one who, when we were all so tired and weary on a march that we could scarcely stagger, would stride down along the line and strike up some old nonsensical song that would immediately bring us to life. I well remember one of his favorites. It goes like this:

"I'm tired of living alone;
"I want a wee wife of my own;
"Someone to caress me, someone to undress me—
"I'm tired of sleeping alone."

Things having quieted down a bit and the Major having gone back to his dug-out, I meandered along the line, stopping now and then to check up on the various M. G. crews. Just as I arrived at the gun emplacement at the junction of the O and P trenches I heard a sharp challenge from the sentry on the firing step and, immediately after, saw a German soldier come crawling over the parapet and drop down into the trench, the sentry all the time keeping him covered with his rifle. Seeing me, he, (the sentry) said: "Here's a prisoner, Sergeant—and don't forget that I got him."

I took charge of the German and escorted him back to the Major's quarters. The Major was much interested, but, as he had no German, was at a loss to interrogate the fellow as he would have liked to do. My German was not anything to brag about, but, upon trying to talk to him in his own tongue, the boy—for that was all he was—about eighteen or nineteen—answered in English. He said: "We go bombing: we get lost: the shells come so quick I know not what to do. I look back and it is so far: I look here and it is so near. I think this is the better way so I come." Can you beat that?

But here comes the "coincidence." He was a youngster named Caspar Meyer, from Sachsenhausen, Waldeck, Bavaria, and I had visited with his family when he was a babe in arms and had, at that time persuaded his elder sister to take up the study of English. It seems that the boy also took it up when he became old enough. Well, he went back —a prisoner of war—but he seemed to be pretty well satisfied at that.

That was, I think, the first prisoner taken by the Twenty-first Battalion. The next was one whom I "captured" as he came over our parapet early one morning—a week or so later—and who turned out to be one of our Intelligence officers but, as he was wearing the full German uniform, I held him up and sent him back under guard. (You ought to have heard him swear.)

After that we picked them up, now and then; perhaps from a patrol, sometimes in a raid; but the first time we saw them in large numbers was during the St. Eloi fight. The Fusiliers and the Yorks grabbed off several hundred and sent them back through our lines. It seems that there was a story current in the German army that the Canadians always killed all prisoners and when these fellows found that they were to go through the Canadian lines they begged like good fellows. However they had to do it and, lo and behold, at every cook's dug-out, they were served with tea and whatever else was available. Captors and captives fared alike and one poor little rascal who was so worn out that he could hardly struggle along, found a bed in my dug-out and slept there all day—with my connivance, of course— and then made his own way back to our reserve lines.

In the actual heat of battle, when it comes to the final, hand-to-hand struggle, men revert to the elemental level of wild beasts and display the ferocity of a trapped tiger, killing remorselessly and indiscriminately, but, once the prisoner has been taken and sent to the rear, all such animosity is forgotten and he is treated very much as one of our own. Of course I know nothing of the conduct of the Germans in this respect or of our men who were taken prisoner (by the way, here is a good place to remark that the 21st never lost a man by capture), but I suppose it was about the same. Of course prisoners in the hands of the Germans did not get much to eat but neither did their captors—according to *our* standard of living, so they could not complain much on that score.

Later on—during the Somme battle, I saw them literally by the thousand (that is, German prisoners), and they all seemed to take their fate very philosophically. Evidently they had been well instructed as to how to act if captured. I have talked with many of them and have been present when they were interrogated by our intelligence officers and I never saw one who refused to give his name and regiment. (That is all any prisoner can be compelled to tell.) Sometimes they would tell a lot more—possibly true; perhaps not, but they all appeared to take the fact of their being captured as just a part of the war game and did not seem to grieve over-much about it. Some, I was inclined to think, were damn glad of it—glad to get out of it so easily. I can readily understand that attitude, although I never quite got to the point where I wanted to try it myself.

They went back to the barbed-wire stockades and from there to the permanent prison camps. Most of them were put to work on the roads or the docks at the sea-ports and appeared to be quite content to stay there and let the war take care of itself.

At first our men were so eager to get "souvenirs" that most of the prisoners went back sans belts or buttons but we always paid for them. We would exchange French script (money) for German marks and gave them a fair price for anything we took. Later, we had no time for such trifles and, excepting for weapons, let them keep everything they had. I suppose the military police and other non-combatants back at the rear probably cleaned up on them, however.

Chapter 12

Duds, Misfires and Stuck Bolts

THIS is not supposed to be a history of the war but a story for riflemen, so we will have to skip along, sketching in the general operations and looking for places to "take a shot."

During the latter stages of the St. Eloi operation there was scant opportunity for the rifleman. It was mostly a case of bomb 'em out of a crater and then get shelled out, yourself, the next day. All these minor actions took place at night but the days were not dull, by any means, as our positions were most persistently bombarded all the time.

I just happened to look at the calendar. Next Sunday will be Easter—and April 20th. A friend, sitting beside me, remarked that it was the latest he ever remembered Easter to come. Well; I remember one time it came a day later—April 21, 1916.

At that time, our line was simply a scattered lot of shell-holes, approximately where our *real* front line had been before the battle started. In each hole was a machine-gun crew and, sometimes, a few infantrymen. As the whole terrain was under direct observation from the enemy line, it was impossible to communicate with these detached posts in daylight, so we had to make our reliefs at night. Of course the enemy knew all about this and regularly swept the whole back area with both machine guns and whiz-bangs all night long, which made it a very interesting operation to get in and out. As sergeant, it was up to me to change these posts every night. The entire expanse of ground over which we must travel was literally leveled by shell fire. I say leveled, well, that is not quite right. It looked level, from a distance but it was one continuous field of shell-holes, just as close as the cells in a honey-comb—yes, closer, as these holes were locked and interlocked, one with another. Not a foot; no, not an inch of that ground had not been upturned more than once—and every depression was full of water.

To even find the various posts challenged the skill of an expert navigator—working by dead reckoning, alone. During all the time we were there, it rained continuously. Never a night was a star visible and the compass was useless, probably due to the fact that the ground was literally impregnated with iron and steel fragments from the shells. That we did manage to get the reliefs made at all was a matter to be proud of. Even the Germans, themselves, starting from a point much nearer than we did, often got lost and straggled into our lines. A whole platoon of them wandered into our line one night and were captured without a struggle. And, I want to record, right here, that, during all this time, we never lost a man by capture.

Well, as I started out to say, the night of April 20th, one of our detachments (I think Corporal Johnstone was in charge) missed its objective and went on through the line and, after hunting around for a long time the men found themselves right up under the parapet of one of the craters, which was occupied, at that time, by the enemy. By that time it was getting daylight and the Corporal, after sizing up the situation, decided that the only thing to do was to dig in right there and wait until the next night, and that is just what they did. Stayed there all day within twenty feet of the Germans—Easter Sunday, 1916. Well I remember it, for I was out all day looking for them. During the day our artillery took a notion to shell that particular crater, which made it still more interesting for them.   They all came back safely, soon after dark.

It was during one of the earlier stages of this battle that we learned that a rifle can be very much like a woman and that the lovable sweetheart of pre-nuptial days may fall far short of being the trustworthy and reliable helpmate in wedded life.

The first time we were called upon to repel a determined attack, and sustained rapid fire was in order, it was found that the Ross would not stand up under that kind of treatment.   Wonderfully accurate weapon as it was, it was never built for fast, rough work.   Never will I forget the time: one night when Heinie tried to rush our lines in one of his many charitable attempts to chase us out of our muddy muskrat holes and back on to the high and dry ground in our rear and we, with characteristic soldier perversity, declined to go, that I heard, during a little lull in the firing, a great voice, supplicating, praying, exhorting and, above all, cursing the whole Clan Ross.   Investigation showed it to be "Big Dan" McGann, assiduously trying to open the bolt of his rifle, using a big chunk of wood as a persuader.   During the short time allowed me to listen, I heard him specify each and every member of that family from away back—from the time of the "begats" down to the present generation, all designated by name and number, together with the most lurid and original adjectives it has ever been my pleasure to hear.   It was marvelous, entrancing—just to hear that man swear—but we soon found out that he was only doing what we should have liked to do, had we his extraordinary ability.   The bolts *would* stick and all hell could not open them.

We had trained intensively with this Ross rifle, both on the Barriefield ranges in Canada and at Hythe, England, and had found it thoroughly reliable and accurate.   Even in the strenuous rapid-fire tests, where fifteen shots per minute were required, it never failed. During a competition, one man fired thirty-three aimed shots (all on the target) in one minute, while many others exceeded twenty-five shots. In accuracy, up to six hundred yards, at least, it equalled or excelled any rifle I had or have since fired—the Springfield *not* excepted.

I have seen as many as forty consecutive bull's-eyes made with it at three hundred yards—on the six inch bull—and correspondingly good scores at five and six hundred yards. We had no regular practice beyond the latter range but, on several occasions, I have used this rifle successfully at ranges up to one thousand yards or more.

Mindful of all this, it can well be understood that we went into action with all the confidence in the world in our rifles. Every man in the original battalion had fired hundreds, yes thousands of rounds, each with his own pet rifle, and knew just what he could do with it. He also knew how to take care of it, which is another very important thing. Cleaning accessories were difficult to find, but somehow or another, every man found some means to keep his rifle in serviceable condition, although it often meant the shortening of his shirt-tail by several inches.

The first complaint against the Ross rifle was based on the ground that it was too long and unwieldy for satisfactory use in narrow trenches or when crawling over open ground where the cover was sparse. It was difficult to handle it so as to avoid exposure to the enemy—especially with the bayonet fixed. However, as the French Lebel was equally long, and their bayonet much longer, this point did not carry much weight with the higher command. But when they commenced to freeze up on us, it was acknowledged that the matter was serious. They tried all sorts of stunts to remedy the trouble, sending the rifles out back of the lines to the armourer sergeants, who reamed the chambers out larger so the cartridge would not fit so tightly, and all that, but it was no go, and the ultimate solution was to take the Ross rifle out of the trenches and issue every infantryman the regulation Short Lee-Enfield rifle.

At that time and for several years after the war, I believed that all that trouble was due to some fundamental defect in the rifle itself, but since hearing from members of organizations in the First Division who participated in the earlier battles without noticing any such trouble, I am now inclined to the opinion that it might have been due, in part, at least, to the ammunition.

During the earlier stages of the war the ammunition was all from the old, established factories and arsenals—and it was made strictly according to standard specifications. Later, however, it became necessary to build and equip many other factories in order to keep up the supply, and as these establishments were, necessarily, manned (mostly with women) by new and unskilled workers, and their machines, tools and gauges also hastily built, it was no wonder that much of this ammunition would not function properly. We noticed it particularly in the machine guns. Some brands would not work at all and many others were woefully deficient, causing many stoppages and breakages, often at extremely critical times.

Dominion Cartridge Company and Kynock were generally dependable brands. Winchester was *always* dependable. U. M. C. and U. S. just about as good, and all three of these latter brands we prized highly. But there was some particularly rotten stuff coming from a factory up on the Hudson river, a "National something or other," that was simply fierce to use even in rifles and was utterly impossible to even consider for use in a machine gun. This same corporation also made up millions of the same rotten stuff for the U. S. Army when they got into the war, and many thousands of rounds of it floated around for some years after the war.

This matter of insuring a sufficient supply of dependable ammunition is well known to our army leaders but it should be impressed upon the minds of those members of Congress who make the appropriations. Frankford Arsenal can easily produce all that is needed for our troops in peace time and can, no doubt, vastly increase that output in an emergency, but the moment war is declared this demand will increase at least fifty-fold. This figure is merely a snap-judgment, based on an army of from five to six million men, but if I am any kind of a prophet it will require more nearly ten millions in the next war in which the United States engages any first-class foreign power.

We must not be deceived by the fact that we got into the last war so easily—after three or four other powerful nations had fought the enemy to a stand-still for more than two and one-half years. Next time we are liable to get the brunt of the first onslaught and, as always, the attacking power will be better prepared in advance. The attacker always has this advantage. He knows what he intends to do. The attacked can only guess.

We have wandered off the track again, so let's get back to that Ross rifle argument and finish it. When we learned that particular weakness, we commenced to use a little discretion in the matter of rapid fire and managed to do very well with them until they were exchanged for the Enfields. Our snipers, however, stuck to the Ross all through the war because of their better accuracy and incomparably better sights.

Before someone else asks the question, I am going to answer: "No, I never heard of a Ross bolt blowing out or coming back in a man's face, until several years after the war was over." I have said this many times, possibly previously in this same book. As we used those rifles for nearly two years, it is my opinion that it just never did happen, and that all these accounts told throughout the

United States regarding the likelihood of such a happening have been based upon one or two isolated instances—possibly due to a wrongly assembled bolt or reloaded ammunition.

Well, let's skip along. We made our own fun when and where we could. On the second day of June, 1916, the machine-gun section, having just completed an arduous tour of duty in reinforcing the lower stories of the buildings in the town of Dickebusch, was engaged in a little "field day" of its own. We had drawn for our quarters the best building in town (it had been a bank) and had thoroughly reinforced it with sand-bags and, here and there, a layer of railroad iron, so we felt pretty safe. George Paudash and I had started a game of "duck on the rock" in the public square, which was immediately behind our quarters, when Heinie started shelling us. He was using those eight-inch rifles— the ones that shoot so straight and with such a low trajectory that you never have a chance to dodge. He was looking for a big 15-inch howitzer which was mounted on a railroad car and was, at that moment, operating from a position just about one hundred yards behind our position. The first two or three shells were short and one of them killed a lot of men of the Nineteenth Battalion which was located just across the street from us. Then a few shells dropped into our "dooryard" and scared most of the recruits into their holes. George and I, however, wise in such affairs, kept on with our game and soon others of the section came out and joined us. *We* knew from past experience that it was useless to try to dodge those fellows. If one happened to light where you were, it was going to get you. Those shells, evidently from naval guns, had delay-action fuses and there was never a dugout or other place in our line that offered the slightest protection from them. We carried on with the game and, as I said, others came out and joined us and we were right in the midst of it when the word came to pack up and move up North.

That was the day of the great surprise attack on the "Pats" and the Mounted Rifles—June 2, 1916. Heinie slipped one over on the Third Division and simply blasted these two battalions out of their position, which extended from about the village of Hooge, south to Hill Sixty. For the short time it lasted it was about as hot a fight as was ever pulled off. The Germans succeeded in penetrating our lines to a distance of some seven hundred yards and almost annihilated the two organizations mentioned. It was the second time for the "Pats," as they had been almost cleaned out on a previous occasion. Both outfits put up gallant fights but were simply overwhelmed, first by a tremendous concentration of artillery fire and then by a powerful infantry attack.

We did not get into it until that night and then only as supports—just to hold on at our G. H. Q. line, where the attack was stopped. There was little opportunity for any real rifle work. Those of the infantry who were engaged did all their fighting at such short range that a shotgun would have been better than a rifle, anyway. When you get down to that kind of fighting, it don't make any difference what kind of a weapon you have—if you have *guts*. And, let me tell you, it takes just that (or those—which is it?) to stand the gaff when it comes to the real show-down.

To regain the ground lost on June 2nd, required a little time. We went in, opposite Hill Sixty and The Ravine, and got well established, while the Higher Command was mobilizing enough new batteries to insure against a recurrence of the St. Eloi affair. One thousand guns against one thousand yards of enemy trench was what they prescribed—and a lot of those guns were of twelve and fifteen inch calibre. Say, didn't they give Heinie a dose of his own medicine? For long, weary months we had been looking and praying for just that and I want to say that that fight (in which I participated as a sergeant, although I had been commissioned a first lieutenant several weeks before but had not yet found it out) was the most enjoyable I ever attended.

Wow, when all those guns opened, *our* guns, mind you, it was like music to our ears. So long had we endured the overwhelming weight of German metal. *Now,* for the first time, we had the best of them in that respect. It was a lark —even though we were still receiving all that the enemy had, and suffered severe casualties, just the knowledge that we had them out-gunned, seemed to put everybody on edge.

The attack went through like a hot knife through butter. All the lost ground was regained and then some—and consolidated. Our battalion suffered severely from the activities of a heavy trench mortar which was secreted down in the railway cut, just below Hill Sixty. This was the most awful thing I ever experienced. Even in the later and greater battles down South never did I encounter anything in the way of destructive agents to equal it. It fired a plain tin can filled with 160 pounds high explosive—probably T. N. T. (We got one that did not explode, so know all about it.) The effect of those damnable things was worse than that of any shell. Even the big Austrian eleven-inch howitzers or the naval guns of like calibre could not do such execution. Coming as they did up out of that cut less than a hundred yards from our line and dropping almost straight down, our parapet offered no protection whatever.

We had a machine gun down at the left end of our line where this thing was operating and I got word that the gun crew and a whole platoon of infantry had been wiped out. Well, it was up to me to find out about it. We had a gun crew in reserve and they were sent down, and after making a hasty inspection of the other guns along the line I went down there myself. Bouchard, of course, came along. That boy followed me around like my shadow.

Just as we were starting out, a particularly intense shelling began over our whole area, one big shell striking right on top of one of our signaller's dugouts, killing the occupants and seriously wounding Captain Caldwell, who was standing in the doorway, dictating a message, I think. Bou and I went along until we reached a "dead-line"—that is, the officers in charge had withdrawn all men from that particular sector until the heavy shelling had subsided. All but the machine-gun crew; they were still out there—somewhere. Colonel Hughes was there with a couple of staff officers. (Depend on that man to be where the trouble was.) I explained to him that it was necessary for us to go down to the M. G. at the end of the line and away we went. We wished the sentries on guard the same as they wished us which was something like "hope you get your heads blown off," embellished with a few of the apt but not printable adjectives then in common use.

Beyond this point, all was chaos. That deadly trench mortar or, as the Germans called it *Minnenwerfer* had completely wrecked things. Our parapet was just about obliterated. We had to crawl most of the way but soon arrived at the old M. G. emplacement, right on the bank of the railroad cut and directly opposite Hill Sixty. The gun crew were still there but, as there was scarcely any shelter and nothing for them to fire at just then, I sent them back, outside the immediate shelling area and then stayed there with Bouchard, just to keep an eye on things and summon the crew if it became necessary—that is, if the enemy attempted an advance.

The dead were everywhere. Of the original machine-gun crew, Simpson was laid out on the firing step, covered with a rubber sheet. Head was back at the mouth of a communication trench, both legs blown off and otherwise shot up—dead, of course. The others were unrecognizable. Bodies and parts of bodies were scattered all around, mostly mangled beyond recognition. I spent some time going around and endeavoring, by means of identification tags, to get their names. I located several, but in many cases the destruction had been so complete that no tag remained. While I was doing this, Bouchard was keeping a close watch over the parapet and when he called, "Here, Mac, hurry—here's a good chance to get some of them," I hastened back to where he was standing.

From there we could see through a gap in the enemy line, made by one of our big shells, a column of German soldiers going to the left (over toward Hooge where the fight was still raging fiercely). I rustled up a rifle and had Bou go on a hunt for more—and started shooting. It was something less than two hundred yards. I kept it up for some twenty minutes or half an hour, the kid loading and passing up rifles and I shooting all the time. By that time the "targets" had all disappeared—probably found another way around, but so far as we could tell they never knew where this fire was coming from, which was not surprising considering all the other noises.

While doing this shooting, I was standing on the only bit of firing step which remained—astride the body of Simpson—and I remember thinking, as I knocked 'em over, that he would be delighted to know that his death was not going unavenged. Yes, there will always be chances for the rifleman to get a little shooting, in any war—big or little.

Numerous queries have come to me as to the comparative excellence of the various rifles used during the late war. Before going any further into this subject, I want to say a few words in explanation of my apparent (and real) ignorance in this matter.

Of one rifle—yes, two, I can speak with authority. The U. S. Springfield, vintage of 1903 and the Ross, Marks 3 and 4, (III and IV). As to the former, all readers of this book are able to judge for themselves and the latter has been so freely discussed—praised and berated—in the foregoing chapters that we can dismiss them.

Now, I hate to say anything in disparagement of our Springfield Rifle (Model 1903—with 1906 ammunition). It does not require my recommendation. Too many people know all about it. But, why don't they put a sight on it? As it now is, I would certainly pick one of the S.L.E. (Short Lee-Enfields) for the ordinary, short-range work of actual battle. Argue all you want to about ballistics but what a man needs when he gets into a fight is a short, "handy" weapon—something with which he can take a hasty, snap shot at a target which only shows for the fraction of a second and then disappears. And he wants a sight that you don't have to hunt around for—just something that you look *through*—not look *for*.

But, when it comes to discussing the merits of the foreign rifles—Mausers and Lebels—the best I can do is to refer the anxious inquirers to Captain Crossman or any other of our well-qualified experts. You see, it is this way—when you get into real war—right up there in front— you have no time to do any experimental firing and no inclination to fuss around with any strange rifle. You have trouble enough with your own without looking for more.

During the course of any engagement, if your side is successful and you get into enemy territory, you will be sure to find rifles scattered all around, and, if fighting over ground that has been contested for a year or more, as we were during the first winter, you can pick up any number of arms which have been used by the various combatants. These things were so common that we paid no attention to them other than, perhaps, pick up this or that one and play with it—just to see what made it tick, as you might say. As we never were associated with any French troops, I know nothing about their use of the rifle beyond what I saw one morning at the capture of Combles, when I was temporarily attached to a unit of the Gloucester Regiment, and that was at a distance of some three or four hundred yards. I have fired the Lebel on a number of occasions but simply at some mark just for fun, you might say.

The same thing applies to the German Mausers, the only exception that occurs to me now being one which I took from a young and cocky Yager who had been wounded and taken prisoner. That one was a beauty. Short and trim—a regular "sporter" in fact. The former owner vouchsafed a supercilious smile when I held it up beside my own heavy Ross, and I don't blame him. He had a real, honest-to-goodness *battle* rifle, beside which ours were just clumsy clubs. I never had a chance to really give it a good try-out but did take a few shots. It had a decided wallop both fore and aft with the regulation 8 mm ammunition which was picked up here and there. The initial velocity of this stuff was, I understand, about three thousand feet per second, as against the 2440 of ours. In one way, this worked to our advantage, for where the lines were close together we had a defiladed space or "safety zone," behind our parapets, much greater than the enemy had and we could get along without a lot of overhead traverses.

And, believe me, anything that lessened the work of filling sand-bags and building up parapets and traverses was welcomed by the Canadian soldier. He was always willing to fight, but hated, like hell, to work with a shovel. Some of this feeling was due to the fact that it was almost impossible to dig anywhere within our lines without disintering bodies of men who had been buried by previous occupants of the position. That whole Ypres Salient was one vast graveyard. I do not know what disposition has been made of it, but were it in the United States I am sure it would be declared a National Park. There, in October, 1914, the flower of the old British Army—the so-called "Old Contemptibles"—effectively checked the German advance, just as they, with the assistance of the

Canadians, did again in April 1916. Gurkhas from India and Indians from Canada mingled their blood with the flower of British manhood on that field, together with legions of French and Belgians. It should be an international shrine. There are a few other places, notably Verdun, where every foot is holy and consecrated ground but none, I believe, can compare with Ypres and the Ypres Salient.

I just cannot seem to keep going along any single track. We were discussing rifles, were we not? Well, I know of nothing more to say about the ones that were used in the last war, so let's do a little figuring on something for the next.

There is a gentleman who, so far as I know, never wore a soldier's uniform, but who has shown by his writings, a better insight into the *real* business of soldiering than any general or other officer it has been my pleasure to meet, and I wish to quote just one little stanza from one of his poems.

"When half of your bullets fly wide in the ditch,
"Don't call your Martini a cross-eyed old bitch.
"She's human as you are; just treat her as sich
"And she'll fight for the young British soldier."

(Of course, you know who I mean—Rudyard Kipling.)

The following is probably a repetition of what I have said elsewhere in this yarn: "The only way to learn a game is to *play* it."

Do you know of any good football coaches who never, themselves, played the game, just as—well, what we might call, "privates?" Or, in any other line of sport or endeavor. Can you think of any of them who have not, literally, "come up from the ranks?" Why should this great, glorious game of war be an exception?

What a blessing it would be if all the officers who have authority in our army had first taken a course in *soldiering* in the ranks, in active warfare. Having been an officer before the war, then serving for more than a year as a soldier during some of the toughest campaigns and finishing again an officer, I have an insight into a lot of things that never would be suspected—or admitted—by the gentlemen who have always sported commissions.

This is just a preliminary to the general attack, which will be directed against the proposal to arm each and every infantry soldier with an automatic or semi-automatic rifle. Up to date, no soldier has been able to carry enough ammunition to take him through a day's fighting—that is, in a real battle. They say they will reduce the calibre and thus reduce the weight of the ammunition. Yeah? How much can you reduce it? You can probably cut it down from say, ten pounds to eight or, to make it more plain, by reducing the calibre from thirty to twenty-six (and keeping up the same velocities) you will have made a reduction such as may be represented by the difference between sixty and fifty-two or thereabouts. Let the school-boys figure out the percentage; it is not worth our while.

What with the machine-guns and automatic rifles already in use, there is absolutely no reason for this innovation. I tell you, and I know what I am talking about, that in a battle you cannot keep those men supplied with ammunition for more than fifteen minutes of real fighting. Having handled machine guns and automatic rifles during periods of desperate fighting, I am sure of my ground—I am not guessing or trying to figure anything out with a slide rule or a mil scale. (By the way, did anyone ever hear of any soldier, in active battle, making use of that mil-scale? I had a standing reward, for several years after the war for any machine gunner who would testify that he had used it, with no takers.)

During one protracted action where we were continuously engaged for fourteen days, I had twelve machine guns—that is, we started in with twelve. As they were wiped out, we got up reserves as soon as possible. One time we had eight German guns working, but assuming that the twelve of our own were working all the time, which of course they were not, I have memoranda, made at the time and on the spot, which shows that we required sixty thousand rounds of ammunition a day. As our machine-gun crews consisted of but six men, and numbers one and two were constantly on the gun, while the others were reloading belts, it can readily be seen that we could not conceivably have brought up our ammunition. Not by a damn sight. What I did was to—well, "holler for help," if you want to consider it that way—simply passed the word to headquarters that if they wanted those guns to keep going, they would have to send the ammunition up to us. It required the services of one hundred and twenty men just to do that—ten extra men to a gun. Now, mind you, we never did have the full twelve guns going and, as before mentioned, at one time had but four of our own, but just the same we ate up sixty thousand rounds a day just as easy as you eat your two eggs for breakfast. One gun, I remember, fired twenty-eight thousand rounds in one day. (For the benefit of ordnance officers, I will remark that that gun never fired a shot after that.) It was a Colt; the barrel was literally welded to the bands and when it finally cooled off it was of no use whatever. I have often seen those guns going—at night—with the barrels glowing cherry-red.

No officer, I don't care who he is, can sit back in his headquarters and say that this man or that squad can do such and such. To even get up to where the real fighting is requires almost incredible endurance and devotion to duty. Always will these men have to go through one or more barrages of artillery fire, and rifle and machine gun bullets will be continually picking off men, here and there. Probably it will be raining—it always seems to do that when there is a fight on—and the mud will further handicap the burden bearers.

There is one way the situation might be relieved, to have special tanks to carry up the ammunition; but, hells-bells, if we have enough tanks for that, why not let them go over and rout out the enemy, themselves?

No, gentlemen, what with all the machine guns, automatic rifles, bombers, wire cutters and what not, you'd better let the little old rifleman carry on with his simple magazine rifle. Out of every hundred men in the infantry, perhaps ten are really qualified to rate as *riflemen*. And you cannot make these riflemen by merely designating them by name and number in orders from headquarters. They must have learned the game by long months of practice and experiment. If, in addition to thorough range training, they have had the experience of hunting big game—especially goats and sheep—so much the better; lacking that, if they have devoted much time to the pursuit of the festive woodchuck in the East or the jack rabbit and coyote in the West, they will be well prepared for the final course of instruction which, as before mentioned, consists of actual war experience.

Take these men (assuming you can find ten out of every hundred who can qualify) and arm them with the very best type of "Sporters," equipped with both telescopic and modern iron sights and turn them loose during an engagement. Their functions will be to afford a protective screen for the machine guns and trench mortars and to take advantage of every opportunity to harass the enemy. They will also prove effective in *abating* enemy machine guns whenever there is no tank available, or on ground which is inaccessible for a tank.

The full war strength of a company being two hundred and fifty men, when you have taken out your twenty-five riflemen and all the other specialists there will not be very many left, so if you want to arm them with automatic arms, well and good. In defensive positions, where large reserves of ammunition may be accumulated, this probably would be quite satisfactory, but in any attack where the line is continually moving forward I am of the opinion that it will be found impossible to supply these men with sufficient ammunition to make it worth while. We found that it required the services of six men to keep one automatic rifle going (Lewis gun), and, as above described, it took sixteen men to the gun to supply the heavy machine guns with ammunition. What is going to happen when each man has an automatic?

I have been asked to state how much ammunition a soldier can carry. Well; I have often carried a case—1200 rounds —from the ordnance depot to our tent, at Camp Perry. Stronger men could probably carry more. Any individual can decide this matter to his own satisfaction by going out and trying it. See how much you can carry, on a hot day.

With his rifle, his haversack, water bottle and bayonet, a soldier already has quite a load. Add to that the regulation hundred rounds of ammunition which he will carry in his belt and an extra bandolier around his neck—which is always getting in the way and frequently "ditched"—well, you do not have to actually go to war to be able to figure out just about what will happen.

Nothing is impossible. Now, of course, that is merely a much overworked platitude and I do not know whether it is strictly in accordance with the theories of Dr. Einstein or the decrees of Congress, but what I mean is that, with our limited knowledge of the laws of Mother Nature and the daily discoveries of our research scientists, it seems to me to be the height of folly to declare, flatly, that there is anything within the limits of our comprehension that "cannot be done."

Have you ever noticed that practically every new invention has had its place in war? It may have been evolved for some of the prosaic occupations of peaceful times but let there come a war and all these little tricks are quickly adapted to the use of the fighters. Outstanding among the more recent innovations are the airplane, the radio and the tank. The latter, originally designed to enable the farmer to drag a gang of plows over rough and muddy land, has now become one of the most formidable factors in warfare. I well remember the day they made their initial bow to the world in general and the Germans in particular. September 15, 1916, during the great Somme battle, these monsters first took to the field. Crude as they were at that time, they must have caused almost as much consternation in the enemy ranks, as the gas did to ours when first used. If my memory serves me right, there were thirty-five of them, great, ugly, ungainly things, and our own men were just as much surprised to see them as were the enemy. They waddled and snorted across the field, trampling down machine-gun emplacements and generally making themselves useful until the enemy guns found them, and by direct hits managed to put several out of commission. One, in particular, I remember, half capsized alongside the road. It did not appear to be seriously damaged but was, temporarily, at least, out of commission. As I remember it, a shell had knocked off one of the trailing wheels which, I think, were the "rudders" of the thing and another shell, bursting under one side, had toppled it over into the ditch. On its side was inscribed, in large letters, the name *Creme de Menthe,* and all the others bore equally ridiculous appellations.

That was the beginning. What the end will be nobody knows. Recent developments in the line of mechanizing the army have been so rapid that it will not surprise me in the least to see battles fought by whole fleets of these land "Dreadnaughts" accompanied by their fast "cruisers" and squadrons of the little "whippets" taking the place of the destroyer screen, following the same tactics as the armadas of the navy. Armed, as the larger ones now are, with rapid-fire guns of heavy caliber, they could certainly put up a fight worth going miles to see.

But all these cumbersome fighting machines—and that includes the whole category of tanks, airplanes and rigid and semi-rigid aircraft—must have certain bases from which they can operate. They are susceptible to many and varied indispositions which must be nursed and treated by a corps of experienced practitioners. To enable them to operate efficiently for a week, they must have at least a day or two in the shop. These infirmities will, no doubt, be minimized, but probably never entirely eliminated. Well, who is going to ride herd on these cripples when they are in the home corral? More tanks? Hardly. Those in condition for action will be needed elsewhere. No, it will be the everlasting, ubiquitous doughboy, with his little rifle. who will inherit the job of standing off any attack.

It is quite within the bounds of reason that this same foot-soldier will be armed with something more efficient than the present-day rifle. Some genius may evolve a method for squirting the juice of the grape-fruit into the other fellow's eye at a range of two or three miles or one of our up and coming radio fiends may find a way to extract static and use it for a lethal weapon, but, of one thing I feel sure, it will be the individual soldier, with his individual weapon, who will have to come in and take charge after the ruction is over; so, until something more efficient has been perfected, let us do the best we can with our rifles.

Upon receiving notice that I had been commissioned as a First Lieutenant (June 19, 1916) I also received my orders to report at our old base camp at Sandling—in England.

A brigade, in the British service, consists of four battalions of active troops, with another, so-called reserve or depot battalion. Our Brigade—the Fourth—comprised the Eighteenth, Nineteenth, Twentieth and Twenty-first as active

Service Battalions, with the Thirty-ninth as the "Base" Battalion. Now this base or reserve or depot battalion—whatever you want to call it—is the training place for the "replacement" troops for the others and from it are sent the officers and men needed to fill the gaps in the active units.

That was the kind of job I inherited, working as an instructor at the base camp. It was not a bad sort of a job for one who just wanted to go to war without actually getting into it. (I had the same sort in the U. S. Army in 1917 and 1918.) But it just did not appeal to me and I was glad of the opportunity to get back to France and the scene of action, during the latter part of the Somme battle.

Chapter 13

The Somme

WELL, here we are, down on the Somme. "What's that? Didn't know we had moved? Thought we were still up at Ypres? Hell, no. We moved down here in August, while you were over in Blighty, in hospital or something; probably running around and having a good time with the girls. Had a month or so back of the lines trying to learn something about these new Enfield rifles after they took the Ross away from us."

That is about the way I was received when I rejoined my outfit in September, 1916, after having been absent since June. But before I found my own people I had an interesting experience. At Boulogne, as I received my traveling orders from the R. T. O., it happened that I was the only Canadian in a bunch of officers, the others being from the Gloucestershire regiment and from the Ox and Bucks (Oxford and Buckinghamshire) regiment; so, by a queer quirk of fate, I was given orders similar to theirs and, a day or so later, found myself, just at nightfall, at the headquarters of the "Gloster" outfit. A few minutes' conversation acquainted me with the fact that I was miles south of where our corps was located; but, as there was no possibility of getting up there at night and these Glosters were scheduled for an attack in the morning, I made bold to ask the Commanding Officer, in effect, "is it a private fight, or can anyone get in?" When I told him I was an "Emma Gee" officer, he threw up his hands and said, "The Lord doth provide." It seemed that their machine-gun officers had all been put out of action during the last few days and no replacements had come up.

Thus it came about that for a short time I was a member of one of the oldest and proudest regiments in the British Army. The Glosters and the Ox and Bucks were brigaded together. The insignia of the Ox and Bucks is a silver swan (it seems that there are some particular swans around Buckingham palace and it comes from that, but I never did hear just how it came about that the device was conferred on this particular regiment). The Gloucestershire regiment (Gloster, for short) wear a bronze sphinx and I noticed that they wore it, not only on the front but also on the back of their caps and, on asking "how come" was told that it was because of a fight that the old regiment had gone through in Egypt. Fighting a great force of tribesmen, they suddenly found themselves assailed by another force, from the rear. The commanding officer simply ordered the rear rank to face about and, in this formation, they had won the battle. For this, they were granted the right to wear their regimental insignia both front and rear. It was only the first battalion, however, which had this right. During the war, all the British Line regiments were augmented by many new battalions—for the duration of the war. The originals were the Regulars, enlisted for from seven to twelve years. This outfit which I went in with was the original, *Regular,* Gloucestershire unit.

I found four guns and a willing but rather inexperienced lot of gunners. The best thing about them was that they knew all the various kinds of "jams" and how to clear them. It made me chuckle (to myself) when one gunner, his gun being silent for a moment, explained to me, as he quickly stuck in a finger and pulled out an empty case, "It's a number three, sir." All the various causes for "stoppage" of fire, in machine guns, were classified by numbers and the gunners were taught, in the schools, to refer to them in that way. Number three was the correct designation for a failure to eject the empty cartridge case.

Our objective was the town (or city) of Combles, which the French had been trying to take for two months. They were now at its doors. The attack was carried on, simultaneously, by both forces, we squeezing in on the north side of the town and the French, on our right, coming at it from the south and the front (west).

The operation went through successfully and the place was taken. While it lasted, it was a pretty good fight, the enemy putting up a very determined resistance until we had them outflanked and could take them from three sides. They then gave up, of course. Who wouldn't? That was the first, last and only time I ever saw French troops in action. The Canadian Corps was always sandwiched in somewhere along the British line and, from the time of the first gas attack, at Ypres, until the end of the war, I think they never were in direct contact with the French.

It was during this action—at Combles—that I first saw the little so-called "Infantry-Accompanying Cannon"—the little thirty-seven millimeter fellows. Soon after the action opened and we were working around into position, I heard, amongst the bursts of larger shells, a peculiar "small burst," if I may so describe it, something like the old "pom-pom," and soon noticed that some sort of small shells were pouring in on one of the nearest buildings of those held by the enemy. Being held up for a few minutes, I scanned the country off to the westward and soon picked up the source of this fire.

A French detachment, with one of these little "cannon" were working their way forward, stopping at frequent intervals to fire a few shots. By the time they had arrived at about six hundred yards, they were simply plastering the front of that particular building and at about four hundred

yards they were putting most of the shots right smack
through the machine-gun loop-holes. That was what really
chased the Boches out, and when we caught them in flank
with our machine-gun fire—well, there was nothing for
them to do but quit. We were never nearer than four or
five hundred yards from the French, but I believe there was
another British outfit—the Warwicks if I am not mistaken
—who actually joined up with them and who accompanied
them into the captured town. Our crowd never did actually
get in there; we were just one arm of the "pincers" which
squeezed them out.

This was one of the few occasions where I personally
saw one of these "specialist" weapons being of actual use
during an advance or in the midst of a battle. All of these
accompanying cannon, light trench mortars, anti-tank
weapons, and what not are all very well in the trenches
where their ammunition supply can readily be replenished
and where they can be "serviced" every day or so. But
just as soon as you step off into an attack or make any
sort of advance away from the supply-detail they all have
the same story to tell—time and time again when you locate these outfits on the battlefield and need them badly,
they are "out of ammunition." They soon shoot away
everything they have and are then out of action for the
rest of the day, leaving the infantry to push ahead with
nothing but their rifles, Emma Gees, and ammunition as best
they can.

The great battle of the Somme opened on the first day
of July 1916 and continued without intermission until
October. It embraced a front of more than fifty miles, the
British, on the left, holding from Combles north for some
thirty miles and the French operating to the southward
from that point. It was the Fourth British Army, under
General Rawlinson.

Our Division (Second Canadian) had remained in the

Ypres salient until August 24th, when they turned their sector over to the Fourth Division and started a march which, after four days, took them to the 2nd Army training area, at Zouafques, where they remained until September 5th. Four days later they were at Brickfields, on the outskirts of Albert, which was about the center of the Somme battle front. During the next few days they advanced, first to the reserve trenches in Sausage Valley, near La Boiselle, and then, on the 14th, to assembly positions in the front line near Pozières.

At 6:20 A.M. on the 15th, they attacked, accompanied by the first tanks ever used in warfare. By 7:03 A.M. they had taken the strongly defended Sugar Refinery of Courcelette, which was the limit of their objective for the day. At 6 o'clock that evening, units of the Fifth Brigade continued the advance and captured the entire village of Courcelette—the 22nd Battalion (French Canadian) took a leading part in this assault.

The tanks undoubtedly were of great assistance. Crude though they were, as compared with the later types, they must have caused considerable consternation in the enemy ranks. All the ground fought over was furrowed with trench after trench, with many communication trenches by way of which the Germans retired from one line to another before the irresistible advance of the Canadians. Some of these fighting trenches were so wide as to make it difficult for the tanks to cross them, and one, at least, of the ironclads got stuck and remained there during the remainder of the fight. I believe there were six of them in this particular area that day, and on the whole they acquitted themselves nobly. They would waddle over and straddle a trench and then proceed to enfilade the occupants with machine-gun fire. Encountering a machine-gun "nest" or strong emplacement, the occupants of the tank would proceed to deposit one or more bombs (lay an egg, as they said) where they would do the most good, and then move along. In a very short time, each tank was followed by a cheering procession of infantrymen, but this formation was quickly dispersed when the enemy began to concentrate his artillery fire on the monsters. Two that I know of were put out of action in this manner—perhaps more. One of them, bearing on its side the name "Creme de Menthe" was overturned in the ditch alongside a road, but, apparently, not much damaged. They had two wheels sticking out beyond their tails and these appeared to be the most vulnerable points—like Achilles' heel. I suppose these wheels were part of the steering gear. At any rate, when one of them was broken, the machine was out of business until repairs were made.

So much for the official record. The designated objectives were captured, held and consolidated, therefore, the operation was a success. As a matter of fact, this was the greatest advance, in which all captured territory was permanently retained, on any part of the Allied front, up to that date.

What did this Somme Battle cost? Oh, well, that is another matter. I have some of the figures for the Twenty-first Battalion. They lost, in killed alone, six officers and seventy-four men. As to the wounded, I have no record, but they usually run about four or five to every man killed, so it can readily be understood that it was a real battle. Other battalions, I am told, suffered even more serious losses.

There is an old, old saying that history repeats itself. Undoubtedly in many instances this is so, and I am now going to relate an occurrence which happened at just this time and which will prove that Napoleon was not the only soldier to be betrayed by a sunken road. This sunken road did not cost an army the battle however, but it did cost them the lives of many valuable men, and I am relating the incident to show just how costly the lack of a little *practical* knowledge may prove to be.

Away up there, beyond Sausage Valley, beyond Pozières, in that welter of smoke and chalk-dust, was a road. At one time, ages ago—so it seemed—it was the main highway, the Route National from Albert to Bapaume. It was clearly shown on all the maps, and as it was in direct line with his objective, the young lieutenant tried to find it. This was his first command—fresh from Canada, he had been sent over to replace some one of those who had gone wherever good soldiers go.

The platoon which he commanded was composed of about half veterans—men who had been in the game from the start —and half replacements—new men like himself who had just been sent out. All that the military college could teach, he knew. From the campaigns of Alexander the Great, on down to the last Balkan War, he could describe minutely, the movements of the troops and the errors of strategy which had won or lost those battles. BUT—here was something neither the text-books nor his instructors had mentioned; a barrage so deep and intensive that it appeared not even a snake could crawl through it, and right along where that road was supposed to be. It was not so bad on either side, although the machine-gun bullets were whipping all around and the whiz-bang shells were searching the whole field.

The previous night, upon having been assigned to his platoon and being shown his position on the map, he had noted this road and right then determined that he would make for it and follow it to his objective. Orders are orders and soldiers obey those orders.

Brave? Why yes, he was all that. In spite of his youth and inexperience, no one could challenge his courage. So, having located the road, he led his men into it just as soon as the German barrage slackened up a bit. No sooner had the whole platoon gained the road, however, than the heavy guns opened up again. The platoon were at this time just entering a deep cut in the road, and the lieutenant immediately ordered them to take cover against the bank—toward the enemy side where they would be "sheltered." The older men where aghast and the two sergeants started up to remonstrate, but both died on their feet as the hail of shells came into them. This was all ground from which the enemy had been driven but a few days before and they knew the ranges to an inch—and they also knew all about this cut in the sunken road. Their shells struck on the stone *pavé* blocks and burst, and the splinters which knew not front from rear simply mowed down the men who were, as they and the lieutenant thought, *under cover*.

The only men to escape were a few of the old timers who had been through the mill and who recognized the place for just what it was—a trap. They had refused to go into it and had scattered around outside, taking a chance of being hit by a stray shot rather than walk into what they knew was certain death. Out of the fifty men in the original platoon, but five were able to walk out. Thirty were killed outright—including the lieutenant.

Even in the midst of a great battle this small tragedy was noticed and commented upon throughout the rank and file of the surrounding units. Hence, I have spoken of it here, as an example of what the lack of *practical experience* may cost a junior officer. Any one of those old sergeants could have taken that platoon across that bit of ground and into their position at comparatively little cost—if they had only been consulted.

A few days later, my own Twenty-first Battalion moved forward and occupied the "Sunken Road" along the outskirts of Courcellete, and they remained there for several days until relieved by the Twentieth Battalion.

It was here, in the Somme country, that we made our first acquaintance with real dugouts. Up in Flanders we had to be content with built-up huts of sand bags, as it was too wet to do much digging. Down here, however, the soil was underlaid with a solid bed of chalk and the Germans had constructed a wonderful system of subterranean galleries and chambers at a depth of at least thirty feet. Many of these rooms were furnished with all the conveniences one would find in an ordinary residence. Some of the furniture was rather crudely constructed, on the spot, but much of it was looted from the surrounding villages. One such place had a huge plate-glass mirror (pier glass) standing at least six feet in height, against the wall. I was told of another in which was installed a piano. Those Heinies sure did believe in making themselves comfortable, and the worst of it was that we did not stay there long enough to enjoy the fruits of their labors. We had to keep moving—and keep the enemy moving.

This fighting came about as near to being "open warfare" as any during the war and, probably, as near it as will ever be experienced in any future wars, for wherever an enemy stops, if only for a night, he will dig in and construct some sort of entrenchments. With present-day artillery and the lavish expenditure of ammunition for which the last war has prepared us, there will be no possibility of any considerable force remaining *in the open* and at rest for more than an hour or two. They would be shelled out of existence if they tried it.

By this time all the Canadians were armed with the Lee-Enfield rifle and most of the time spent in training before joining the Fourth Army was utilized in becoming familiar with it. There was some target practice, on an improvised range, but most of this was at the newly-conceived "marching fire" in which the men were required to fire at a strip target, about three feet high, while advancing from two hundred yards to twenty yards. This firing was done from the hip and was, primarily, designed to keep the enemy down behind his parapet until the advance came within bombing range. Later, as the automatic rifle (Lewis guns) were increased in number, this style of firing was largely discontinued. It never was much good, anyway. In practice, on a comparatively level field, it appeared to be quite effective but, like a lot of other things, when it came to the real business of fighting, marching, stumbling and crawling over the shell-torn and barbed-wire-encumbered battle-field, it proved to be altogether different. This is a point that cannot be mentioned too often, and every officer—yes, every soldier—should understand that, after all the training he can possibly get in peaceful surroundings, he still has a great deal more to learn and that it can be learned only in actual combat.

While the Enfield was some six inches shorter in the barrel than the Ross, the bayonet was correspondingly longer, so that the over-all length, with bayonet fixed, was about the same. Bayonet instruction was gone over again—to get the *feel* and balance of the new arm—and it was found that the Enfield, with more of the weight right in the hands, was much easier to handle than the Ross with its long barrel and correspondingly heavy muzzle.

Bayonets may be a necessary evil. I am not sure that I would throw them away entirely, but, if I were running things they never would be fixed until within a few yards of the enemy. They are a serious handicap when it comes to accurate firing and are certainly of no use when a hundred yards or more away from the enemy, yet it was (and still is, so far as I know) the usual practice to have them fixed from the beginning of an attack, no matter how far back it started. If every man had a pistol, I would unhesitatingly say that the bayonet could be discarded as an unnecessary encumbrance. On the rifle they are practically useless in a trench. There, the bayonet alone, used as a sword, is much more effective, and in the open you will seldom come to grips with an enemy as long as you have a good shooting iron and know how to use it.

Now, while I am quite willing to agree that some sort of an edged weapon is a very useful part of the soldier's equipment, I do not believe that the proper place for it is on the muzzle of the rifle. For the fast and accurate work which is necessary during the short-range stages of a fight, the rifle should be as short, light and *handy* as it can be made without otherwise impairing its efficiency. To hang a pound or more of metal on the end of the barrel is the surest way I know to handicap the rifleman in the use of his weapon *as a firearm*. Where the difference between life and death is dependent upon one's ability to fire an accurately aimed shot in one second or thereabouts—anyway, before the other fellow can shoot—this handicap may well prove the deciding factor.

A machete or bolo makes an excellent weapon for actual hand-to-hand fighting; or, if you like, the regulation bayonet, well sharpened, can be used in the same way—as a short sword. The point I am trying to emphasize is that it should not be attached to the rifle unless, as may happen in some cases, the rifle has become disabled or ammunition exhausted. I have often watched men going into action with rifles slung over the shoulder—but always with the bayonet fixed, even if it was a mile to the nearest enemy position, and, a few times, have seen the bayonet actually used—to intimidate prisoners—seldom for any other purpose. One of the rare occasions was when one of our men, crazed with blood-lust assaulted a small group who had their hands up in the air in token of surrender. He stuck two or three before being overpowered by his friends. Now it did not make a bit of difference to that fellow whether he had a bayonet or a club. In similar circumstances, one of our men brained a German with a pick. Among the few souvenirs which I brought home is an ordinary table knife, well sharpened, with which a wounded German killed a wounded Canadian, whereupon a second Canadian, also wounded, took the knife and finished off the German. All three were lying in the same shell-hole when this occurred, with the battle raging all around them. As I was in need of a knife—having lost mine—I took that one and used it, for other purposes, during the remainder of the war.

The only instance that came under my personal observation, where opposing troops actually used the bayonet, *en masse,* was when a company of Highlanders engaged a strong force of Prussian Guards. It was a terrible struggle for the few minutes it lasted; and as I sat and watched, powerless to help, although I had a machine gun, my memory carried me back to the stories I had read of Bannockburn and other bloody battles of Scottish history. Those brawny Scots were simply invincible and soon there was not an enemy man on his feet—and not a prisoner was taken.

Glorious? Yes, it was all that, *but* there I sat, ready with a good machine gun, within less than one hundred yards, and had those "Ladies from Hell" simply remained in their trench I could have wiped out the entire enemy contingent, without any loss whatever.

It was on the Somme that the Canadians first came into contact with the Australians. Of course we had often seen individuals, here and there, on leave in London and elsewhere, but had never seen them as an organized force, at the front.

Now, there is something I have never been able to understand about that ANZAC bunch (Australia-New Zealand Army Corps). While they all came from "down under" and were incorporated in the same corps, there was a vast difference between the men from the two countries. With the New Zealanders, as with the South Africans, the Canadians were always on the best of terms, but Canadians and Australians always seemed to antagonize one another. Many a bitter and bloody fight has been staged back of the lines between detachments of the two factions when they happened to meet—at some *estaminet* or other place of recreation. If there ever was any real reason for this, I never learned what it was, but it was an indisputable fact. They just did not mix, that's all.

Before coming to France, as the world knows, the ANZACS had taken a tough dose of punishment at the Dardanelles, where so far as I know, they did a very good job. The task set them there was simply impossible but they acquitted themselves admirably. After being withdrawn from the Eastern theatre and having had a long period of needed rest, they were sent to France, where they were assigned to the Vimy Ridge sector, which the French, after months of desperate fighting, had finally succeeded in wresting from the Germans, but their unlucky star seemed to follow them, as they very quickly lost the position, which remained in the enemy's hands until retaken and definitely held by the Canadians in April, 1917.

Their next assignment was in the big Somme Battle and they had been hammering at the Germans in the vicinity of Pozières for several weeks, making some small gains but unable to accomplish anything that could be called a real advance. Their losses were very heavy—as they were everywhere. Their failure to get anywhere was certainly not because they did not try, but the fact remains that when they turned the position over, the Canadians, within two hours, had pushed the enemy back farther than the Aussies had been able to do in a month. It is all a matter of history and I do not need to dwell upon it.

So far, I have spoken of it as "The Somme." Perhaps I should explain that, while this whole great battle has been so described, the particular region in which we (the Canadians) operated was really not on or along the Somme River, proper, but on one of its tributaries—the Ancre. But that is the way of battles on the grand scale. They are usually designated by some feature of the terrain, a city or a river or a mountain, but, due to the extensive character of the operation, probably spread out for many miles on either side. Just compare some of the "major engagements" of the World War with other, previous, great battles of history. Gettysburg, Chickamauga, Antietam, Missionary Ridge and Lookout Mountain combined, supposing that entirely different troops, on both sides, participated in them, did not have as many men engaged as this Somme Battle, and it, in turn, was dwarfed by many of the later battles. And when it comes to artillery fire—well, you might as well throw up your hands. In many of the big battles more weight in shells was thrown within a period of twenty-four hours than during the whole Civil War or by Napoleon's aggregated armies during all the years he was running wild over Europe. If my memory serves me right, the Japanese, at the Yalu, had a front of some thirty miles and something like two hundred thousand men engaged. That was probably the record up to the time of the later unpleasantness, but it looks small as compared with the later figures.

I have no authentic records of the numbers engaged nor the mileage of the fronts during the last year of the war, but, even in 1916, at the time of which I am writing, Rawlinson's Fourth Army had four hundred thousand combat troops and I suppose the French, who were also in it, on our right, had as many more, and the *active* front extended for at least fifty miles, with probably an equal distance on either flank more or less engaged in order to keep the enemy from detaching troops from those positions and sending them into the real battle sector. On the Russian front the figures are simply staggering. The captured, alone, sometimes ran up into the hundreds of thousands. With this to contemplate, what do you think the next war will be like? Can we expect to get along with the four or five hundred thousand men which our present establishment provides? *Ich glaube nicht.*

Chapter 14

My Final Score

I WAS in neither at the beginning nor at the end of the
fighting on the Somme. During the early part of it I
was "down the line," involved in the hazards that frequently
beset a man once he has been detached from his unit. I
had been detached after we had come out of the line in the
vicinity of Hill 60. It was not a bad time to leave, in a
way: The war was picking up; I had had the satisfaction
of hearing a real barrage, coming from the right side; and
we had been introduced into a real trench-system, which
was a welcome novelty after the muskrat holes of St. Eloi.
On the second attempt, after going back to the relief of the
Twenty-seventh, we succeeded in getting out, and I was
advised that I had been commissioned. I was ordered back
to England and was there attached to the staff of our train-
ing-camp at Sandling.

I soon began wriggling out of this instructor's job. It
required a lot of wriggling. First, I was side-tracked into
a job conducting troops to France. Then they let me stay
on the right side of the Channel, but put me on despatch
work between various headquarters. From this, I graduated
to court-martial and other duties at Le Havre and Rouen.
Finally, the big battle well under way, room was made
up front, and I was ordered to report again to the Fourth
Brigade. I missed my train and found myself too far southward, as elsewhere recorded. But it was the front; so I

joined the Gloucestershires for a scrap before proceeding
northward to find the Second Division. Here I learned of
the work of the Twenty-first Battalion about Courcelette.
And I learned also that during this fighting, Bouchard and
several others of my old section had been killed. In my
new capacity, I was no longer with the section and was,
moreover, decidedly busy, for the fight was still going on.
But I got what information I could and on several nights
went over the scene of the fighting in which my old comrades
had been killed. On the last of these night-excursions, having previously located the remains of my old friends as best
I could, I set out to mark their graves. I awoke some days
later in a hospital at St. Pol, fifty miles away.

So I was again out of it, off on the circuit of hospitals,
convalescent homes and medical boards, in France and England, which led at last to my being marked fit for duty.

Duty this time took the form of commanding a pack-train.
This sounds familiar enough to many a Westerner. But
it was not at all like pushing into the wilderness or jogging
contentedly and leisurely—however laboriously—up hill and
down on a mountain-trail, stopping at nightfall, enjoying
the view and a good breakfast in the morning. We began
work at nightfall—and had to be finished by daylight—and
we had such pack-animals as we could get, mostly horses.

This work had been started while I was away. It had
become necessary during the latter stages of the battle—
which lasted from early July to late October—because the
front lines were far advanced, separated from the furthest
reach of motor-transport by a trackless morass of shell-
holes and barbed wire, cut by battered trenches, old gun-
pits and dugouts, and strewn with the usual debris of battle.
By day it was a desolate waste, inhabited, if at all, by
dwellers underground or under other cover when this was
available; or small detachments of engineers, artillerymen,
pioneers—all about their various business of maintaining

communications, establishing lines of transportation, new battery emplacements, etc. They moved cautiously by day, looking over the ground, and at night they directed the work of various labor details. Sometimes, for hundreds of yards in these areas, there was no sign of life, save perhaps a solitary signaller sitting at the top of a battered dugout, like a prairie-dog on its mound.

At night the place stirred with life; but it was isolated, detached, like men adrift on an uncharted sea. No one could tell you how to reach any particular unit, because there were few recognizable fixed points, no established trails leading anywhere. Attracted by the sound of shovels or voices, you turned aside to inquire the way to a certain farmhouse or village which the map indicated as a point of reckoning for your further progress toward your destination. You might learn that you were even then in the village; but, get down as low as you liked, nothing resembling a village could be made to show against the dark sky. Everywhere were the same grotesque, blurred shapes, at indeterminate distances, like a mad scene in a fantastic nightmare. Farther on, having caught a glimpse of a faint bar of yellow light, you stopped again, hoping to be able to orient yourself. The light showed again, as somebody moved aside a screen-blanket, defining a cellar stairs and two or three timbers at odd angles about the entrance. "Yes, sir," a brigade-signaller would tell you, "this is the best *estaminet* in town. You are on the right road. It is a little difficult to follow here because they have just finished filling in the shell holes made by the heavies. There is a working party down in the valley who can put you on to the hedge you are looking for." Resuming your way, you were almost at once at sea, guided by instinct, striving to make a crazy pattern of shadows look like a group of trees which were to be a useful landmark. You soon learned to distrust your judgment as to distances traveled.

It was a chaotic world, but it offered some good instruction in another aspect of war. It is not always a soldier's privilege to see much of war. And when he has the opportunity he doesn't investigate very far. He takes things as they come, going in and out of the line on his own particular job, and soon becomes but little concerned about the other fellow's job. He accepts the unexpected, both in surroundings and in new implements of warfare, without astonishment. Even the tanks caused little real astonishment, though they were a never-ending source of entertainment and gleeful satisfaction. The soldier, possibly had never thought of such a thing; but then he had never thought of such a grotesque place as the modern battlefield, and after a few weeks of this, taking it as it came, he was quite prepared for any monstrosity it might produce. He accepted them as quite natural developments.

I had much opportunity to observe this and a great many other things during the next few months. I was soon recalled from the packtrain work and again found myself with the Fourth Brigade, though no longer with the Twenty-first Battalion. We were established for the winter in the country north of Arras. Established is the word: war had become a business, not an adventure of a few months or a year; and we settled down to it in a business-like manner, rotating smoothly from Corps or Divisional reserves—in billets just back of the lines—through the reserve trenches, the supports, the front line and out again. We had good trenches, which were, as trenches go, fairly dry. This was in the mining and hill-country which begins in the vicinity of Loos, and, except in limited areas, drainage problems could be solved.

Moreover, I had now a more comprehensive view of the business, due not only to its having become, definitely, a business, but also to my larger field of action and responsibility. I was to have become Brigade Machine-Gun officer, but going on the casualty list had interfered with that. It remained, however, my particular interest and the field to which I might naturally expect to be called. The place of the machine guns had already been pretty definitely fixed; but Lewis guns were now displacing them for use with the infantry, there finally being two of these with each platoon. All the heavy guns were thus left free to be used in their own place in the scheme of offense or defense. In this work, the battalion frontage was too small, as machine-gun fire, whether from the front line or positions further back, is nearly always cross fire, enfilading wherever possible. The machine-gun officer, therefore, was directly interested in a mile or more of front, whereas the platoon officer was restricted to two or three hundred yards.

Familiarity with front-line conditions over a frontage covered by several battalions and a careful study of the topography of a large area were necessary to the effective locating and handling of these guns. It was interesting work. They constituted but one item in a deadly and fascinating scheme: the rifles and automatics up front, along with grenades and the light trench mortars; then the machine guns and heavier mortars, followed by the 18-pounders backed up by their bigger brothers right on down the line until you came to the big naval gun in a convenient copse somewhere miles back of the lines. There it was, all spread out in place, stocked up with ammunition—waiting, and, at the same time, working, improving positions, making new emplacements, providing for concentration of guns and men in an emergency. The machine guns and artillery entertained themselves, kept in practice and got in a bit of effective work by strafing and shelling vital points and positions in the enemy lines. Comparable activity on the part of the infantry took the form of trench raids. The regular duties of their positions consisted of strengthening the trench system, protecting certain points with outposts, establishing

listening-posts and in maintaining constant surveillance of
no-man's-land through organized patrols. But for effective
work that was satisfactorily like war, they had to put teeth
into some of their patrols and stage a raid occasionally. This
work has been covered, in a manner, in the chapters devoted to patrolling and trench-raiding.

Meanwhile, it was necessary to look forward to the time
when the whole vast machine should again be unlimbered
and got into action. For the northern part of the line the
first step in this work was to take Vimy Ridge. This was
the job to which the Canadians were assigned, and we set
about systematic training and preparation for it, ending up
by timing the whole assault, all obstacles to be overcome
and the various lines of defense to be occupied and consolidated and the attack pushed on strictly according to
schedule. The Germans, of course, learned a good deal
about these plans. Vimy was, in any case, a point at which
an attack was to be expected. They considered the position
impregnable and had had a long time in which to make it
so. At the time of the action its defenders outnumbered
the attackers by about two to one.

When the Battle of Vimy Ridge occurred I was on my
way to New York, and the training-ground again. The
attack went through *according to schedule.* It was not
exactly according to schedule that the tanks did not even
get as far as the first line of defense. They had been counted
upon, but the going was too much for them. This did not,
however, upset the schedule. Their place was taken by
men, more men. The going doesn't get too bad for them,
if they are properly trained. I was on my way to a new
job instructing men in the business of war. In the idle
days of the crossing I sometimes found myself taking stock
of what I knew about it. Usually I didn't get any farther
than visualizing probable happenings along the Western
front at the moment. Vimy would be in the hands of the

Allies. Possession of this strong position was necessary before any general advance could be planned. Winter was over. It was the open season for soldiers. They would be expecting anything at anytime, whether in the way of offense or defense for a soldier simply waits for either one, knowing as little about the plans of one side as the other. Waiting is a little less apprehensive when there are signs that his side is preparing for offense. He will, at least, not be unexpectedly smothered by a barrage, against which he can do nothing save dig himself out and dig his guns out, while the hours pass, until, suddenly, it lifts, and he knows that all that he can certainly count on to protect him against whatever the gathering light brings is the rifle in his hand and the few men whom he can see in the smoke and fog on either hand. That's all. If things go well, he discovers in a few minutes that there is more. But for the moment, there is only a man and a rifle, against everything that may come over the parapet within his reach.

On the offensive it is a little better. He will be on hand to receive the counter-barrage. But he has first heard the music of his own, and seen the signs of activity as he came up the night before: the concentration of guns, with their grim files of steel messages for delivery in the initial stages of the attack, ammunition in the bays up front, handy for the machine guns; signallers with their coils of wire, and stretcher-bearers waiting innocently beside stacks of stretchers. It is comforting to remember these things while waiting for his barrage to lift, and to know that the thing has been planned and *must* be carried through to the first objective, even though all communications are cut before the zero-hour. If it is raining, as it seems, usually, to be, and he has to wait for several hours, this knowledge may be rather cold comfort, but it is there just the same, and does a good deal to boost his confidence in himself.

This is the point that I was always coming back to in

my meditations, miles away on the Atlantic. I had been a machine-gunner nearly all my time in France; but when I thought of battle I thought of the man with the rifle in the front trench. I was on my way to undertake the training of men for this job, and that's the picture that my thoughts revolved around: the man in the front trench before the zero-hour. I hope something of my notions about the things which count then have gone into these chapters. The artillery is but to make a way for him, the machine guns but to aid and cover his advance, the tanks but to crush the traps laid for him; and not much can be done in the way of official control or command after the barrage lifts; the result, then, is largely in the hands of the man with the rifle. All that has been done and all that anybody can now do will be nothing if he fails. The wheel is to spin, the die is to be cast, which, when it comes to rest, will read either life or death, victory or defeat. This is the moment and this the man on which the value of all training and preparation depend.

I liked to think of undertaking to help in the training of United States soldiers with an eye solely to this moment, in an effort to insure, as far as this is possible, its being not a gamble but a sure thing. There was not much doubt in my mind, on those days when I first realized that my actual participation in the war was over, as to what was essential and what unessential. With this sudden perspective, the essentials stood out, and there was no room for trifling—possibly fatal—unessentials. My enthusiasm for war as an adventure gave place to a keen appreciation of and admiration for the human material that won its battles. It was startlingly clear how all the vast organization—the thunder of the guns, the congested lines of transport, the roaring factories, the fatherless homes—all waited upon the fate of this thin line.

I had every reason to appreciate fully the value of training; yet, with all the training it was possible to give, this seemed to be expecting a great deal of men. It remained a gamble, a desperate and critical game in which a man needed to be given a break; the result was not scientifically certain; it was human. And there were many little things in the practices of the British Army in which this was recognized. It is difficult to name them; they were not always provided for in the regulations; but the effect was there. I tried to summarize it on those mornings of early spring while others were waiting to go over the top in a war which for me was finished. Training? Cold, wet and benumbed through enforced long waiting, strapped up and loaded, in cramped positions, they are by no means the same alert men who a few weeks ago turned out smartly for physical drill. The instructor can't finish with men and say: "Now you are ready for battle." The British war organization doubtless had its full share of theorists, little men with big, impractical ideas and good-intentioned fellows who didn't know exactly what they were talking about; but somewhere in the set-up was a practical and efficient hand which was never bound by red-tape, precedent or regulations and which, in the final show-down, did not allow these to interfere with the real business of war; it went on quietly keeping in touch with the essential realities of the situation as they affect the soldier all the way from Aldershot to the Somme and the zero-hour and the final jumping-off place.

I don't wish to idealize the British—or any other army; I merely wish to say that in so far as this effect was achieved, it is worth knowing about. It is vital. The rum ration of the British will serve to indicate what I am talking about. I intended to say something about this, anyway, for its value in itself; but it may also be taken to illustrate this larger effect, this determination to give a soldier every possible chance to win—and live. This will, of course, arouse the indignation of the perfervid and patriotic guardians of purity, but we are talking about war and the *men* who carry it on.

The rum ration has been issued just before the zero-hour, and is getting in its effect by the time the word comes along to be up and away. If the men are alert, mentally and physically, their chances of reaching the scene of the first actual encounter are incalculably greater than if they are tired, benumbed with cold, and apathetic. After that, their blood will be up; they uncover new and unsuspected sources of energy that will take them through the day.

It is this first minute that is important, the initial attitude of men who are awake and ready with the quick parry, the sure thrust, the dead-certain shot. This is a truism. As to the effect of rum in this emergency, there is room for just two opinions: that of the man who has tried it, and that of the physician and physiological chemist who knows the effects of fatigue and exposure and of alcohol in temporarily and quickly overcoming them. Yet, there has been in the United States another and very loud one. It could not very well be called an opinion, because an opinion should rest only upon full and unbiased information and should be qualified in so far as the information is not full or the viewpoint prejudiced. There was no such temperance in the mouthings of these temperance fanatics. The least damaging part of their noise was the charge that the men were made drunk and sent in to die. This doesn't deserve an answer; but it may be stated:

The rum ration of the British Army consisted of one-half gill (one-sixty-fourth of a gallon) of pure unadulterated Jamaica rum, the real article, thick, syrupy stuff, such as is not generally known commercially, particularly in the United States. It was administered by an officer or sergeant in person, at a stated time, and had to be swallowed then and there, or not at all. It was not invariably issued, to all troops at all times; but it was expected by all troops on active service during most of the winter or under any unusual conditions of fatigue or exposure. We did not get it in England or Canada. But we nearly always got it at just about the times when we needed it most.

In the trenches it was issued as a routine matter just before daybreak, at stand-to, when every man needed to be up and on the alert to guard against surprise. Men were not only sleepless; but at that time in the morning, even after comfortable sleep, man's vitality is at its lowest ebb. These men had not slept comfortably. Some of them had not slept at all, but had just returned from patrols or other duties in which there is hardly a moment that is not tense and fatiguing. If there was nothing doing, they counted upon getting their sleep during the next few hours. Sleep is the great restorer, and this single shot of rum made refreshing and invigorating sleep possible at times when it would otherwise have been impossible. If sleep was not to be considered under the circumstances, then the rum soothed jangled nerves and revived tired muscles inspiriting men for continued activity. It was accepted gladly, even by most of those who did not drink, as the best compensation available for the loss of sleep and rest which could not be avoided.

There is little complaint about hardships when men believe that everything possible is being done to minimize them. I am convinced that a distinction of the British Army, and an important source of its strength, is the conviction among the soldiers (above all grousing and grumbling) that their health and well-being are of intimate concern to those higher up, not simply matters unfeelingly provided for in K. R. & O. (King's Regulations and Orders). This was a secondary and not unimportant effect of the rum ration. It was a great mediator between human endurance and military exigencies, between what seemed unreasonable demands and the obscure necessity for them. The sergeant with the little brass nose-cap (fuse cover of a shell), replenished as required from an ordinary water-bottle put to nobler use, was an emissary of good-will and understanding from the Brass-Hats who lived in comfort back of the line: "I can't get you out of the mud to-day, Tommy; there's nobody to take your place. This will help to pull you through. Cheerio!"

When the United States entered the war, the powers that be did well to study what two years of warfare had developed. The intention, presumably, was to profit by the experience of others. How, with this sound and laudable intention, they managed to adopt such trifles as the Sam Browne belt and that silly chin-strap for the campaign hat and pass up such splendid institutions as the rum ration and the bagpipes is beyond me. I suppose that in the case of the rum there is no doubt that the rabid reformers are largely responsible. That is why I have had something to say about it, because it is not a matter for reformers of any sort. It has nothing to do with the muddle of prohibition. It is a matter for those charged with national defense in time of war, with maintaining efficient armies in the field; and for them to allow themselves to be influenced by irrelevant considerations of politics or so-called morality and temperance is the same as to allow such considerations to decide what powder shall be used.

I hope it is clear that I regard it as an important matter and one that has nothing to do with anybody's opposition to alcoholic beverages. I am convinced that in the British Armies many lives were saved by the timely issue of rum, and this may mean the difference between success or failure in the initial stages of an attack, which are often the critical ones. If this sounds like making the fate of empire hang upon a drink of rum, even so; it is only necessary to point out that life or death frequently depends upon a difference of a very small fraction of a second. Ask any athletic coach what top form means. What is the meaning of "fresh

troops"? Well, you don't have them on a modern battlefield.
They are exhausted or shelled into insensibility in reaching
it. In offensive operations, generally, the men that begin
them come nearer to it than any others. A battalion that
goes in on the succeeding day has quite likely been shelled
and bombed from the time that it reaches the area, far back
along the transport lines. It has probably reached this point
only after forced marches. In the evening it begins its
tedious progress toward the point from which it is to continue the advance. In the strongly entrenched areas, this
route lies over a trackless waste, much worse than open
country would have been. There are no roads, few recognizable landmarks. The communication trenches have been
shelled to pieces, or, if usable, are filled with the wounded
coming back. The lines of communication, quickly extended
to keep in touch with the advance, are maintained with
difficulty; and these are the ligaments which bind the loosely
jointed war-machine together as well as the nerves which
enable it to function. It all has to be moved up together,
sensitive always to the varied and uncertain fate of the front
line, which melts away at one place, is pushed back by a
counter attack in another, while at a third it has encountered
a stubborn redoubt, and at a fourth has pushed suddenly
forward leaving an ominous gap which may mean disaster.
In this tangled and uncertain flux, the battalion is but a
small detachment, and it spends most of the night waiting
about in little stretches of trench which afford a measure of
shelter from machine-gun fire and shells. No one knows the
cause of the delay or when it will end, what is happening in
front or where the front is. With daylight, perhaps, they
are able to guess at their bearings and learn a little of what
is happening, from questioning wounded or stretcher-bearers
or signallers, who know little themselves. It may be another
night before they take over their position. If there is no
night attack (which is always hazardous business) they keep

watch until day, then take up the advance. They cannot, of course, be called fresh troops. The fight has been going on for three days, and they have for most of this time been subjected to the most exhausting of its inconveniences and discomforts. They are tired, chilled and sluggish; their boots are heavy with mud and their eyes with lack of sleep. With daylight they are to face troops which may well be well-fed and rested, for they have come up over shortened lines of communication. They will have little artillery support, or none at all. Once in the fight they will take care of themselves. But the first few minutes may reduce their strength by as much as twenty per cent. In close fighting, the difference between life and death is measured in terms of hundredths of a second. That's all. There is no second chance. Either you get him or you don't. If you are on your toes, your eyes open, your whole self on the job, you get him.

These cramped, uncomfortable muddy men have no appearance whatever of being on their toes. For two days they have been living on bully and biscuits. The fortunate and resourceful ones may have found opportunity to make a cup of tea; but a hot meal for all hands is out of the question and they do not expect to connect with a regular ration supply for two days more. There are few complaints, not much conversation of any sort. The platoon officers pass along, checking up on the supply of ammunition, grenades, etc., and acquainting them with the nature of the attack, so far as they know it. The sergeant follows, pouring for each man the allotted portion of rum: "All right, rouse up there, Johnnie; you'll be water-logged." "Righto, Sergeant: When do the fireworks begin?" "This is about all there'll be till the sun gets high enough for observation." "Well, this is not so bad; they're wicked-sounding bastards. Cheerio."

Presently he returns, shaking his water-bottle, in which there still remains four rations. Tomorrow and next day there will be a much greater excess, because the casualties will not yet show on the strength-return.

"Say, Sergeant, I think I ought to have one of them; Smith was my buddy."

"I'll give it to you in a few minutes. You probably won't know it, but I'll hold your head up and pour it in."

"Hell you say; damned if you catch me getting a Blighty today; too much trouble to get out of here."

"Who the hell said there would be no more artillery; listen to that."

"All right, men; shake yourselves out; stand to."

There is a lively little echo of this, varied between man and man, back and forth along the line. Everybody is ready. There is a deadly interest in what is to come, hardly a thought of the misery of the past two days. If they could have had a good hot bath, a change of clothing and a substantial and leisurely breakfast, much the same result would have been achieved. Hardly practicable? But the rum ration is practicable, and it was adopted out of a very sensible and laudable desire to give men a chance to take care of themselves, to utilize fully their training, to achieve, with a minimum of suffering and death, the ends for which they were sent into the field.

There is no denying the practical, immediate value of this; but what I should like to get at is the purely human side of its issuance, in which it is recognized that all the devastating machinery of war—the tons of shells and bullets, the hundreds of ponderous guns and the vast array of men, motors and materials serving them—is dependent upon the work of a few elemental human beings who must face a similar concentration of destructiveness on the part of the enemy and whose energy and powers of endurance must often be severely taxed before they can even begin to do the actual work of battle.

I do not mean that the drink of rum was adopted as a

dramatic and empty gesture recognizing this. The tot of rum is an old custom with the British. I do not know how long it has been observed in the army, but the morning grog of His Majesty's Navy has long been an institution.

But I do mean that the issue of rum at this particular hour illustrates the use of common sense and that the occasion may serve to emphasize the imperative necessity for common sense in the handling of men on a modern battlefield. In the first place, soldiers of today are men not only of common sense but of intelligence and education. In the case of the United States and the principal British colonies, aside from the purely technical and formal knowledge gained at officers' training schools, representative men from the ranks will match a similar group from among the officers in all branches of human knowledge. This is something that has become true within the last few decades and will be increasingly significant in the future. To fail to take it into account is the same as to refuse to take advantage of the scientific and mechanical developments in the business of war.

These common-sense men are, moreover, in the war for their own ends. They are free agents. In the last analysis, nearly all have of their own accord put aside their accustomed pursuits, to face, of necessity, a disruption of their normal way of life. They are not professional soldiers serving some conqueror for personal aggrandizement. The day of Alexander the Great is past. The soldiers of Attila trusted their leader and sought the hazards of battle because by the outcome they lived. They fought for flocks, pillage, women, for the sake of fighting, and to further the ambitions of their leader, which they in a measure understood and appreciated. They prospered as they were successful. The soldiers of today mistrust their leaders as being fallible, limited creatures much like themselves. They know that the blunders are made by the leaders and that the men pay for them. They recognize this as a necessary condition of modern war, even assuming that a Napoleon is at the head of it. The genius of a Napoleon is lost between headquarters and the days of preparation and the miles of chaos incident to launching and carrying on a battle today. Quick strategy and tactical acumen are resources not always directly available to the G. O. C. These qualities must be exercised largely through hundreds of ready heads on the shoulders of subalterns and sergeants and privates. The general officer who recognizes this and looks to key men all the way through his ranks is in a fair way to *commanding* his troops. It is the only way. The rhetorical chroniclers of battles must look for other phrases. "Flinging his legions against this wing * * *," or, "General Blank, perceiving at once the advantage which this maneuver gave him, threw two divisions," etc., no longer, except in rare cases, have a shred of meaning or applicability.

So far as I know, these phrases have been little used in describing the battles of the late conflict, though if our historians are to match some of our generals, we may well expect them. But General Blank, if he was wise, counted upon the cool heads of Lieutenant Smith and Private Brown, knowing that his legions were not to be flung anywhere, that they would dissolve into a thin straggling line lost in smoke and confusion beyond his reach, and that they would advance as occasion offered, in small groups, by their own resources of courage and skill. He not only counted upon them, but he let them know in advance that he was counting upon them and did what he could to enable them to assume the responsibility in close cooperation with the general plan of battle. This was only to avail himself fully of the resources at his command.

If this sounds ridiculously non-military, that is because the cult of the military is still lost in notions of regulations and orders and obsolete ideas of discipline and methods of exercising control. They have not made the jump from the parade-ground to the battlefield and from the nineteenth century to the twentieth. It always seems to take a year or two of war to get clear of the rubbish and deadwood and make room for the leaders who are alive to the realities of the situation. A few real barrages and the concentration of machine-gun fire that goes on *quietly* beneath them will do wonders toward silencing the childish orders of the favorites of post commandants' wives and the armchair theorists recognized through political and social intrigue who manage to find themselves charged with the grave business of conducting a war. This would be all right if these men alone suffered the consequences of their folly. The pity is that they escape.

They are not all politicians. Most of them are honest students of military science fallen into the common error of becoming academic. They lack experience and first-hand knowledge to bring them back to practicalities. But it does seem time that we utilized the high general average of common sense, intelligence and initiative characteristic of the people of these United States. That is exactly what is called for in war today; and men do not become imbeciles and children simply because they have put on a uniform; they still have their native intelligence—and a first interest in the efficient and intelligent conduct of their armies.

Now England is commonly held to be the example *par excellence* of hide-bound precedent, of dependence upon authority, of acting according to orders, of the complete paralysis of common sense until an order has been secured to enable it to function. This may or may not be true. The little apostles of regulation may have had fairly complete sway and a pretty firmly fixed hold on the military machine. But somewhere in the labyrinth of the British War Office there lived a human genius of common sense. He could not get rid of all encumbrances, but he did succeed in rendering them harmless at critical points and he had a sort of tacit understanding with the men in the field that together they would try to do as well as they could under the circumstances. This genius made use of all intelligent and courageous field officers, and he must have had a few of higher rank to enable him to rescue the essential business of war from the busy hands of officialdom.

It is useless for me to attempt to analyze his efforts or to waste words on the various things that hampered him. The net result toward which he strived was that which would immediately occur to the man of common sense familiar with the conditions of modern warfare, and the odds against him were the usual accumulation of bunk and inefficiency in addition to the stupendous responsibility of an almost superhuman job. When nothing else could be done, he contented himself with the endeavor to acknowledge that the job was impossible without the hard work and cooperation of the men in the field.

And 'when the tumult and the shouting died' this genius still had his eye and hand on the essentials, already busying himself with the one great, dramatic element in the spectacle of demobilization—thousands of men suddenly, in a disorganized world, suspended, rendered, for the moment, useless, unattached. Sinews of war! A fine phrase by which patriotic orators refer to copper or steel or cotton. But these are the sinews of war—these men and their personal necessities; all else is superfluous, refinements—munitions to be expended, guns to be moved laid and fired. These will now rust, rot or corrode, unimportant, useless. And "organization" becomes a mere stack—miles of stacks—of useless papers, another incidental, a mere mechanical convenience. The whole may be tossed into the fire and the army remain as before—to be dissolved.

The bond is a very slight one. I had about come to the conclusion that officialdom had lost sight of it, and I was agreeably surprised to find that it was still known, and to have it simply acknowledged now that it was dissolved. My connection with the British Army had ended some years earlier. Most of these years I had spent on the training-ground, where, much to my annoyance, the very purpose of the training-ground seemed as often as not to have been lost sight of. Finally, disgusted, but probably much to the relief of my immediate associates, I was mustered out of the U. S. Army and had hied to the tall timber of Oregon, well back out of the way.

One day there was an unexpected visitor at my camp, miles and miles out in those Oregon backwoods. He announced himself as the British Consul, charged by his Majesty to advise me of the final disposition of affairs at the conclusion of our mutual exigent enterprise. A substantial gratuity was provided to enable men to establish contact again with normal pursuits.

The whole business was clean-cut and simple—and human. It might have been handled through the mail. A packet of forms, in quadruplicate, initialled here and there by uniformed clerks, locating, identifying and disposing of one McBride, an item of cast off war material, would have served the ends of some organizations. But the genius of common sense in the British War Office was humanly dissolving the bonds which make armies. You can't put them on paper. It is a universal understanding between men and I accepted the two medals as mere formal tokens of this, possessing a meaning exactly matching my understanding of it.

Chapter 15

The British Army

A RIFLEMAN at war is a soldier, and a soldier is one of an army. Something of his identity is imparted to the aggregate, something acquired from it. It is in the aggregate that he achieves victory or suffers defeat. His own state of mind and spirit is sensitive at all times to that of the whole. His record is determined not solely by his individual qualities, but, as well, by the qualities of those on either side of him, and by the organization which binds them together, directs their efforts and consolidates their gains, and by the spirit which this organization instils and fosters and the stimulus and incentive which he gains from it.

I should like, therefore, to say something about my comrades-in-arms during something like half of the not-so-recent war. Mine is not to be regarded as an illustrious record of service. I can see, now, many places where it might have been improved, but responsibility for its shortcomings is largely my own. The other fellow didn't fail me, and I think the record gains rather than loses from being part of the record of the British Army. It gave me plenty of opportunity to show what I could do. If I felt, in the beginning, that there were some things that might have been managed better, I discovered many other things that aroused my admiration. Organization for war is a vast and complicated business. No ministry of war or general staff

266

is omniscient. The first few weeks following the little incident in the Balkans witnessed not only the usual revolutionary change in the manner of life of the average man, but a change hardly less revolutionary in the methods of warfare itself. The civilian not only had to become a soldier, but the soldier had to become a different sort of soldier; and the ministry of war had not only to provide for his equipment and training, but to familiarize itself with the new conditions for which he was being equipped and trained.

I was better acquainted with the English and English customs than is the average American; yet, at first, I thought they were pretty slow at getting things done. I was a year late getting in the game; yet, one of the first things I ran across was a precious trio of snipers, blithely sniping away at ranges of a thousand yards and upwards. This rather dismayed me; particularly so since one of the trio was an officer. Here they were, diligently carrying on "according to orders," unconcerned, apparently, by the obvious fact that they were accomplishing nothing, when they might so easily have got themselves into position to do some deadly work. The whole business seemed peculiarly inept—and peculiarly British. An American (only the so-called typical one) armed with the same authority would have been killing Germans in numbers, hardly knowing that he was disregarding orders in getting within range. But this is by no means to say that an American Army, under similar circumstances, would have had a well-organized and equipped sniping service. I have every reason to believe that it would not have had one, though a lot of individuals—if they could have got hold of the equipment—might have been having a great time with some real live targets. Besides, the Englishman has his own way of going about things, and eventually he did effective sniping, even if he had to get a General Order to bring him within range. And he probably had this by the time he had the equipment to justify an organization.

But it was not individual action that won the war; it was organized action. And even confining ourselves to the individual, this isolated instance tells us little about the Englishman, because it illustrates the characteristic in which he is notably weakest. It takes many other qualities to make a good soldier—and many soldiers to make an army. If you will look at the matter from all angles, I am willing to risk the charge of odium that is proverbially supposed to attach to comparisons. I hope there will be none, because I foresee that I am going to be constantly involved in comparisons. I spent a good many years with the American Army and did all my fighting with the British. And I am the more inclined to stick to my admiration for the British because it grew as my acquaintanceship lengthened. This does not, of course, mean that it grew at the expense of the United States. It is simply that I came a little nearer to understanding the Englishman. From the viewpoint of the average American he takes a good deal of understanding. And let me add here—for the other side of this matter of international amity—that he acquires a good deal of understanding before passing judgment. At his best—and you will find many of them—he is not even disposed to pass judgment. Rare virtue!

And the British Army requires a lot of understanding, even in its outward aspects, the mere catalogue of the various units. Any visitor to London has seen the Horse Guards down on Whitehall, and I am free to admit that, just common, every-day Hoosier that I am, I never see those magnificent living statues that I don't get a thrill. Other Guards Regiments are the Coldstreams and Grenadiers and the Scots, Welsh and Irish Guards. In peace times a Guards Division is usually kept in London, forming the backbone of the garrison there and being available for the frequent ceremonies that mark the annual routine of the capital. They went to France with the first contingents, and I don't know how many times their number flowed through their ranks—in as replacements, out as casualties—before the end.

Other regiments of the British Army bear the names of the cities or districts from which they are recruited. Many of them have histories running back for hundreds of years, and they carry on their colours the names of battles that mark turning points in the course of Empire, and of civilization, throughout many centuries. But the names of cities or districts is only the beginning. There are—to mix cavalry and infantry indiscriminately in the few names that I recall—Fusiliers, Dragoons, Foot, Horse, Rifles, Lancers, from various places and with various further designations, as King's, Queen's, Royal, etc.

The Territorials correspond roughly to our National Guard. They, too, are locally recruited and maintained—usually by counties, sometimes by cities. But they also run to diversity in the matter of designation, including such organizations as the London Scottish—which, by the way, sent the first Territorial Battalions to fight in France.

Scottish, also, was the first Regular Regiment offered the war-time British Army. This was the Royal Scots. Many of the Scottish Regiments are designated by the name of the clan whose tartan they wear; or are otherwise closely identified with proud tradition: Argyll and Sutherlands, Seaforths, Black Watch, Gordons. The parade becomes colorful not only in name and battle-flags, but in dress. During the war all the various regiments were greatly augmented. Some of them had several battalions in France, all bearing the same name, but further designated by number. And each regiment maintained a training battalion in England.

And now the real diversity begins—after leaving the British Isles, having said nothing of the various auxiliary, vital, but not so glamorous organizations, such as the Royal

Engineers and the various Pioneer battalions and service corps, and not mentioning the display of artillery. This diversity is first simply the stamp of a different environment—the English Colonials; but it is further a diversity of race, color, creed, tradition and spirit. Pathans, Sikhs, Gurkhas joined men from Newfoundland and the Union of South Africa. There were African natives and Fijians, men from New Zealand and Australia. They came up and over from the farthest islet of that Empire on which the sun never sets. And it seemed to me they were all British. The fiercest Sikh sergeant had about him an unmistakable British stamp. It was a treat to watch these fellows, and other native Indians. They were natural-born fighting men, and they seemed to take more pride in their work than any of the others. No matter what one of them happened to be doing, on the approach of an officer he would spring to attention—and I mean spring, and to the perfect position of attention—and execute the salute as though he himself were being honored. Seeing them, a man thought two or three times about that colossus which was Britain at war.

Much of this variety was lost sight of, unless we scan the makeup of brigade or division, or remember the various special and service organizations. But the more populous colonies contributed and maintained their own army corps, as the Anzacs and Canadians. Of the Anzacs (Australian-New Zealand Army Corps), my impression is that there was a decided difference between the men of these two neighboring colonies. It seemed to me a quite obvious difference; yet, one that is by no means easy to define. In my case, it may have been due to the initial impression made by particular individuals; though I can't see that this has anything to do with it, for my first contact with the Australians leaves me with nothing more—nor less—than a very agreeable memory of a lot of good fellows who gave us something to eat at a time when we needed it very badly.

Among the New Zealanders I was always fancying that
I could recognize something of the Midlands or of Perth;
they seemed closer to the British Isles than did the Australians, despite the fact that in their ranks was to be found
now and then the strong close-knit figure of the Maori, a
diverse element to which I remember noticing nothing
similar or comparable among the Australians. This impression was heightened by the difference in uniforms;
though in this connection I must say that I am not specifically familiar with the uniform of the corps and of the
various branches of its service, and it may be that I am
contrasting the Australian supply service or artillery with
the New Zealand infantry. Anyway, for me, the uniform
of the Australians was dark and was not cut on the rigid
and severe lines dear to the heart of the old British drill-
sergeant. And if it had been so cut I doubt if it would
have been worn so. It ran more to loose-fitting careless
comfort and was topped by a somewhat soft broad-brimmed
hat turned up on one side against the crown. I remember
the New Zealanders for a uniform of cut, color and material
more like our own.

Whatever be the truth of the matter, the men from these
neighboring islands are in my mind differentiated by their
uniforms and general appearance in a manner which somehow agrees with differences in temperament and personal
characteristics. I fancied that in civilian dress I could dis-
tinguish between them. Most Canadians will wonder why
I am coming at this so gently. They will tell you in a
minute that there was a difference—a hell of a difference.
Whenever the average Canadian thought of the corps, he
thought of the Aussies. He accepted the New Zealander
as a quiet, efficient soldier; he knew him; he understood
him as a man not unlike himself despite the fact that he
lived in a land where September is spring and apparently
spent most of his time shearing sheep. But the Aussie

was an anomaly, or something worse. What he thought of the Canadian, I don't know. But they didn't get along. Either of them, I think, would have been glad to have the other on the flank in battle; but back of the lines they were antagonistic. Frequently, when they encountered each other there, there was trouble. I never had much personal experience of this, but the stories told at first hand were numerous. Even if some diplomat smoothed things over and blended antagonism into a semblance of conviviality, it was not enough; the evening, more likely than not, would bring disturbance to the quiet of Madame's respectable *estaminet*. I never heard of trouble with the New Zealanders. That with the Australians was probably of the same sort that results in the instantaneous bristling when two excellent dogs come together in camp. It disappeared when they had something else to do, and neither side was the worse for the antagonism.

Of all the colonials, the Canadians most closely resembled the soldiers of the United States, though there were among them a great many who were English or born of English parents. Except for this element the two were much alike in physique, carriage and physical characteristics, as well as in temperament, habit of mind and other qualities which determine the response to discipline, and which, therefore, should decide the methods of training. But of the Canadians, as of all the colonials, it must be remembered that they were, first of all, British. Even those far-flung possessions, and near-possessions, of the Empire which were inhabited by peoples of alien race found something in the British character (not in the British bayonet) to which they quickly and whole-heartedly responded. I am not well informed in the various particulars, but I do know that this response was something upon which the Germans had not counted. They had, in fact, counted upon something quite to the contrary. Their contempt (hardly real contempt) for the British army sprang not only from its small numbers and its deprecated fighting qualities, but from the belief of the German High Command that Britain would not always be free to use it on the Continent. Much of its effectiveness would be dissipated in scattered efforts to keep order in the various colonies and dependencies. It didn't happen that way. The dependencies, generally, not only didn't require the presence of English troops; but they and the colonies proceeded at once to take care of the Marshall Islands and other German possessions in the South Seas. Southwest Africa ceased to be German Southwest Africa without appreciably hampering England in its Continental activities; and German insurrectionary intrigue in British South Africa didn't prevent this colony from sending troops to France.

I think it is something more than a fancy with me that the bearded Sikh sergeant had a good deal about him that was decidedly and staunchly British. There is a great significance in the fact that a Colonial three generations removed from the British Isles frequently refers to England as "back home." This feeling of close kinship throughout the Empire is but a large expression of a peculiar sense of solidity in England itself. An understanding of this sense of solidity is necessary to an understanding of the Englishman and to an appreciation of the British Army and its methods of training.

Someone has said that an Englishman's house is his castle. This is commonly taken—and was so intended, I believe—as expressing his love of home and his disposition to shut himself up within it. It is a just observation, but to the uninformed outsider it reveals very little of the Englishman or his home; for the castle is England; it does not exist for and by itself. Aside from its comfort and privacy (and the absence of heat) it is filled first of all with the consciousness that there are thousands of others like it, all sharing

in the vast and powerful accumulation of English tradition
and in the intimate necessity for importing tea and in maintaining contact with a cousin in Jamaica and an uncle in
New Zealand, in Hampstead Heath and Hyde Park and in
the Horse Guards at Whitehall. This is what I mean by
solidity. It is closely related to another characteristic
commonly called English stolidity. The Englishman is
stolid because England is solid and has proven herself so
throughout so many generations that she has acquired a
quality of inevitability. She has grown up, emotionally, and
the homeward bound Londoner accepts with equal uncon-
cern the cries of alarm on the part of some excitable individual and the figure of Nelson atop his monument in
Trafalgar Square. The one is quite effectually canceled by
the other, and the Englishman, who doesn't love war and
excitement, goes on his way home. It takes a lot to disturb him, and when he finally is disturbed he fights that he
may be undisturbed again. He resents being disturbed and
is likely to do a lot of grumbling about the failure of the
government or the opposition to protect him forever in the
peaceable enjoyment of his tea and port, beef and plum-
pudding, and England's inexorable schedule of holidays.
But these things must be protected, and he accepts the
necessity. There is nothing of *la patrie* impersonated by a
woman, a woman insulted or in danger or suffering, or (and
this is enough) beautifully and imperiously calling on him
for service, which moves the volatile and quick-witted French-
man; nothing of the excitement of parade and display which
inspires the Italian; no welcome opportunity for individual
exploits which is at the heart of the typical American. It
is simply a matter of moving again to protect his island
and his castle and the trade-routes of Empire on which
they depend. War becomes his business for an indefinite
time and he settles down to it in a business-like way, making himself as comfortable as possible. Anyone who has

seen him in the trenches will testify to this. A redoubt is *Piccadilly Circus;* a funk-hole becomes *Marble Arch;* somewhere near, along *The Strand,* Tommy can be found in his dugout, *The Three Lions,* making a cup of tea. It is this characteristic which is responsible for the observation that an Englishman is at home anywhere.

In all this I do not mean to imply that Tommy is conscious of fighting to protect his supply of tea and to maintain English institutions. He is not; he is fighting because it has become the business of England and he has been ordered to fight. He grumbles and does what is required of him, not troubling to inform himself further, any more than at home he informed himself of the policies of the government. The government is an ephemeral sort of thing, a matter of speeches, and of elections and cabinets which come and go. But England is a fixed and enduring condition, the result of a long process of accumulation and integration in which Tommy, and the King, fit as stones in a building. It *is,* and will continue to be; though now and then the governmènt finds it necessary to order Tommy out with a rifle in order to make others realize this. He must go in his place; the thousands of him comprise the base of the structure, and it is not in the nature of things for them to rise to the top. The whole is nicely articulated and must move together. This is what makes it invincible. Willingly and unwillingly, war-party and anti-war-party, Cavalier and Roundhead—but never a revolution that hasn't yielded to and strengthened the traditional order of things.

Tommy would not know what to do outside of his place, because to take him out is to destroy the structure—and Tommy. He is not an individual; he is first an Englishman. With a full realization of this fact, we will, I think, cease to worry about his lack of imagination and self-reliance or his failure to possess the necessary quick resilience and adaptability to overcome the unexpected or to take advantage of it. He doesn't lack self-reliance, and few men more readily adapt themselves to conditions. What he does lack is a feeling of independent self-sufficiency and aggressiveness and the concomitant impulse to push on alone, defiant of danger, glorying in individual achievement. Instead, it is instinctive with him to stand with his fellows. He is disposed to attach a great deal of importance to orders, and to conform strictly to them, because the issuing of orders is the business of the higher-ups, and all his life he has been accustomed to obeying orders or the decrees of government. Orders are a sign that everybody is on the job and things are being done in the correct manner.

But this doesn't mean that the English soldier is demoralized and helpless when the officer is killed or momentarily absent. If leadership has been sound and inspiring it outlives the officer. The officer is a symbol, just as at home the King is a symbol, the *crown* of this graduated structure which is England. I do not mean that the intelligent officer, schooled by birth and breeding in poise and self-command and trained in the essentials of leadership, is not missed in a difficult situation. He is missed, and would be missed with any body of soldiers, else we shouldn't waste training on officers. If his leadership has been good, the men will carry on in response to it after he is dead, and even more ardently. This is more strictly true of the English, I think, than of any other soldier, because no other is so proud of a really fine officer; he is a justification of the English system and of the soldier's habit of obedience; for the English soldier does not aspire to the officer's place, but only to serve under the best sort of officer. He is, in this manner, peculiarly dependent upon leadership.

This imposes a great responsibility upon the officers, and I think it is here that the British Army was weakest. I don't mean to indict the British officer. Far from it; the British officer at his best—and there were many of these—

was a remarkably fine soldier. He was intelligent, and schooled by birth and breeding in the first essential of command: self-command. The old, regular officers were, of course, highly trained at Sandhurst (the British West Point). There were some who held commissions without having undergone this course of training; but, still considering the best, they rapidly acquired an acceptable substitute. They fell in with the traditions of the regiment, with which they probably were already familiar, and with the fine traditions of the British officer, which leave nothing to be said. They were a fine lot, distinguished at all times by something which perhaps may be called aplomb. They were always right side up, unruffled under the most harassing and disconcerting conditions.

The weakness to which I refer has nothing to do with them—except that, if it obtains, as I think it does, it resulted in their numbers being shot through with a lot of men not all of this sort. It is a weakness which seems to me to inhere in the British system—though I think it can be, and perhaps is being, overcome. The line between officers and men in England is not drawn by military decree. It has been determined by the circumstances of birth, habit, custom—all that goes to make up the English social system—through a thousand years. It is recognized in the broader authority of the sergeants as compared to ours. The sergeants, under the sergeant-major, attend to nearly all matters of camp and drill routine, and any special orders are executed through them, the officers merely indicating to the sergeant-major what is to be done. The idea is that the soldier may put on "company manners," bring out his best just as he would like to do at home, however poor it is, if he were to be visited by someone of a station above him. The distinction may be made clearer, perhaps, by saying that it is not the business of the officer to train men, but to command and lead them. They are to be presented fit to respond to command. This is what is wanted. The ranks are not filled, as they are likely to be with us, with men who believe that they would be better officers than the lieutenant in charge of them. They do not aspire to lead, but to be well-commanded. The line between them marks the class distinction about which developed the weakness to which I refer.

The officers came from the classes, the higher-ups—of traditional necessity. But the traditional line is maintained more or less in defiance of the procreational methods of Dame Nature who goes on, indifferently, producing above the line a fair number of freaks with a minimum of grey matter. Many of these find their way into officers' uniforms. The Chinese have a proverb: "You can't carve rotten wood." These fellows have the manner, but no way has been discovered to give them the matter; and the manner thus becomes a caricature; hence the stage-Englishman. On the stage he is all right, except that, in the United States, where the genuine article is not so well known, he reflects upon a lot of the finest fellows in the world.

But the battlefield is no place for a joke of this sort; though even here, so far as the manner goes, they carried it off pretty well. They could carry a "stick," and many of them had the necessary self-command and calmness of manner. But that, of course, was not enough. In the hands of the real and splendid officer—and they were splendid— the stick was a symbol of his business to lead, to command, not to fight. It was a glorious sight. Armed with nothing else, they walked out ahead of their men into almost certain death, for they were easily spotted and picked off. Because of this, it was forbidden. Officers were required to remove the distinctive braid from their sleeves and to substitute dull bronze insignia on the shoulder, and were encouraged to carry a rifle. In the hands of the "dud," the stick was not only a symbol of the right to command; it became also a symbol of his failure to possess anything more than the arbitrary right. He was fittingly armed, and if nothing more than his own life had depended upon it, his conspicuousness would have worked out well enough. The order to remove conspicuous insignia and to carry a rifle was a triumph of common sense over tradition. The officers who possessed this rare commodity appreciated the order, not for their own safety, but because they realized they were more valuable alive than dead—and I think, too, they realized that there were too few of them. But orders could not confer common sense upon the dud.

He should, of course, have been in the ranks but this was not always possible. After all, tradition is a hardy growth; and, though it coudn't outwit Nature, it could and did outwit the High Command. It was not only difficult to get rid of him; it was difficult to replace him. For, although, while producing the duds above the line, Nature produced the same fair measure of fine material below it, this could not always be used. Tradition again. The English upper classes have among them a goodly number of families only a generation or so removed from the condition of poor bakers, brewers, soap-makers and distillers, and these have somehow and in some acceptable measure managed to acquire the approval of tradition. A generation and a lot of money can do wonders. But in England you can't take a man from the ranks and make him an officer—generally speaking. He has the common sense, but he can't carry a stick. Again, the High Command is helpless. In this case it has at hand the common sense, but can't impose the manner; it can't disguise this fellow so that the men will not recognize him as somebody who has been taken out from below and stuck up into a higher place, a violation of the order of things: "Aye; I knew the bloke when he was a bloomin' sergeant."

This, I think, marks a real weakness in the English Army.

It is a situation with which the United States will not be faced. The qualifications here pertain more strictly to the individual, and we have no limited officer-class to be depleted. There is such a class in England. It contains some of the finest men in the world—and some of the greatest asses. This class was sadly depleted of its best during the war. I suspect (and would very much like to have first-hand information about it) that if along in the spring of 1918 the war-weary Tommy (whose ranks were also shorn of their best) showed signs of flagging morale, this condition had much to do with it. It is a pity; for Tommy, if he has the right sort of officer—even if this officer is killed in the first minute of the attack—is damned near invincible.

This insistence upon the importance of the officer should not be taken to mean that in the British Army it was held that battles were won by orders, by masses of men trained to strict obedience and sent forward as a machine to conquer by sheer weight. On the contrary it was an axiom with the British that the greatness of an army rests with its men, not in the individual exploits of the men, but in closely organized action. This, of course, is not to be secured by constant direction by an officer, however efficient and ubiquitous he may be; it is not a matter of strict obedience to orders. It depends to a great extent upon the various qualities covered by that convenient blanket-term, *esprit-de-corps*. It is through this that any real unity of action is secured. This, of course, is a truism; yet it is often the obvious that is missed, and, if seen, is quite likely to be unappreciated and inadequately understood, its very obviousness making it seem a simple effect to achieve.

Whenever I pass Vancouver Barracks, it always seems perfectly clear to me that we have missed it. The Seventh Infantry happens to be stationed there at the present time. My father's father served with that regiment—and died with it, in Mexico. It has a glorious record of achievement; it

may be a fine regiment now, and quite fit to carry on that
record; but the record does not belong, peculiarly, to the
present members; the regiment is no longer the Old Seventh
Infantry, built of the pride and fine spirit of a particular
locality, handed down from generation to generation, a ready
atmosphere for the new recruit, with a minimum of racial
antagonism and sectional prejudice. General Pershing ob-
jected—and rightly—to simply using the various *units* of the
United States Army as feeders for the older and better
trained—but strange—organizations of the French and
British services; yet that is exactly what was done with our
men at home. It didn't matter whether they came from
Florida or Oregon, they were split up and slapped in with
men from Maine and Kansas. This action, presumably, was
based upon an assumption of *national* unity. Such a unity
is fine from a civic or political viewpoint or as defining the
civilian attitude toward the army. But as a basis for building up a fine military organization it is worse than useless.
A fine army is not made up of men, but of crack army corps
composed of divisions each proud of its own distinctions,
distinctions which rest upon the excellence of its command
and of the various brigades and services of which it is made
up; and the brigades look, not to the men, but to the command again, to the regiments and the several complements
of its establishment, and these are matters of pride only as
the companies are up to scratch. It is here, and in even
smaller units, that the men come in. Men aren't proud
of an army, but of the high standing and smart appearance
of their particular section and company. If this gets the
Old Man's eye and stings the other companies to come up
to it, then you are in a fair way to having a fine regiment,
and so in turn a good brigade.

Of course, this is more of the painfully obvious; it is the
simple fundamentals of organization; it is inescapable. And
it is a thousand times more important when we move from

this purely mechanical business to the effort to achieve the various abstract and indefinable qualities that go to make up what is *esprit de corps*. Yet, here we have ignored it, ruled out the essential and set up an arbitrary scheme for something which certainly cannot be imposed arbitrarily. It is not simply a matter of our refusal to allow the military organization to take shape readily and easily from civil life, of disregarding natural sectional feeling and interposing sectional strangeness and antagonism. In doing this we have also destroyed the continuity of the regiment. Soldiers die or are super-annuated, but tradition and history live on and grow with the years, accumulating and solidifying. Let the Second Ohio forever remain the Second Ohio, always recruited from the same localities. A soldier is little concerned with the personal qualities of a soldier in another division, but his own excellence depends to a great extent upon the man next to him. When, of these two, one is a hill-billy from Kentucky and the other an East-side Jew they cannot be expected to get along very well together. In a peace-time establishment they may be counted upon to wear off the edges, come to some measure of appreciation of each other's peculiar qualities, and overcome the arbitrary and foolish handicap. But peace-time establishments should provide the framework for full war-time strength, and it is here that the value of tradition comes in. If the regiment is always recruited from the same localities, the new recruit, hastily trained in an emergency, fits smoothly and harmoniously into an organization with which he is already familiar; on the part of the old men he is willingly received, and for his own part, anxious to justify this reception.

The value of this is perfectly exemplified in the organization of the British Army, and I am going to devote a paragraph or two to this, not because I think the British soldier is superior to ours, but because I am convinced that the United States soldier is potentially the finest soldier in the world and that he was not given a chance to realize his potentialities. But first, and in order to illustrate this, I want, briefly to make the comparison a triple one. In the German Army the emphasis was upon orders, carried out by mass formations. They abandoned this, or attempted to, perhaps largely because of the exigencies of trench warfare. But that was the theory; the German soldier was but a unit in the mass, and when the mass was broken up he was inclined to surrender. He did not depend upon himself and his comrades, as such, but upon the mass; the German unit of *morale* was the Fatherland, the arbitrary and pretentious will of the Kaiser and his henchmen, even though the divisions preserved their sectional integrity. There was little effective unity of action once the mass was broken. The result was German prisoners, in great batches, with their hands up. The Americans were never in danger of doing this. But what is the danger which is being invited by this hasty scrambling together of men widely different in temperament and character, antagonistic as to racial and personal habits, and with no common tradition of achievement back of them? What is the greatest danger to which such an ill-assorted unit, in which half the men mistrust the dependable qualities of the other half, may expose itself when the attack is checked and enemy machine-guns find their targets held up for murderous fire? Well, here is what is being invited: The few men who know each other get together in such numbers as find themselves in touch—two, three or a half-dozen—and proceed to do something about it: "All right, fellows, let's go; to hell with that gang; we can't stay here and be shot down with a lot of god damned Kykes." They may cover themselves with glory. But the company, despite their heroism, may suffer disastrous defeat. In any case, the essential unity of action is destroyed. I have thought this matter over many times since my little period of service. Frequently, it took the form of visualizing just what could be done with a regiment of real soldiers, every man exemplifying those individual qualities that are considered typically American, and all working smoothly together, each depending not only upon himself, but also upon the added strength that comes from the sure knowledge that he can count upon every single man in the company. We are *not* getting this effect as long as we take pains to destroy this solid sense of mutual dependability in the very outset.

Precisely here lies the strength of the British Army. The regiments are recruited by localities, availing themselves of all the common associations of civilian life. In war-time, the regiment may send out several battalions. They all *belong* to the regiment. Their achievements become not only a part of the history of the army but of the locality. The new recruit is not taken into a hastily formed organization; he is admitted to an institution, along with a lot of others whose qualities he pretty well knows. They are raw. While the drill-sergeant is turning them into soldiers, a lot of other things—not forgetting a stirring necessity within themselves—is turning them into a unit. Their first night in barracks, is quite as valuable as their first day on the drill-ground, for it is there that they begin to realize what it means to "belong to the regiment". The regiment has the names of a hundred battles, the history of three centuries, on its colours. His great-great-grandfather, possibly, died with it. Unity of action cannot be secured by commands in the field, and *esprit de corps* cannot be imposed arbitrarily. It is a thing of growth.

The British go much further in their efforts to take advantage of local spirit and pride. The Scotsman wears his native costume. This is a departure for which we have no occasion; yet it may be considered, as illustrating the strength to be gained from sectional prejudice and racial pride. Its allowance is not a mere negative matter, a concession to local feeling. The Scot could probably have been brought to adopt the khaki trousers, and the Gordons would then have appeared in something like uniformity with a regiment from Devonshire. But this semblance of uniformity would do much to destroy the vital unity. The kilt is not a whim, nor merely something that added color, and excited some curiosity, in the British parade.

It did excite a good deal of curiosity, by the way. Many a good old French woman, sometimes with not six sound teeth in her head, turned out as often as the Jocks passed through the village. Her curiosity might have taken many turns, but it was usually expressed in the not entirely innocent wonder—to judge by the sly smile—if there was anything underneath it. Sometimes she endeavored, with her stick, to lift the skirt in order to find out. With the real Scot, of course, there wasn't—nothing, that is, in the way of trewes, for although these were issued they were not always worn. Later in the war, I believe, it was considered necessary to order that they be worn in London; or else the gallant Scot, on leave, was kindly asked to take an inside seat in the London bus. The upper deck of these vehicles— in case you don't know them—is reached by a steep circular stairway from the rear platform. Passengers on the platform, and the nearby crowd on the curb, had no trouble satisfying any curiosity as to the presence or absence of trewes underneath any kilt ascending this stairway. I am told that trewes were a nuisance, besides unnecessary and an affront to Scot hardihood and pride. As illustrating the hardihood—and possibly the pride—a friend told me of one night crossing the Irish Sea during a Northeast blizzard with a good deal of sleet driving along the deck of one of those narrow little packets. A Highland soldier spent the entire passage on deck. My friend did, also, but he was well buttoned up in a nice "British Warm", which he had bought while on leave. His old coat was at hand, and after a time he offered to lend it to the Scot, who, declining, assured him that he had one in his pack, just in case it should be required when, later, he went to Inverness.

But to get back to the importance of the kilt: The Scot was not only brought into the army as an individual and allowed to serve with those whom he knew; but with him came the kilt and the sporran and the glengarry and all the associations of tradition and history and racial pride of Scotland for a thousand years. Forcibly deprived of these things, submerged in regiments which were not *theirs*, not a little of that fighting stuff which established the reputation of "The Ladies from Hell" would have been lost. We have no occasion for anything comparable to the kilt; but we do have sectional feeling and sectional pride, not as sharply defined as that between Scotland and England, but there just the same, and not to be ignored in any scheme to give the American soldier a chance to realize fully his superb qualities as a fighting man.

We do have bands—and what a hell of a mess we make of them. Again, to take the extreme example, a Scottish regiment would be humiliated if required to march to music made by men assembled from Cockney orchestras. It not only must have bagpipes but bagpipes played by Scotsmen, not recruits from a London vaudeville. Why? Because it is necessary to his pride in his regiment and in himself. All our regiments may have brass bands (though I am partial to the pipes for martial music), but the music and the musicians should *belong* to the regiment. A band may be excellent in itself, but it is not going to complete the excellence of the organization if it is not in all respects at one with it. A bunch of weatherbeaten Tennesseeans will forever have a thorn in its side if it must forever be confronted with a band composed of Wops, though they might readily concede the excellence of this band with another regiment to which it *belonged*. It seems absurd to be arguing about this; but the condition exists, and it seems to me equally absurd to have to point out the importance of remedying it. Perfect discipline—a fine spirit in the company—not only imposes a duty and sets an ideal for the soldier; it pre-supposes that everything will be done to realize the finished ideal. If it is not done, there is a failure on the part of the command, a breach of faith in a tacit compact with the private soldier.

It is in these things that the British Army won my admiration. That the men come first, was not only a *cliché* of the newspapers and a honeyed phrase for home consumption; it was a fact. The British soldier groused and grumbled and said all sorts of things about all sorts of Brass Hats; but at bottom he had a good deal of affection for the organization that showed an intelligent regard for his peculiar qualities and feelings.

Nor was this organization so hide-bound and hopelessly devoted to precedent and custom as is commonly supposed. K. R. & O. (King's Regulations and Orders) was the Bible for all British soldiers. Yet many of the Colonials took it as a sort of a point for departure rather than strict con-formity—and got away with it. We probably distressed a good many dyed-in-the-wool English officers; but on the whole, the system was not so inelastic. It made Britishers of Sikhs and Gurkhas and still left them Sikhs and Gurkhas. And for the most part it allowed the Canadians sufficient latitude to remain Canadians without being very badly hampered.

A little further word about the Canadians is necessary, for it happens that, during the years since the war, I have frequently been complimented by the remark, usually made in introductions: "Mac went over with the Pats." and a lot of other stuff along the same line.

Now; just to set at rest a lot of these "fairy tales", I want to record the fact that I never, at any time, belonged to that organization—much as I should have liked to.

The Princess Patricia's Canadian Light Infantry was the first Canadian organized force to share actively in the conflicts on the Western Front. Membership in that organization, even after it had been whittled down by successive engagements, was a mark of honnor which we, of the other Canadian contingents, fully appreciated. When I left the front, they were incorporated in the Third Division, under command of General Shaw. Another unit of this Division was the King Edward Horse. The others were mostly recruited from India—sort of a mongrel outfit, if you want to consider it that way; but they sure were fighting fools.

The "Pats" had, during the war: EIGHT commanding officers.

That is a separate paragraph and is inserted for the information of the uninitiated and the edification of the "soldat".

You, the reader, may not understand why I am spending all this time telling about an outfit with which I was never connected. Well, I'll tell you. Soldiers are soldiers and to all of us who are worth—what'll we say? Hell room?—anyway, they were our living examples during all the rest of the war.

Oh, sure; I know some other outfit probably lost more men and all that. And, also, you may rise up to remark that these same "Pats" took a hell of a licking the first time they tried to take St. Eloi. Say, boy, they took a worse one on the second day of June, 1916. But they came back to take Regina trench in October of the same year—didn't they?

The Canadian soldier was never *licked*. Say what we may about our own fine American troops, I, as an American born and with more than twenty years service under the Stars and Stripes, am here to certify that the men from over our Northern border are just as good at this fighting game as we are.

From the first day Canadian troops went into the line— it was at St. Eloi, that first time—until the end of the war, when they had their front lines East of Mons, they never were *licked*. About the only time they had to give up a bit of ground was on that June second operation, in 1916. That was a slam, all right, but I'll tell the cock-eyed world we took it all back, again; didn't we? Yea boy; we took it all back and plenty more—before Heinie had a chance to even think about it, we had all our own trenches back— all the way from Hooge to Hill Sixty. That was the time I wrote to my father, an old Civil War Officer: "Remember what Kit Carson said at Chantilley? 'Lovely fighting all along the line: go in anywhere'". Sure: plenty fighting for all of us.

The casual American reader of "War Stories", is very apt to think that the "Pats" were the only soldiers that Canada sent to the war. Well, I'll tell you something about that, too. It is just about the same as the story that the U. S. Marines won the war at Belleau Wood. The "Pats" were a magnificent fighting regiment. So are our Marines. No man on earth has more respect for their quali- ties than I have, but, just the same, you want to remember that they were not fighting the whole war by themselves. That Second U. S. Division was composed of two infantry regiments and two of the Marines. Some enterprising war correspondent, writing the story of their fighting during those critical days, forgot to mention the fact that these two Marine regiments were but a part of the Second Division— the others, as I recall it, being the Ninth and Twenty- third Infantry Regiments.

In my opinion—and after thinking it over for some six- teen years—the men who really *won the war* (if it was actually won by anyone) were the members of the First

Canadian Division. I was not a member of that Division—though I tried hard enough to be.

Their superb courage in withstanding the initial ordeal of poison gas is, in my estimation, the outstanding event of the war.

But I don't want to get excited about this. It was an exciting time—war at its best and worst, its most sublime and most pitiful and horrible; but I was going to give you some idea as to the make-up of the Canadian Expeditionary Forces, after those first units, led by the Princess Pats, which were sent out at once to do their bit while Canada was getting ready. A First Division was in action during the first winter of the war. The Second followed in the spring, and later two others, until as the organization was completed and filled out there were in France four divisions, with the fifth constantly in process of filling up in England and as constantly being sent out in small detachments to reinforce those in the field.

Service was voluntary in Canada until the last year of the war, and new units were steadily being authorized and recruited in various centers throughout the Dominion. I am not in possession of official information here, but I suspect that it was much easier to secure recruits for service units being formed in various localities than it was to get replacements for the battalions already in the field. In any case, many were formed which never got any further than England, though they left Canada as complete units, not always up to strength, perhaps, but with a full complement of officers. When these were broken up, they were not scattered indifferently to all units in the field. So far as possible they were kept together, men from one new battalion going as needed to replace casualties in a particular battalion or in two battalions in France. Thus was done all that could be done to maintain and make use of the bonds of community, to give a man every chance to fit smoothly and proudly into his organization for war.

There was a much further departure in this same direction: Men were allowed to wear a uniform to which they were by racial tradition and sentiment attached. I wonder how many Americans know that the Scotsman in Canada might wear a kilt. Not only might he wear a kilt, but several choices were provided, so that, although he might not find the tartan of the clan of his own name, he might nevertheless wear one to which he was sentimentally or otherwise attached. The Royal Highlanders of Montreal sent out the 13th Battalion clad in the kilt worn by the Black Watch (42d) of Scotland. In that same brigade, the Third (of the First Division), were two other Scottish battalions, the Fifteenth and the Sixteenth. The Fifteenth was from Toronto, sent out by the 48th Highlanders, who wore the Davidson tartan, allied with the Gordons. The Sixteenth came from some place in the West, I believe, and wore the Seaforth kilt. And there was at least one other Scottish unit, also from the West and wearing the kilt of the Seaforths. Of the later battalions, which never got to France as units, I recall two that were Scottish. There may have been others, but since this is in no sense intended to be either a history or a complete record of the Canadian service, I have not gone to the trouble to inform myself.

But I am informed as to the wisdom of letting the military organization take shape as naturally as possible from civil life. The idea that it must be as arbitrary and violent as it can be made—and that a feeling of solid unity can be *imposed* upon it—is of a piece with the notions of little minds regarding authority. We have all seen these little fellows, who, not having within them the quiet consciousness of authority, are at pains to display the outward semblance of it, foolishly supposing that thereby they prevent themselves being seen for what they really are.

Well, the records of the Canadians probably will be conceded to have some bearing upon the quality of their organization and training. And one of the most radical departures
from this precious uniformity—those Scottish battalions—
did their part towards earning and maintaining the reputation of "The Ladies From Hell."

But I must get on, back among the boys—old and young—
of my own battalion. In age, they ranged all the way from
sixteen to fifty-two. At both extremes there was probably
considerable lying done, but that's the kind of lying that
I believe even old St. Peter himself would overlook. By
hook or crook, those boys were determined to get into the
game. Some that I came to know very well in later days
showed me medals for Indian campaigns which were over
long before some of the youngsters were born. The same
way, many of the really young ones confided to me that
they had to resort to all sorts of subterfuges before they
were accepted.

A very large percentage of both officers and men had been
in the organized militia, and many had served in South
Africa, the Sudan and other campaigns. Our Colonel dated
his active service from the Riel Rebellion, in 1885, and I
am not sure but that Major Bennett (Second in Command)
could claim the same honor. Many others of the officers
and N. C. O.'s carried the ribands proving long and meri-
torious service, but here and there in every company would
be found some of the very, very young ones.

The first time I took any particular notice of these kids
was when, during our training in England, we went in for
a course of signalling. The instructor of the class to which
I was attached—a corporal—had been a Scoutmaster and he
had picked out several ex-Boy Scouts as likely candidates
for the signallers section. At the very first day's instruction
it was painfully apparent to myself and a few others who
knew nothing about the signalling game, that we would

have to get up and hustle. Those boys already knew the
Morse alphabet and most of them knew the flag codes—
both single and double—while we had to learn the whole
business from the ground up. However, by perseverance
and endurance we managed to catch up. I can only speak
for myself, but I am willing to admit that I did more real
studying during those few weeks than I had ever done in
my life.

From that time on I was rather partial to the youngsters.
Of course I had some up and coming nephews, back home,
who were Boy Scouts; and I had, one time and another,
taken enough interest in their work to boost them along
whenever any matter came up in the way of camping,
hunting, fishing and all that sort of thing, but had really
never taken them very seriously. Now, however, I realized
that the training they had received was just exactly that
needed as a foundation for the making of real soldiers. Intelligence, straightforward honesty of purpose, devotion to
duty—they had them all, and many's the time during the
following years that many of us older ones had reason to
be glad that we were supported by those same boys. Boys?
Yes; they were that, in years; but no man, of whatever
age, has ever excelled them in the patriotic way in which
they did their duty through fair weather and foul. Courage?
They were the very exemplification of it. Clean, upstanding, forthright men, they never shirked or dodged a hazardous enterprise, but took their chances with the best.

The crew of the first gun which I commanded was composed entirely of these boys: Bouchard, Wendt, Toms, Mc-
Farlin and Shangrow. The combined ages of the oldest
two of them was at least two years less than my age at the
time. I believe (and sincerely hope) that McFarlin and
Shangrow are still living. They were both wounded and
sent home and I do not find them among the list of those
killed. The others are peacefully sleeping in their graves,

close to where they made the great sacrifice—"For King and Country".

During the time, in the summer of 1916, that I was back in England and attached as instructor to our Reserve Battalion at Sandling, I had occasion to take numerous detachments down to the Hythe ranges for musketry instruction, and there I came into contact with some of the *real* Boy Scouts of England. They were taking the places of the older Coast Guards and were on regular and *active* duty, patrolling the shores of the Channel. I would judge that their ages were between thirteen and seventeen, but they, each and every one of them, were doing the work of a man. More than one German submarine was caught by their vigilance, and I doubt not that they also were responsible for the frustration of many attempted air raids.

I have often thought that General Sir Baden-Powell must have, during his epochal defense of Mafeking, noticed that the young boys were more susceptible to instruction than the older men of the available forces and that it was there that he conceived the Boy Scout idea. Of course, I may be all wrong about this but that is how it looks to me. The young men *do* learn easier and more quickly than the older ones (how well I know it).

Yes; I remember those youngsters very pleasantly—over this interval of a decade and a half. Then I realize that not all of them are alive now, that within the year, perhaps, after I last saw them, the oldest among them had gone to join the colours—and the dead. But, still, the memory of them is not a depressing one. We are depressed with the death of a soldier only when he has died unnecessarily— when he has been sacrificed to inefficiency, sent into battle poorly equipped, inadequately trained or falteringly supported. I do not believe that those fellows were thus sacrificed—this despite my feeling that toward the last many of their officers lacked the stuff—and the experience—to develop that inspiring leadership, the cool and consummate courage and sureness, that characterized a great number of British officers at the beginning. But the battalion had something which held them together and pulled them through. This something belonged to the battalion—and to the British Army. It could not be destroyed by the war, which destroyed the best men and the best officers.

It is this something I have tried to get at in this chapter about the British Army. And it is this something that I should like to *get across*—in addition to the value of rifle-training—as I try to sort out the experiences and impressions of my "military career". Of this career, there are a score or so of years that need not be counted, except in so far as they familiarized me with the rifle and gave me the rudiments of military training. With this equipment I went to Canada, where I taught something of the little I knew, and learned a lot myself. A little period of active service enabled me to test this—to see what counted and what didn't count. Then I found myself back in this country—with no very high opinion of myself as an instructor, but with a very definite knowledge as to what mattered on a modern battlefield. I had rosy visions of a magnificent army—built to fight and to stand up to it, shoulder to shoulder, each man proud of the next man.

Well, the contrast between the early days of Canada's preparations and the early days of our preparations was painful to me—as an American, as a soldier, and as a man of a bit of common sense—and to my budding pride in this coming American Army. I had come back with a great deal of admiration for the British; but not the least part of my feeling was this anticipation of an even greater admiration for the United States. I was sure of this. I had seen what Britain could do with material not as good as ours. With two years in which to observe and with this vast resource of dynamic energy, self-confidence and adventurous spirit on which to draw; the United States, I thought, might well startle the world with a model and magnificent army.

I soon became convinced that those who were in charge of things had somehow lost all touch with the realities of the situation. The finest sort of beginnings for a real army were deliberately destroyed. It was like a madhouse. The important thing seemed to be a lot of theories which did not even have the virtue which should belong to theories: that of having evolved from logical thought. These had evolved from a lot of wrangling, petty jealousies, animosities—and I don't know what fancy ideas—and they had resulted, largely, in destroying the very basis on which a fine army is built.

I suppose I rubbed the apostles and supporters of these theories the wrong way; but my regret is that I did not have the power to rub hard enough. I should have liked to rub them out. There is no place for factionalism and petty jealousies in an army, particularly when it is being hastily enlarged to meet an emergency. There must have been some aim which, in its fine-spun, roundabout intention, was good, but I don't know what it was. If it was to eliminate factionalism (such as might be supposed to develop between Marine Corps, Regular Army, National Guard, etc.,), it will not bear much examination. This sort of factionalism is of the very stuff out of which armies are made—if the general officers are equal to their jobs. A good officer does not mistake uniformity for unity any more than he depends upon gazetted authority for his right to command. Unity belongs to the regiment, not the uniform; and the right to command is a quality of the officer. If he is a general officer he welcomes individuality in the various units of his command. Whether this individuality is marked by differences in uniform, doesn't matter a snap to him—just so he has the individuality. That's the stuff fighting spirit is made of. It's up to him and his subordinates to use

it. That's why I wished for the power to rub harder. If
they can't use it, let's get them out of the way, not sacrifice
the makings of a fine army (and later literally sacrifice the
resulting mob) to a few little notions and petty jealousies.
I can put up with these things in politics, but in war, lives
depend on them.

That's one big lesson I learned with the British. England
was full of all sorts of obstructionists, strikers and long-
winded members of the opposition. Adequate supplies of
munitions were long delayed, partly because of them. But
no one found it necessary—and crack-brains were not given
a free hand—to reorganize the army, turn the Scots Guards
into a battalion of pioneers, put the Royal Marines to driving lorries, and scramble the remainder together in con-
formity to impractical, or insincere, notions of a fond and
fatuous national unity.

Once again: the unit on which *morale,* and fighting efficiency, depend is small. *Esprit de corps* begins with the
pride of the individual soldier in himself and as one of a
small unit on *all* of whom he knows he can depend, each
one of whom challenges and supports the best that is in
him. If you will provide officers to command regiments and
brigades built of this sort of stuff you will be in a fair way
to having an army that is a United States Army.

And you certainly can't get it by mixing raw recruits
representing all strains of a widely diverse people—except
with unlimited time and the best of leadership. With these
it would be possible to do things the wrong way. But if
we had plenty of brains and leadership in the right places
there would be no inclination to do things the wrong way.

Well, the war is over. I should like, graciously, to re-
frain from speculating upon what would have happened if
the United States had not had a full year—after the declara-
tion of war—in which to get into action. Another time, it
may be that we shall have to fight, instanter, with no foreign

power to shield our befuddled preparations. If this should happen, I hope that the armchair Napoleons and the jealous little minions of uniformity will have mastered their technique of producing armies presto! out of the hat, and that their assortment of East-siders and cowpunchers, Boston Irish and hot-headed Southerners, Wops, Poles and hillbillies, will each feel proud of his tent-mates, glad to have them on his right and left, and that they stick together and carry on as well as did the "Limeys".

Chapter 16

Notes on Sniping

IN THIS chapter I propose to give some of my own personal opinions and experiences relative to sniping in the trenches, or from a fixed position while on the defensive; and will follow this with a chapter devoted to the individual rifleman who uses his rifle while advancing over the modern battlefield. There is a vast difference between the two situations and in the equipment, methods, and what might be termed the individual qualities which must necessarily be employed.

I do not make any pretense as to this being a text-book, but it might not be amiss in this chapter to give my readers an idea or two as to just how we went about what turned out to be the very first efforts made by the British Army at anything like organized sniping. Well, anyway—I am going to take the role of "Old Man Experience" and tell you some of the details. In various other chapters of this story I have had occasion to say a great deal about our experiences, and I fear I shall be accused of repeating a great many things simply to fill space. However, I shall try and minimize these repetitions as much as possible.

It is a common but erroneous belief that the only necessary qualification for a sniper is to be able to shoot accurately. As a matter of fact that is only half of it—perhaps less than half. I have known, and know now, many expert riflemen who would be of little or no use in war—at least not without a lot of additional training and experience.

Before the sniper can "snipe," he must be able to get into position within range of the enemy, and as this game works both ways, he must be able to do so without allowing said enemy to locate him, and perhaps get in the first shot, for if this should happen it is quite likely that *our* sniper would be through before he started—in other words, a wash-out. Since we no longer have an open season on Indians, about the best way to acquire the skill to advance over varied ground without being detected is by stalking wild game. And by stalking, I mean to get right up close to the animal before taking the shot, and not merely to crawl into some position at long range from which it is possible to take a shot over open ground. Crawl, roll or push yourself forward until you are within relatively close range of the target, and learn just what sort of Indian-cunning and patience the art of proper stalking calls for. The practice may be gotten on anything from a moose to a goose, both of which take a lot of stalking at times.

I suppose that in this day and age, the most readily available live animal upon which to practice will be the common woodchuck or ground-hog. From personal experience I can testify that excellent stalking practice may be gotten by anyone who will really *stalk* woodchuck, and not merely use them as a long-range rifle target. In recent years I have talked with a great many woodchuck hunters, many of whom told me what excellent "hunters" they were and what splendid shots and kills they had made, mostly at the longer ranges running up to three hundred yards. I never bothered to explain to them that it was *rifle* practice they had been getting and not hunting practice at all. Those of you who wish to learn the art of stalking under such conditions must hold your fire until you have stalked forward to within thirty or forty yards; which may readily be done in any hilly or rolling country, or where the grass or other cover is of any height. Too easy a shot, do you say? Well then:

use a light .22 rifle and hold for the eye, or else take a running shot offered in the few yards distance our 'chuck will be from his den. The idea I am trying to put over is that you must get your rifle practice on the paper target and your stalking practice on the woodchuck or other available live game.

When the British finally did get around to organizing anything like a real Sniping Corps (in 1916) they made good use of the game-keepers, guides and men from the Scottish deer forests. They called 'em "Lovat Scouts" possibly because Lord Lovat may have been instrumental in the organization or equipment of the force—I don't really know. But I do know that Major H. Hesketh-Prichard was the man who really boosted and built up the game. Further along I shall have something to say about his organization and methods.

Another odd slant which many expert riflemen have about this sniping game, is the belief that their superior ability as a rifle-shot will gain for them such special privileges as relief from disagreeable duties or hard work, and added security through being given care or protection by higher authorities, or in the language of the trenches, being put on a "bomb proof" job. As to the first of these suppositions, I can only say that in both the Canadian and United States services it takes a lot of "rank" to get any pick-and-shovel work out of the men for anyone but themselves, and even then they are very apt to shirk much such necessary labor. My personal experience during the first few weeks of sniping was that the operation called for much additional hard labor on my part, and that often the only way to have that special work done right, let alone done at all, was to do it myself. As to the job of sniping offering additional safeguards to the sniper—why hell's bells man, it calls for far more exposure and chance-taking than ever falls the lot of the average soldier. It's just a lot of extra work and misery for the sniper, that's what. So, if you are looking for a soft job in the dugouts, take up something besides sniping.

When we started our first serious sniping, in November 1915, up in the Ypres salient, we were within close, easy range of the Germans and they already had many expert snipers in their line and at work. They beat us to it at the start, but I am personally satisfied that we overtook and surpassed them in the end. As far as I know, there were at that time no text books on the subjects nor any other literature that might have been useful to us, so we had to work out our own system and "technique".

It was at this time and place that it was first decided to organize a corps of snipers, and orders were issued for each company and detachment to submit the names of two men who were supposed to be well qualified for such work. The order stipulated that all must be "volunteers." Now, whenever you put that phrase into an order, it is a cinch that all hands will immediately prick up their ears and take notice. Naturally, it implies that the duty is extra hazardous, and it might be supposed that the average soldier would be glad enough to "let George do it," but the truth is that it works out just the opposite. After a few months of the monotony of routine warfare, nearly every man is anxious to make some sort of a change. The question of the "hazards" never enters his mind, he knows full well that he is liable to get bumped off any minute anyway, no matter what he is doing, so that consideration never enters into the thing. For example—we recruited our machine-gun men from the infantry companies. Now at that time the life of a machine gunner was figured as a very poor insurance risk, in fact, the M. G. outfits were commonly called "suicide clubs." But just the same, there was always a long waiting list in every company, eager for the chance to get with us.

So it came about that company and section commanders were besieged with applications from men who wanted to be snipers. It must have been a difficult matter for some of them to make their selections, as there were many really "expert" riflemen in every company. So far as my observations went, however, they made good selections, taking men who, in addition to their known shooting ability, had had considerable experience in big game hunting. And that generation of Canadians was very fortunate in this respect.

One in particular—John Paudash—a Chippewa Indian, comes to mind. By birth, inheritance and inclination, he was a hunter. He never would have an observer, preferring to work alone as he made his devious ways along behind the lines, watching for a chance to take a shot. He seldom (perhaps never) had any permanent "nests" but moved about continually. Each evening he would turn in his report, and I for one believed him, which is more than I could say for any other *lone* sniper.

His brother, George, was a Corporal in our Machine Gun Section and was also selected—together with myself—to represent the Section. Together, we went back to the Sniping School and got our rifles and equipment, but poor George never had much chance to use his. You see, I was a Sergeant and he a Corporal, so I had the edge on him and he stayed with the guns mostly. No doubt he would have done as good or a better job at it than I did, but I just simply could not give up the fun I was having. However, a few months later, when the sniping business was really organized, we both had to turn in our special rifles and telescopes. But we had plenty to do in our own line from that time on.

I mentioned above a "Sniping School." Well, that was what it was destined to be, but at that time it was in the first stages of formation. There was an improvised range of some two hundred yards and that was about all—but it was enough for us. All we did was to check up the telescope sights against the iron ones, and sight in enough to learn that we had accurate and dependable rifles. We only spent a few hours there, having left the front line that morning and returning soon after dark. As I have said elsewhere, we made our own medicine as we went along, and in the end it appeared to work out very well.

A while back, I spoke about John Paudash—the lone sniper—whom I considered to be the very best man I have known to work alone. In my opinion, the individual sniper does not get very far except for short periods of time—such as at daybreak, or at sundown, or for sniping at very short ranges where cover and shelter is apt to be scarce. For continuous sniping and observation, extending over a period of hours or days, it is much the best for the sniping force to be paired off in teams of two men.

The mental and physical strain of having to be continuously alert for long periods is entirely too much for any one man—and this is particularly true when a large portion of the observing has to be done through a high-power telescope. No one pair of eyes will stand up to the occasion for very long. With two men, the telescope can be taken turn about, and one man can take it easy while the other keeps the enemy under continuous observation. Also, this observation must often be kept up while the rifleman is sighting and waiting to take his shot. Very frequently you take a shot at a head bobbing up and down behind a trench or looking out from some gap in the sandbags, and when looking through the sights *you* cannot tell whether the target is in the clear or not. Under such circumstances, you "draw a bead," get the slack out of the trigger, and squeeze off when your observer tells of the head again coming into view.

The situation is exactly the same as that of a pair on some rifle team shooting over the 1000 yard range in a bad wind— or better still, that of a man firing his string with a good coach at the spotting scope. The coach has all the work and worry, while the rifleman merely holds steady and touches off when the coach signals that the wind is right. And furthermore—as is very often the case with the sniping team—the coach (observer) may frequently be the more important of the two men.

No—the lone sniper has a bit too much to contend with at times—particularly the one who wanders about the front lines looking for a favourable target. Not the least of his troubles may be the expostulations of some nervous Sister Annie who insists that no firing be done from *that* section of trench for fear "they will retaliate."

The paired teams are much the better for sniping from fixed positions or while on the defensive, and in the Canadian Corps this was the system we started out with. It worked from the start too. With a pair, it is not absolutely necessary that both men be crack shots—the best rifleman can stick to the rifle and keep the other man observing with the glass, only relieving him for brief periods. The great benefit of the pair, to my mind, is that it breaks the monotony of long hours spent away from other troops and gives two kindred spirits the constant opportunity to talk about their common interest—in addition to other topics. Then again, conditions may be such that it is much easier to train observers than to train rifle shots. In my own case, I did all the shooting and kept Bouchard at the glass for most of the time, doing the greatest part of my observing through a pair of binoculars. No, these last were not issued—there are some things which can be gotten in active service without an indent.

Once paired off, and the equipment drawn, it behooves our team to get started at their sniping. The first thing to be done is to make certain that the equipment is all right—particularly that the telescope sight is properly fitted to the rifle and *lined up right*. The greatest handicap to such sights is the total lack of understanding *anything* about them which is invariably displayed by the authorities who issue or try to tell you what shall be done with them. The average ordnance officer or sergeant will probably know next to nothing about this equipment, and finally, the men to whom the 'scopes are issued may not have the slightest idea of their use or possibilities. This was one of the great handicaps to the use of rifle telescopes in the British service; they were handed out so many to a battalion and given to men who never before had even seen a telescopic-sighted rifle. Give the average man a rifle so sighted and he looks through the glass, sees how clearly everything is "brought up close" and don't see how he possibly can miss. Such an individual may shoot for days with a rifle whose 'scope is several feet out of alignment, yet think he is never missing a shot. This last statement is no exaggeration whatever—his bullets may be striking so far from the point of aim as to be outside the field of view of the telescope, and just because every "target" shot at will naturally duck back out of sight our "rifleman" modestly assumes that he is hitting them all.

I mention these things because they were faults which seriously handicapped the sniping game in France in its early stages. Fortunately, in the Canadian Corps we had no such troubles as these, because we had plenty of skilled riflemen who had previously used telescopes and who knew their peculiarities, faults—and virtues. One such man to a division may indeed be priceless at a time like this, and we Canadians had several such to the battalion. Our Ross rifles were promptly sighted in *right* with both 'scope and iron sights—and kept that way until turned back into ordnance stores again.

Having checked up on the alignment of the telescope and seen that it is right, *tight* and proper, it now remains to get hold of some suitable ammunition—*and enough of it*. Not all the ammunition issued to troops in the field will be suitable for use, in fact, very little of it is likely to come within the requirements of accuracy as demanded by the sniper. I have spoken elsewhere of our troubles along this line, suffice it here to say that if you *do* locate some accurate ammunition *grab on to it*—enough to last a long while too. There may be a bit of competition when it comes to "grabbing off" this good ammunition. Amongst my immediate associates in the 21st Battalion were any number of really good riflemen—experienced big game hunters and guides who honestly knew good ammunition from bad. These men always selected their ammunition with the greatest of care, and when we happened to locate a case of some reliable, standard make they would promptly gather around and load up with it, often taking many times the amount actually required. They knew that the time would come when it would be impossible to obtain *any* good ammunition.

The spotting telescope is an important part of the team's equipment. The ones issued to us were splendid, about 36 power I believe, which was much too high, so we put in the extra eyepiece which came with it—this was around 20 or 25 power and worked all right. The care and *proper* use of this spotting 'scope is something to be learned, and some chaps become very proficient with it. The important points are to keep the lens clean and free of grit, grease or fingerprints—then keep a *clean* bit of soft cloth handy so the objective lens may be kept in proper shape. Scratches on the surface of this objective lens will soon ruin it for clear observation. Keep the draw tubes lightly oiled with some heavy grease, and mark the first draw with a line scratched around so it will indicate the exact place at which the telescope will be roughly in focus. The use of that sun-shade on the front of the glass is of the greatest importance and this must be kept *extended at all times* to avoid giving your position away through the flashing of the large objective lens This was very necessary with us at early morning when the sun shone directly into our eyes. As soon as the spotting telescope is received, it should be camouflaged with a covering of khaki cloth or brown sandbag, and this cover is best kept on permanently. One always uses the observing glass from a comfortable, steady rest, and it pays to take your time and examine the enemy ground slowly and closely—a small bit at a time.

Continuous observation through a powerful telescope is very trying on the eye, and in my opinion the shooting member of the pair had better not engage in too much of it. I much preferred to do most of my general observing with a pair of good binoculars, and only used the big telescope to check up on a bit of target after my partner had found it; this was seldom necessary. By keeping Bouchard at the big glass most of the time, and spelling him with personal observations through my binocks, we both got along very well. At times, it may be necessary for the rifleman to put in a stretch of close observation; but it should generally be done as a preliminary to the actual shooting and not mixed in with it too much. A pair of good binoculars is not nearly as trying on the eyes as a telescope, at least that is my experience. But the telescope is much the best for real, honest-to-God observation at long ranges.

Having obtained our equipment, and rigged it up in proper shape, it now remains to hunt up a few places from which we can snipe. This may turn out to be a considerable job, frequently calling for much hard work on the part of both members of the team. In general, one's sniping from a trench or defensive system falls into two classes—close range, rather restricted shooting from a loop-hole or nest built into or ahead of the front lines; and more elaborate and pretentious accommodations arranged farther back of the lines, where better concealment and a far more extensive field of fire is generally available. Maybe I better discuss the two systems a bit.

Shooting from a loop-hole in a front trench is apt to be a

decidedly limited proposition. The ground which may be covered with fire is likely to be restricted to that part of the enemy lines directly in front of the loop-hole, quite possibly to the front trench alone, and often only a few yards of trench at that. It naturally depends upon just where the trench is located. Such sniping is more of an irritant to the enemy than a source of real danger: they soon learn to avoid that particular bit of trench or to keep heads down when in it—and if it gets too hot for them they call on the artillery to bust up the entire front section from which you are shooting. I always thought this sort of "keep your head down Allemand" sniping could best be done by the ordinary rank and file—and done all along their line too.

And when it comes to crawling alone out in front of your own trenches, probably dressed up in one of those "sniper robes," I am off that stunt also—by preference, that is—although I have done quite a bit of it. Here, a man is strictly "on his own" and is apt to be pretty much up against it if anything goes wrong. His field of fire is much limited, no moving about can be indulged in, and generally but one or two shots may be fired before the show is over for the day. Then comes the long, fearful wait until darkness sets in, before the crawl back to your own trenches may be begun. A fellow feels pretty helpless lying out there all day in the open under a hot sun,—I know, for I have done it and I think I have about as much nerve as the average man. Still; this sort of thing must occasionally be done. But a little shelter and cover go a long way towards making one feel more secure during that "aeon" from daybreak until darkness—even if only to roll over in and go to sleep.

As I said before, another great handicap against a man working alone is that often he cannot *see* when to let off his shot. You are generally shooting at some very small loop-hole or opening, and once your eye is down over the sights, cannot tell whether or not your man has his head exposed.

With a pair, you hold "ready" with the sights aligned on
that place of exposure, and when the "target" slides his
head out so it can be hit your observer signals and you let
off immediately. Then again, once the shot is fired, no individual rifleman, and I don't care how conscientious he is,
can ever truthfully say whether or not he got his man. The
rifle kicks up into your face and hides the aiming point,
dust and dirt fly up around the target, and before your
vision has cleared up, the target has disappeared—whether
shot or merely ducked *you* cannot tell. Your observer often
can. During our early days at sniping I was greatly amused
at the tremendous "bag" made by our various lone-wolf
snipers who worked up and down the trenches. These chaps
never missed a shot, to hear them tell about it.

No—having tried both ways I am very much in favor of
the two-man team as a sniping set-up. The pair will actually
pick up and observe several times as many targets as any
individual watcher, and they can keep it up for far longer
periods of time. For these and other reasons mentioned
above, I preferred to do most of my sniping with an observer and from the positions we had especially prepared.

It is generally advisable to move behind the front-line
trenches for one or two hundred yards, and build a series of
sniping posts in suitable locations. In this manner, one can
invariably pick out commanding positions from which a far
better observation of both enemy trenches and back areas
may be maintained. Also the field of fire will be several
times as extensive; we had one post where some 1200 yards
of German trench system could be "commanded." The additional hundred yards or so of range over which one must
fire is of no great handicap to the real rifle shot, and will be
more than compensated for in the far greater number of
shots which will be obtained. Observation on the part of the
enemy and consequent detection of *your* nest is made much
harder and therefore less probable. All in all, the erection

of these sniping posts somewhere back along the support
trenches is much to be preferred.

While about it, make up a string of sniping posts and do
not make a practice of using any particular one of them for
too long a period of time. Continuous fire (if effective)
coming from one fixed direction is bound to result in extensive observation on the part of the enemy and in a deluge of
artillery fire once the post is finally located. Use one nest
for a day or two and then move over into another one located in a different sector.

I have spoken elsewhere about the inadvisability of always
locating these posts in some building, or on a hill top, or in
some other prominent or commanding feature of the landscape. The enemy *expects* them to be located in just such
places as these, has the exact range figured out to each and
every one, and soon shells them apart with his artillery once
trouble comes from that direction. The very best locations
are out in some open field, away from anything on which
he may sight or range his guns. This generally calls for
much hard work and preliminary preparation, all done at
night of course, before the post is properly dug in, concealed,
and arrangements made for getting in and out without being
seen from the front or flanks.

Once the posts are completed, and we are finally inside,
it remains to get the ranges laid out and sighted in before
operations really commence. This consists of making *your
own* range maps of the exact distances to all the various
prominent objects in our own and the enemy trench system,
and in thoroughly checking up these with the more elaborate,
official maps which will be available.

This sighting in is a rather extensive proposition. First,
you and your observer lay out the entire enemy trench system and back areas into general sectors and give each a
designation. The most important thing is to arrange plenty
of reference points. These latter are generally prominent

objects or features of the enemy system and a knowledge of them soon becomes second nature to both members of the team. Your targets will be located with reference to these designated points or objects, as: "That petrol can by the new trench, nine o'clock, third sandbag, see him?" Naturally, both know where the new trench is, and can see the petrol can, but the picking up of the exact target will not be quite so easy through the sights. In addition, the rifleman must immediately judge the exact range to that particular target, set his sight (possibly) and *shoot quickly,* because that target is not going to stay there all day. He will have just one "first and last shot for record," which ends that particular shooting match for the day. Then the team starts all over—at another target somewhere else. The range will be different, the angle of fire probably changed considerably, and worst of all the light will be different. This last, I consider to be the hardest of all to combat, even with a telescopic sight.

The team will have little trouble in agreeing upon a set of designating points, and will soon become so familiar with them that their use requires little conscious thought. The ranges to them become automatically known in a short time, and it does not take long to get trained upon a target. There may or may not be time to change the sight setting; one generally "holds off" a bit and takes the shot just as quickly as possible. When it becomes necessary to transmit a designation or target back to someone else—say the artillery or some other observer, there is but one method—give the exact map reference from the official maps.

The well known firing-point scheme of using the clock face in order to designate targets or objects is applied in the case of new ground where the designation points have not yet been laid out; also occasionally in directing observation on vague locations. Generally, this part is pretty easy and one soon gets a good mental picture of everything in the field of

view and also the exact range to it. This range will be
determined by both map readings and trial shots. The latter
are much to be preferred and one may indulge in quite a bit
of shooting as the day progresses, in order to keep sighted
in with the various changes of light. This, as I said previously, is the most serious thing to contend with, and as the
sun works its way around the position one should keep
sighted in to agree with the difference in light.

This general sighting in is a very easy matter to do at
almost any time of the day. It may not be possible to do
much of it from concealed positions close in to the enemy
(for that matter, it is hardly required at short ranges) but
from the positions in the rear it is almost always possible.
One utilizes small shell holes filled with water, or a bare
spot of dirt in the trench system, or a bit of brick wall—anything which will give off a dust or splash when hit. The
observer can readily pick up the splash with his big telescope. It pays to keep sighted in at all times.

There are any number of small tricks to sniping which
may best be learned by experience—but often this sort of
experience is very costly in lives, so maybe I better mention
something about them right here. It is of utmost importance
for the sniping team to avoid observation and detection by
the enemy, and there are often small and seemingly insignificant things which may give a position away. The flashing
of the objective lens of the big telescope is a common fault,
and I believe more positions in the rear are given away
by this than by any other occurrence. With the light coming
from the front, that lens will flash for a long distance. Then
there is both muzzle blast and "smoke" from the burning
powder to be taken into consideration. "Smoke" do you
say? "From smokeless powder?" Well, maybe not exactly
smoke, but a fairly good substitute. There are often occasions when the discharge of a military rifle will leave a small
puff—about as big as a campaign hat—of thin, dark smoke

in front of the muzzle. Nothing at all like the old black powder fog, but still sufficiently visible to be picked up and identified—and the position given away. This phenomenon is not always visible, but can best be seen on sharp, cold mornings and often throughout the entire day during a spell of damp, muggy weather. It is only noticeable when the muzzle is close to the ground or against cover, and in certain makes of ammunition the fault may be more pronounced than in others.

The muzzle blast, or hot gases being violently expelled from the muzzle, must be taken into account in many situations. This can kick up quite a cloud of dust at times, especially from some loop-hole or nest where the muzzle does not project sufficiently—in these cases they say the thing to do is to keep the hole "wet down" with water, but personally I have never seen this done. Then, if the rifle is discharged with its muzzle hidden amongst thick grass or weeds, this gas will cause a great swirling and bending about of the vegetation and quickly give the position away. These faults I have just spoken of can be noticeable to the naked eye at ranges of a hundred yards or more and can be picked up with a glass at much greater distances, so it will be seen that they can be a serious matter even to the sniping pair in back of the lines. To the lone sniper, out in the open and close in to the enemy, they may easily become tragic.

Another point our sniper should always keep in mind, is to be a bit particular as to what targets he sights in on. Better stick to some available water hole or bit of dirt out in the general direction in which you expect your next target to appear. Avoid shooting through petrol cans, buckets, tins or boxes lying along the top of the enemy trench system —they may have been put there for just that purpose. Any shots fired into or near where you expect a target to appear can only result in greater wariness and hesitation being shown by the occupants of that place. Don't give your position away either by careless actions or promiscuous shooting. Targets will be scarce enough anyhow—make every opportunity count.

I almost forgot to mention that the sniping team should also keep an accurate "score book." Sure thing. This contains the sight settings and elevations of the various lots of ammunition you may have found sufficiently accurate, the ranges to all the various main designating points, official map designations and all that. You might even mark down the "bulls" as you make them—but this will often be a very uncertain matter and you will have to let your conscience be your guide many, many times.

Next to accuracy, the most essential quality possessed by our sniper is the ability to get his shot off quickly. By this statement, I do not mean the skill necessary to make a good "rapid fire" score such as we practice here in the United States, but have in mind the ability to "snap shoot" as practiced by the skilled deer stalker hunting in thick woods. These fussy and particular "old women" whom we have all seen competing in some of the matches at Camp Perry—who insist upon their six feet of clear space on the 1000 yard firing line, and the full minute-and-a-half allowed for each shot fired, are going to fare badly when it comes to sniping. You *must* be able to aim quickly and get your *one* shot off within a few seconds after the target is indicated. First: accuracy—then speed, is the rule for the sniper.

Naturally, with the enemy at long range, or during brief periods when the light is very poor (such as at daybreak or dusk) and your man does not consider himself visible, the target offered *might* be of some minutes duration. But the time of exposure of the average target is apt to be mighty brief, generally lasting but a few seconds—this is especially the case if any shooting has been recently done at that particular time or place. I would say that the rifleshot who cannot locate his target, get aligned on it, and let the shot off in less than ten seconds will prove a hopeless case. Ten seconds is much more time than will often be given, and our prospective sniper had better try to reach the point where he can aim and shoot within three seconds—which can readily be done where the range is not too long.

It might be said that the rifleman of our pair should be in constant readiness to think *and act* at an instant's notice, but the rule for the observer is to *go slow*. Accurate observation with a big telescope is a long, drawn-out proceeding. One will do best to mark off the enemy position into small sections of ground and go over each section slowly and carefully, a bit at a time; work out every foot of it inch by inch and make certain there is nothing there which can be shot at. Don't wait for the enemy to show himself, go ahead and look for him. And keep looking.

The work of the sniper is not entirely confined to shooting. If he is really qualified for the job, he will probably do as much good by reporting his observation of the things he sees going on in and behind the enemy lines, as by killing off a few men. As a matter of record, the snipers in the Canadian Army Corps were a part of the Intelligence Section—working directly under what were, at first, called "Scout Officers," but later "Intelligence Officers."

Any man who is daily, carefully and conscientiously, scanning a certain bit of terrain and who has carefully marked all the noticeable landmarks, is sure to notice any change. It may be that the enemy is constructing additional defenses, or that he is bringing up more troops. Perhaps the artillery are sneaking up a battery. I have lain, day after day, watching through the big telescope the construction of concrete emplacements, the digging of new trenches and the movements of bodies of men far behind the enemy front line. The worst of it was, that when we reported a lot of these things, they were not heeded or believed by our superiors.

That was one of the advantages which the "graduates" of the later sniping schools had over us forerunners; they had a recognized organization in back of them with considerable official standing and "weight" and when they turned in a report covering their observations for the day, that report was given real consideration by the powers who were running things from the rear.   Many a time I have turned in a report to my own Section or Battalion officers— one regarding which they fully recognized the accuracy and great value.   But when forwarded to the rear for consideration or action by higher command, the report was pooh-poohed as being merely "some soldier's imagination."   But those Lovat Scouts reported directly to their own Intelligence Officers, who knew just how much dependence could be placed on each man's observations, and to whom the other staff officers were obliged to give due consideration and attention.

We "volunteer" snipers tried for some weeks to get our artillery to wipe out some German guns which we had spotted during our observations throughout the daytime. One battery in particular, which we knew to be concealed in an orchard at a place called, on the maps, Hiele Farm, had been firing from that position (it was only 800 yards away) every night—strafing one of our roads by which our supply trains and the ambulances came up.   However, we finally got a chance to shoot them up a bit on our own account, as mentioned elsewhere in this story.

I sometimes took a shot at men around that Hiele Farm place while sniping, but we had no observations which would prove that we ever made any hits.   While it was only about 800 yards from our front line it was at least 1200 yards from our sniping and observation post.   My judgment, based upon experience, is that it is futile to attempt any sniping at such ranges.   Up to 1000 yards a man *may*, very rarely, make a hit, but the results in the end do not justify the expenditure of ammunition. Up to 600 or 700 yards I consider it comparatively easy—beyond that, hardly worth while unless you have ample opportunities to sight in and conditions are in your favor, then you *might* possibly make a hit up to 1000 yards. On many occasions I tried to hit men with the rifle fitted with a telescope at ranges all the way up to 1500 yards, but, although I had succeeded in previously sighting in at those ranges, I must confess that we were *never* certain of any hits at such distances. But inside the 500 to 600 yard limits it was "duck soup," and we also made a big percentage of hits at 700 yards or thereabouts.

Since the war I have met a great many expert shots in our own country, and in talking with these and other shooting authorities in the United States I find an opinion prevailing that the specialized sniping rifle need only be a single-shot action; that there will seldom be any need for rapid fire on the part of the sniper, and that it is unnecessary to have the magazine on such rifles in working order as it will never be used anyhow. My experience in actual sniping has been just the opposite from these contentions.

Frequently, even in trench warfare, the opportunity will arise for three or four rapidly fired shots to be poured into a target. In two or three instances throughout this book I have described how the opportunity was offered me to shoot up a working party, and at fairly close range too, who thought themselves well concealed from sight. At my first shot into the target, which may or may not have been a hit, the entire bunch simply boiled out of there and fell all over one another in the attempt to get away. When an opportunity such as this is presented, the sniper can always get in two or three more quick shots, provided the rifle he is using can be reloaded by manipulating the bolt and it is not necessary to grope around and load the other cartridges by hand.

To me, it is ridiculous to think of using the rifle only as a single shot, and one of the reasons why I liked the Warner and Swasey and similar off-side mounts was that with it you could always use the cartridges in the magazine as in rapid fire, and not have the ejecting shell jam the gun. With the scope mounted on top of the action this may be impossible and such rifles can be used for only one shot; by the time you have placed another cartridge in the barrel by hand your target will have disappeared.

Quite often the sniper will have an opportunity to put off two or three quick shots at a target. Occasionally you will catch a man out in the open and can shoot several times as he runs to the nearest cover. Or a shell may destroy the cover or protection of a gun crew, working party, or machine-gun nest, and start several men running for shelter. On occasions like this, a magazine full of cartridges is a great thing to have available and may be the means of piling up three or four dead enemies. Such opportunities will long be remembered.

The big help in being able to load from the magazine on such occasions, is not only the greater rapidity of fire, but is also the fact that you do not have to take your eyes off the target while reloading the rifle. That's a real advantage, I can tell you. You very likely are firing through a small loop-hole, or from some concealed location, and must remain in a decidedly circumscribed position to be able to see anything at all—once you move your face away from the gun stock, or change position in the least, your entire "shootable" field of fire may be gone. It takes a second or two to again pick up the target, and seconds are most precious at such times.

After you have lain in a sniping nest or been at a loop-hole most of the day—possibly several days—straining your eyes for something to shoot at, it is most satisfying to be able to do some real shooting if the occasion *does* offer. Too often it does not. Any sort of a target is generally hard to find, and once found, the cardinal rule is to keep your eye on it until it is shot down or else ducks out of sight.

Our telescope sights were mounted on the left hand side, in such a manner as not to interfere with either the operation of loading from the charger or the manipulation of the bolt and the ejecting of the fired cases. Furthermore, they did not interfere with the use of the iron sights, and this was another great advantage. I always tried to check up both sets of sights every day so as to have it possible to shoot with either the 'scope or iron sights at a second's notice. This was easy as we always had plenty of "sighting-in" targets in the bits of brick wall, or the numerous water-filled shell holes, at known ranges behind the enemy lines. The observer could almost always pick up the strike of the bullet, whether it hit the point aimed at or in the mud alongside.

It pays to have one set of sights on the rifle that you know are going to "stay put" and it also pays to have them ready for use at an instant's notice. I remember one morning, when my very first shot was made as soon as we got into position in Sniper's Barn, it was under very hard conditions of light and background, and was at a soldier who was standing up behind the German lines some six hundred yards from our position. There was no time whatever for sighting-in shots; I just cut loose and put him down cold. Another time I got a similar shot at an officer who was standing up right behind their parados with his back up against a tree and probably thinking himself invisible; my first shot for the day dropped him also. This chap was a Marine officer, we could see this clearly through the big telescope, and I got a lot of satisfaction out of that shot because for general cussedness those Marines had it all over anything else in the German organization, even Bavarians and Prussians, which is saying a lot.

I have never heard a good word for that Warner & Swasey telescopic sight, but I am going to put in one, right now. Having had considerable experience with all the various "breeds" that had been turned out up to that time, including the Winchester 5-A, I found that this same W. & S. was as dependable as any of them and a whole lot better than most. I had to tinker up the mounting a bit to keep it from jarring loose; on my particular rifle I rusted all the screws in and spiked them with a center punch, then by ramming a thin wedge or "shim" (made from a safety razor blade) in between the sight base and its holding lug, I finally got it on so tightly I could not get it off. This "anchored" it properly and the sight thereafter worked all right. We all know that the 'scope sights of that date were crude as compared with the later types, but I do not believe that any better one had been constructed then unless it was some that the Germans were using. They had some good ones, make no mistake about that. The Winchester 5-A was about the best one available in the United States then, and anyone who had much experience with them up to and including 1918 can testify that they could and did "act up" something scandalous at times.

If the light was right, I would use the 'scope sight; if not, the iron ones. The service sights on the Ross rifle were so good that, by using the large aperture, one could see plenty of the territory in the vicinity of the target—a very important point, as the "targets" in such cases were usually nothing more than small round caps—about the size of a small dinner plate and always of some indistinct, neutral color. The telescope sight is not always better than the iron ones, as everyone knows. Never as good in a fog, and sometimes even on bright days when there is a heavy mirage. The 'scope exaggerates everything, including the ground haze and the distortion of the target by the mirage. Those of you who have fired over the 1000 yard range at Camp Perry know how hazy and "wavy" that big bull's-eye can get in a bad "boil," yet that bull is some ten feet above the surface of the ground. Think how much worse it can be when your target is right on the ground and of a color which blends in with it. Everything is so distorted that it is impossible to define your target from its surroundings, and under such conditions your iron sights are much better than the telescope. But in the average light, and especially early on some mornings and late in the evenings the telescope is all to the good.

That is one thing I have been harping on, ever since the war: this matter of sights. Most of my criticism has been directed at the Springfield. I cannot, for the life of me, understand why, in a country that has developed some of the finest types of aperture sights for use on sporting rifles, we cannot have an equally good one on the military rifle. I wouldn't care if they put on nothing but a "battle sight"— built right into the top of the receiver bridge—so long as it had a big hole in it and was close to the eye. That, with a reasonably broad front sight would be perfectly satisfactory for battle use. For accurate shooting at ranges beyond about three hundred yards, of course the sight should be adjustable for both elevation and windage but, aside from the sniper, the soldier seldom sees an enemy at anything beyond what might be termed "hunting" range and our deer hunters well know what that is.

The Germans always had much better constructed trenches than we had. The Canadian soldier hated anything like ordinary manual labor and would put up with a lot of discomfort rather than put in a few hours with a shovel. Consequently, we had but few decent sniping positions in the front line while the enemy had many very ingeniously constructed loop-holes through which to fire. They nearly always made use of some one of the numerous and miscellaneous articles which always decorated the front of his parapet—put there, I always believed, for just that purpose. There would be old boots, tin cans of all shapes and sizes, pieces of cast-off clothing, old knapsacks and bits of board—anything and everything that would serve to break up the flat expanse of the embankment and the sniping holes were usually concealed in one or the other of these objects which, while appearing from our side to have been just thrown there, was really securely anchored to the front of a well-constructed loop-hole. On my trips to his parapet, at night, I have been able to locate several such places and have also detected them with the telescope, from our observation posts and sniping positions. One such loop-hole, I remember was in the sole of an old boot and at least two were through large tin cans.

Such positions however, where the lines are so close together, offer but a limited field of fire—limited, in fact, to the space between the trenches and, of course, the top of our parapet. Of course, it made our men keep their heads down below the top or—well, a few of them tried to find out—and did. It was one sure way of committing suicide.

We fixed up a couple of such places and used them now and then but not often. It was fun to take a shot at the loop-hole of a machine-gun emplacement or observation post just to hear the bullet hit the steel plate—to ring the bell— but there was but little profit in it and I preferred to shoot from the positions in the rear, from which we could actually see our targets and, sometimes, see 'em fall.

Now, for a change let's talk about another most important phase of the sniper's work—counter sniping, or abating the enemy snipers. A most essential part of this operation is to first locate that enemy sniper before you abate him, and there are times when this is a considerable job just in itself. In the first place, the sniper may have been at work for several days, and have downed quite a few of your men before the troops in that section realize they are up against a good sniper. Mebbyso I better explain about this, so you catchem-savvey.

It is an odd fact, and one hardly understandable to the average civilian, but after the first few days, soldiers in the trenches pay very little attention to bullets flying around. Bullets are mostly always flying around anyhow—stray shots coming in from God knows where, long range fire from machine guns, fixed rifles set off now and then, floaters and odd shots let off by dubs all along the enemy trenches and loop-holes. All these come in under the general term of "strays" and you are continually losing a man here and there from them. Also, during the daytime, when there is nothing being pulled off as a rule, the men remain in the dugouts and sleep, leaving sentries at intervals along the trench with what few men who must be up and about on one detail or another. The result is that when an odd man does get hit, no one is about or looking to see him go down, and it may be a long time before somebody comes down that particular section of trench and finds him lying there. When found, the verdict is pretty apt to be "hit with a stray bullet." Then, when another man or so is shot down at that same spot, the outfit wakes up to the fact that a sniper is covering that place and they commence to get to work on him.

The busiest hour of the sniper is at daybreak. At this time the trenches are crowded; morning stand-to is just over with and all the various machine-gun and trench-mortar crews and specialists of one sort or another are busy taking in their guns, ration details are coming up with breakfast, men going to the latrines, observation and staff officers going back to make their reports, and so forth. And I must confess that as a rule the Germans had the edge on us at this time, owing to the light being entirely in their favor at daybreak. On clear mornings we could do very little until the sun had lifted its glare out of our eyes; it was just like drawing one of the early relays at Sea Girt. But at evening, the shoe was on the other foot; we had the light in our favor, and very much so, as a rule. On dull or rainy days conditions were about even.

Having determined for a fact that a sniper is located out in front and working on some particular part of our trench, it now remains to find out just where his sniping post is located. You do this by exceeding close observation, plus a bit of "baiting" him into shooting a few more times. After getting a general idea as to where the bullets are coming from you offer him a target to shoot at, and, by watching for the striking angle of his bullets, trace them back to their source. By showing a target at various places along the trench top it may be possible to utilize two such points as the base of a triangle and locate him at its apex. This is the approved "book" method, but I must confess that we seldom used it, we generally stuck to one place and kept a close observation back along the bullet's path until we had located our man.

As a matter of actual fact, when it comes to close range sniping, the sniper is pretty apt to be very much restricted as to the "arc of fire" over which he can deliver his shots. Invariably his sniping nest will be arranged so that its loophole covers only a very limited area, and it is down this area only that he can fire. They generally build a very small hole, crawl inside, and then pull the hole in after them. Once in position they "stay put" and cannot move about enough to take shots offered off to their flank or from some other position, but can cover only a certain limited section to their front. Hence, the well known story-book method of triangulation does not always work out so well in actual practice. Instead, you generally locate your man by hours, and often days, of close observation from one spot.

At the longer ranges it is all different, and in these cases the situation is similar to that in our own main post at Sniper's Barn. Here you arrange a large and comfortable place from which fire can be delivered over a considerable section of enemy front, with room for two or more men to work in and everything quite convenient. These places are either built into the front trench system, or better still are arranged a couple of hundred yards behind the trench and on higher ground. When you locate such a nest, don't bother trying to determine its loop-holes or shoot into them, just call the F. O. O. and have him flatten it out for you with his guns.

The experienced rifleman has a number of factors to aid him in this work of locating the other fellow. The first is undoubtedly the sound of the sniper's rifle; on a quiet day when there is not much doing, two or three hours may pass without a rifle's being fired; then an occasional shot is pretty easy to trace. The strike of the bullet along the parapet or such other place as it may hit, tells a great deal. Even the sound of the bullet as it snaps past overhead may tell you whether the man is shooting from close range or is back in rear of the enemy trenches.

If observation determines that our friend is shooting from some loop-hole in the opposite trench, there is not much that can be done but to call on the artillery to "level off" that particular spot. Those loop-holes are petty apt to be fixed up with steel plates in such a manner that a bullet cannot enter, so it is no use trying shooting at them unless you just want to "ring the bell." But a great deal of enemy sniping will be carried out from positions in front of their trench line, or from locations hidden out in the open, and against these one rifle is as good as another.

I remember an incident which occurred early one cool, foggy morning; there was no dense fog up in the air, but a blanket of light "mist" lay against the ground and was drifting and streaking slowly about. We had been bothered a lot by a sniper who was working in front of that particular bit of trench, and I had gotten down there early that morning to try and locate him. A careful search of the opposite trench lines and likely places with the big telescope did not disclose anything to me, and I had turned it over to my partner for a look-see and had just taken my binoculars to look again at the same time. I was sweeping the ground in front of the German trenches when that sniper fired another shot—it happened that I had those binocks on his position at the time and I clearly saw the fog blow and swirl about in front of his rifle muzzle. Five minutes later we took the nest apart with bursts from two machine guns, and heard no more from that Heinie.

On one other occasion I was sweeping the open ground between the trenches with that same pair of binoculars. There had been a particularly bad sniper operating from the vicinity, and we had it figured out that he was located somewheres up in the German trench system. There were the remains of an old stone retaining wall just in front of their trenches, and it had been blown over and leveled off somewhat into the surrounding ground. After several hours observation and search of the trench works and upper parts of this stone pile, I happened to be looking at the foot of the stone rubbish when the sniper cut loose at something and I easily saw the swirl of sand and dirt blown up by the muzzle blast of his rifle. It picked up a handful of that dirt and whirled it about like some miniature cyclone. A few more seconds observation with the big glass and we had that chap definitely located and one shot from a rifle at a range of about one hundred and fifty yards finished him for good. Strange to say, after he had dropped down into his nest, we could all clearly see the large, dark hole from which he had been firing; he must have had some nifty arrangement of closing it up or hiding it when he was not in position to shoot. Or possibly he was one of those "turnip top" robed snipers who dressed up to resemble their surroundings—if so he was certainly good at it.

Very often, this trick of locating an enemy sniper turns

out to be quite a hard job, and cannot be done from where one "baits" the chap into firing at a dummy target. Occasionally, you must string up a field telephone from the front trench to the rear and have an observer or two get well in back of the line or off at an angle where higher ground gives better observation, not only of the point where you assume the shots to be coming from, but where you may also get an idea of the bullet's line of flight when it hits —or misses. (This is one match where a miss is worth as much to *you* as a bull, possibly more.) Many times it is an impossibility for the men in the trench, or hidden in from where the target is being offered and manipulated, to see anything at all; they must keep their heads down continually or be shot. Hence it may take an entire squad of men, and much time before one even learns where the shots are coming from.

Along towards the latter part of my experience in France we received some very elaborate and life-like hollow manikins, made of papier-maché or some such material, to be used for sticking up over the parapet in decoying enemy snipers to give away their location. At the time all this struck me as being very funny, just some more junk issued to make the poor soldier's life miserable, and to be lugged in and out of the trenches. The trouble with all that sort of stuff is that when the time and occasion arises to use the trick, the manikin is somewhere else—miles to the rear probably. It all works out very nicely at the sniping school or training camp—adds interest and looks very practical—but just don't always pan out anywhere else.

At this time I might mention that now and then you'll run into a pretty smart sniper whom you cannot fool with these decoys, helmet-on-a-stick, or such tricks. Some are like preachers I have known—they will only bite on live bait. The Germans had such men, and in particular I remember one Dutchman who worked his way up within a hundred yards or so of our front line and fired from there for several days. This chap was so close that he could tell a real target from a decoy and was located so that observation was impossible without a periscope. He could readily tell periscopes, or any thing else for that matter, and even when we stuck up a large and elaborate trench periscope he never shot at it, but passed up the chance for a real one. That Heinie showed sense, he was not going to give away his position for a lot of fool rifle practice. I don't remember that we ever did locate that chap at all, not while I was around anyhow. Possibly one of those lifesize "dummies" would have worked on him; I don't know.

Chapter 17

The Rifleman in Battle

SO FAR, we have dealt almost exclusively with the business of sniping from a fixed position in siege or trench warfare. There is another phase of the sniper's work which differs in a vast degree from this sort of sniping, and that is during a battle when his force is in the open and advancing or retreating.

Then he has no opportunity or time to construct anything in the way of hiding places, but must make use of whatever natural cover he can find. In a withering, sweeping barrage, where it is imperative that the line continue the advance, he takes his chances with all the rest. He may be and often is, cut down before he has had a chance to fire a shot. During this first stage of the attack he is "just another soldier."

But, if he survives long enough to come into contact with the enemy, when the resistance stiffens and our line begins to break up under the fire of hidden machine guns, then he may have a chance to show just how good he really is. His job, and it is a big one, is to work his way into such positions that he can see and fire on individual enemies —not to cower in the most convenient shell hole. If it is a machine gun that is doing the dirty work, it is up to him to endeavor to work around into a position from which he can cut the gunners down with enfilading fire. Difficult— nay, impossible as this may seem, it has been done so often

330

that it became almost commonplace. You have all heard of
Sergeants Woodfill and York. Now I'll tell you of another one—Captain MacCrimmon of the 21st Battalion.
He was a sergeant when I was one and rose to the command of B Company. At the Battle of Arras, having
gained his objective, he found his position enfiladed by a
battery of three field guns, so, taking a rifle and calling
for a sergeant to go with him (I am sorry I do not recall
that sergeant's name) he proceeded to *abate* those guns.
The two of them then rushed the position, shot some more
of the gunners and then stood, back to back, holding off
the rest of the enemy until his men came up. Then, he
calmly took a piece of chalk from his pocket and marked
the guns "Captured by B Company." He had done many
such stunts before, both as an officer and as an enlisted man.

No, impossible though it may seem, it *is* possible for a
cool, resourceful man to circumvent and actually destroy a
large number of the enemy.

But, leaving aside these brilliant exploits, the *rifleman* in
battle has his own work cut out for him. It is not easy;
not by a long shot. Nothing is easy when a man is stumbling and crawling and creeping through an inferno of flying,
howling and shrieking missiles: through dust or mud, straining every muscle to move at all—probably wearing a gas
mask which *will* fog up and *sweat,* in spite of all the dope
that can be put on it. No, no, it is not easy.

I have read Major Hesketh-Prichard's book "Sniping in
France" and find it exceedingly interesting. He describes
at length the methods used in training snipers in the "Imperial" schools. I also had the opportunity, during the
summer of 1918 while on duty at Camp Perry, of observing the sniping school there, which was conducted by Major
Godard—who had received *his* training at one of the above
mentioned schools.

It was all intensely interesting and exceedingly clever;

the way they worked up artificial cover—camouflage and all that—but I could not then, and cannot now agree that their system was sound. For use in permanent locations—perhaps yes, but for troops that are continually shifting—no. It requires too much paraphernalia. In my opinion, the true sniper must "travel light" in order to be able to take advantage of all *natural* cover in whatever situation he may find himself. That, I think, defines the point I am trying to bring out—that to train men to the belief that they will always have a "sniper's robe," long grass and turnip tops, or other similar material with which to construct concealed positions—is to lessen their ability to take cover where none of these commodities are available. Furthermore, when out in the open, as in an advance, you do not have all day in which to get a position fixed up, or to get in position, or even to take a shot. Conditions change very rapidly and the sniper must have been trained to act and shoot at once— or pass up that opportunity.

By taking advantage of "natural" cover, I do not mean to be able to get into some old building and make a nice little nest from which to shoot, although I have spoken a great deal of having done that myself on many occasions. When such locations are available, it is fine business—until the enemy gets suspicious and starts to shell the place—but such locations are generally rare and the sniper must be in position to "carry on" even from the middle of a vacant field. Even when we had our nest in Sniper's Barn, we also had many other places outside—behind a bit of hedge or even just a few sprigs of shrub—once with no concealment other than several unusually long tufts of grass. An enemy will always devote most of his time to scrutinizing what he considers the *likely* places for a man to be hiding. It may be a stump, stone, bit of log—anything that would offer concealment. Seldom will he waste time watching what, to him, appears to be an open expanse of ground.

All my sniping was done from that one sector—I mean the regular *sniping,* and not battle firing—and we were prone to make use of that position in the Barn because it was so comfortable, even though we knew that Heinie would shell it every day. That we were not killed there was no fault of ours. Just luck.

In any sort of an advance, the type of country and surroundings may undergo a decided change. One moves from the flattened-out country of shell holes and blown down buildings over into comparatively open ground, with growing vegetation and standing buildings—plenty of cover of an entirely different color and type. What fitted in closely some ten miles back will draw fire if tried in the new surroundings. Have something ready which *will* fit in, do you say? Hey, who is carrying all this stuff anyhow? Not the Quartermaster Corps, hell no, they are some fifteen miles to the rear just now. No indeed, you and I must lug it along—which means that we left it back at the jumping-off place and are now carrying nothing but our rifles, ammunition and possibly a pair of binoculars.

Under conditions such as these it will be seldom possible for the rifleman to assume the orthodox firing positions he has learned back home on the rifle range. He must be able to adapt himself to all sorts of restricted positions and still deliver accurate rifle fire. A shell hole or small hollow in the ground will be the usual place from which one fires, and as little as possible of one's anatomy should be exposed to the bullets which will be flying about. Under such conditions, the rifleman invariably rests his rifle over the edge of the shell hole to fire, and one soon learns to take advantage of every possible assistance of this nature. I have often felt that we do not give enough instruction in range firing from positions in which the rifle may similarly be rested. Sometimes it is necessary to kneel or squat, or even stand up, in order to see the target at all. In an advance one often has to assume these less secure positions in order to see or fire over top of shelter or cover in the immediate foreground. In thinking it over, I cannot recall that I ever fired any shots from the sitting position—and a good one it is too.

In firing from the trenches, our usual method was to stand on the firing step and rest the elbows on top of the parapet, which gave one a very steady position. But the top of the parapet is the aiming point for which everyone in the enemy line generally fires—machine guns, whiz-bangs, riflemen, and such, and one may not last very long in such an exposed situation. So we soon learned to pick out some place where the parapet had been broken down, or we pulled a sandbag or two out of place and piled them up so as to afford some sort of protection from fire coming from the front. Then we would fire out to one of the flanks.

As to using the sling—well, I doubt if it could be done at all during an advance, or during offensive fighting on a battle-field. It ties down a man too much and hinders his movements and observation, also to be of real assistance it has to be adjusted so closely as to be of use in but one certain position, and you change position very often in a battle. But the sling is of great help to those in defensive positions, or to those who may get fixed in a good location and stay there. I have seen many old timers in my crowd who had much training on the rifle range, fix their slings for firing and leave them in that position. For the benefit of those who are not familiar with the sling on the Ross rifle, I might add that it was designed mainly for carrying the rifle and to be of any use for firing had to be removed from the butt swivel, have new holes punched, and then laced so as to form a loop from the upper swivel only. This made the sling useless for carrying the rifle, but our crowd always fixed and kept it in the shooting position.

The sling is a most valuable aid in accurate aiming and troops should always be instructed in its use.

One fact was very apparent to me as the war went along, and it became more and more noticeable as the Somme fight progressed and our replacements became very numerous. Our older men—that is, those members of the original Battalion who had received long and thorough instruction in rifle firing over the ranges of Canada and England, remembered and profited by their range training. These old-timers would always endeavor to take up a good position before firing, and then they really *looked about for a target to shoot at.* But the replacements, who had had little or no range training, would drop into the nearest hole, poke the rifle muzzle over the edge, and let 'er go. These chaps were always the first to run out of ammunition too. This alone, is sufficient justification for our range instruction and rifle competitions, in my humble opinion.

During the offensive stages of an action the rifleman (sniper) does his best work alone. One man can slip through a lot of holes where a squad would be instantly detected, and it is the *squads,* the groups, that interest the enemy machine gunners. They want a target worthy of the expenditure of a hundred or more bullets, not a single man. And it is while they have their attention concentrated upon some likely target—that is, a group—that the "lone hunter" has his chance to steal a march on them. Of course the enemy has his "hunters" out too, and we must beware of them. In the German army I believe these particular riflemen were called "Jaegers."

The neatest and handiest military rifle I have ever seen was one I took from one of these German Jaegers, and when I held it up beside my Ross for comparison, the cocky little rascal actually laughed in my face, and he had a bullet through his arm at that. It did look ridiculous, I admit—that is, the Ross did; a great big, long, heavy *club,* beside the trim little "sporter" which he had been using. His rifle had been made for something other than a handle for a bayonet. I wanted to keep that beauty, but lost it, as we nearly always lost our trophies—because we could not carry them around with us and had to entrust them to some non-combatant back at the base. They probably got back to Canada all right, but the fellow who did the actual taking seldom had the pleasure of ever seeing them again.

For effective use as a *rifle* in battle, the arm must be just as compact and "handy" as it is possible to make it and still retain accuracy and the punch. It is probably not possible to build a high power, bolt-action rifle that would be as handy as the little .30/30 carbine or "saddle gun," but that is my idea of what a handy rifle should be. No, with the bolt action and box magazine, it would be impossible to get the "balance" just the same and that has a lot to do with the "handiness" of any rifle. Perhaps the Spring-field Sporter could be worked down somewhat. It is not bad, just as it is, yet even it would have appeared "clumsy" beside that little Mauser I took that day.

Whether or not the sniper can get away with the job of handling a rifle equipped with a telescope sight *in battle* is a question for the future. I have never heard that it had been successfully accomplished. The fact is that the rifleman has to squirm and crawl through every little hole he can find; often through deep mud and water, over rocks and through brush. It is a sure thing that he will have "one hell of a job" to keep that 'scope from being broken or so badly disarranged as to make it useless. Of course, there have been and will be battles fought over ground where the conditions would make it comparatively easy to "baby along" a telescope, but we cannot depend on that— it will be the exception and not the rule. The scope would certainly be a great help in picking out the obscure targets— if it could be taken along.

Since the war I have read a great deal about the new types of telescope sights and their improved mountings. Many of our leading sportsmen and big-game hunters are claiming they are just as substantial and dependable as the iron sights. I cannot by any means subscribe to this contention, because my personal experience, gained in the trenches and in battle, is all to the contrary.

The telescopic sight needs a lot of attention, care and babying, to keep it in proper condition and to make it "stay put." I have told about having done so much sniping from our main position in Sniper's Barn, and how often we fired from there when the chances were very good for the German artillery tumbling it down around our ears. One of the main reasons why I liked so well to shoot from Sniper's Barn was that while in there you could take care of and handle the telescope *right*. For one thing, when through firing I would leave the rifle (and the big observation telescope) right there, hidden away under some old bales of tobacco, and there was no danger of its being dropped and the sight jarred out of alignment. I had several wide strips of old woolen blanket and used these to wrap around the entire telescope and action when I put the rifle away. In there I could keep the lens dry and clean. You cannot work a telescope in the rain with any degree of satisfaction, and even a light fog or mist will cloud up the lens continually. The rifle cannot be carried through wet or dew-covered underbrush without throwing water all over the lens. Even the taking of the rifle from a comparatively "warm" dugout out into the open air of a cool or damp day may fog up the lens so badly you cannot see through them. Often on a misty morning one is constantly wiping off the lens in order to see at all. And finally there is the dirt and the mud to be considered, and the wiping of a few specks of mud or grit from the lens of a telescope is a job to be gone about with much caution—

and a clean soft rag, else you will soon ruin the glass from scratches.

NO. I kept my telescopic-sighted rifle in out of the mud and rain, where I would not be obliged to lay it down over night on the bare ground and then find the lens so fogged up with condensation of moisture as to be useless—and inside, where I could not get at it, too. Any sort of telescope—and binoculars also—may do this on very short order.

No, it just don't always work out according to the book. I have looked into this matter of telescopic sights in warfare as much as I could—went clear back to their use by Berdan's Sharpshooters in our own Civil War—and I find that everyone's experience had been pretty much the same as mine. If you are settled down right, sighted in, and get that telescope going good—*you're good* and you can go along like a house afire *for the time being.* But if anything throws you off—and some mighty little things *can* throw a telescope sight off—you are strictly S. O. L. until you can take the time off to again sight in.

Here again, let me repeat—that is why I liked to have the iron sights in position on my rifle, and fixed so either they or the telescope could be used. Then, when conditions prevented the use of the 'scope, or it got "out of whack," I went right along *from where I was at the time,* and used those iron sights. Have issued a second rifle for iron sights only, do you say? Listen here, you, I left that rifle back in the dugout this morning, and we're out here in this shell hole for the whole damn day and can't get back until after dark. Besides, come to think of it now, I "lost" that second rifle, what the hell do they think I am going to do anyhow, clean rifles for the whole damn Battalion?

It never happened to be my personal experience to advance across a battlefield and act the part of a modern rifleman while armed with that Ross rifle and Warner & Swasey

telescope. Hence I cannot give any actual experiences as
to just how the telescope sight *would* work under such
conditions. I do not think it would stand up under the
necessary rough handling but would soon get out of alignment for real accurate shooting, the only sort of shooting
that is worth anything, by the way. But, supplemented by
the regular iron sights, it would be all right and even if
the telescope did get out of alignment or have its cross
hairs jarred loose, it would still be splendid to have along
for purposes of observation. One could easily look through
the misaligned telescope for a target and then hit that target
with the iron sights once it was located. Targets are
mighty hard to locate on the battlefield, too. Also, under
such conditions as these, the rifle must be fitted up so the
magazine is available for use at all times; no modern rifle-
shot, no matter how good, is going to advance very far
with a single shot rifle in his hands.

My own ideas as to the proper telescope for such battle
firing would be one with an absolutely *rigid* mount that
would stand up under any and all conditions of jar and
abuse. For that matter, the rigid mount is the only type
to consider for sniping work of any description—one could
not begin to use these conventional target mounts where
the scope slides forward from recoil and must be pulled
back by hand after each shot. The whole works want to
be *solid and rigid,* with no outside springs, shock absorbers,
or similar gadgets in sight. If these must be used, put them
inside of the 'scope where they will be out of the way—
and out of the dirt and dust also. There must be some
arrangement for changing both elevation and windage,
moved by means of sufficiently large devices to take hold
of, showing settings in both plain figures and "clicks."
I want no range-finding contrivances, etched lines, battle
slogans or anything of that sort on the lens either—what
is mostly needed is the largest possible entirely clear and

distinct field of vision with a definite aiming device in it— and nothing else.

As to magnification, or power. For the general purpose telescope, to be used in all sorts of weather and conditions —and by advancing troops—I believe the three power to be about as high as one can go, possibly the two-and-one-half power is enough, at that. Large field and clear vision is more important than magnification in most instances. But when it comes to real honest-to-God sniping, from a prepared position and with an observer to help, where the ranges may run up to seven and even eight hundred yards, one can use considerably more magnification, and even an eight power telescope is none too high.

A lot has been written about the various types of "reticules" for telescope sights. Well, let 'em fight it out. No matter what kind you have, whether cross-hairs, posts or what-not, the man who tries to pick out a little, obscure target which has been so plastered with mud and dust as to look just like any other part of the scenery, will soon find that the darn thing gets in the way and covers up some part of the view that he wishes to see. Locating the head of a woodchuck at one or two hundred yards is a cinch compared to the job of finding a little round, mud-encrusted cap at two or three hundred. Part of this trouble is due to the fact that after a field has been blasted with shells for an hour or two, nothing looks natural. Everything is knocked cock-eyed and there remains just a mad, futuristic picture that looks like nothing at all.

The battlefield soon takes on a weird and grotesque appearance, and the ordinary objects such as trees, bushes, stone walls, buildings and such become so disrupted and twisted out of shape that they look like such things as one sees in a mad dream. Men crawling through such a background and scene of chaos become as parts of the whole "crazy quilt" pattern itself, and to pick out an individual at any but short range is well near impossible. But the rifleman has it to do. He can, with no great trouble, locate certain individuals with his binoculars or observing telescope, but when he attempts to find the same fellow through his rifle sights, his troubles have just begun. He may have his man spotted—right beside, or above, or below a certain stump, fence-post or bush, but when he tries to pick up that particular point, even if using a 'scope sight, the cross-hairs, post or particular reticule he is using may be such that it obliterates enough of the surrounding scenery to make it difficult or impossible to be certain he is even aiming at the man he wants to hit.

Under such conditions, almost any sort of sighting reticule has its disadvantages, and I don't know but that the ordinary cross-hairs are not as good as any. For one thing, the horizontal wire is of great help in keeping the rifle from canting, and when you are shooting from a restricted position or loop-hole it is very easy to get the rifle out of plumb. Then again, there just ain't anything on the battlefield that will blend in with, or look like, those precisely drawn crosswires which are unvaryingly at right angles—they *always* stand out from the landscape. The post reticule is preferred by many, owing to its greater visibility and strength, but there are times when that post will blend in with the target or surroundings, and the average post reticule blocks out too much of the target, especially if you are obliged to "hold high" for a long shot. Move the sight up do you say? Hell man, no time for that now.

I speak of these various points for the benefit of those who may use a telescope such as the Winchester, where the reticules may be changed at will. On many telescopes there is no choice, as the reticule is etched on the lens, this has some advantages of its own, at that—no danger of your cross-wires breaking. At any rate, I was issued a telescope fitted with cross-hairs, and although they were much thinner

than many other types of reticule, there were many times
when they blocked out the target at which I wanted to shoot.
So, after many trials and much tribulation (I don't know
what that word means, but it sounds all right) I resorted
to the expedient of establishing my "aiming point" right in
the upper, right-hand corner of the cross-hairs, the inside
angle. Not the center cross at all. And it worked—which
was the only thing we cared about in those days. Theories
and theoretical reasoning are all right when you have plenty
of time to kill and nobody is shooting at you, but when you
get up against the active game of warfare, it is the common,
everyday, practical things that count.

The very best thing I ever struck along this line was a
German telescopic sight which we took from a prisoner—
a machine gunner—which had nothing but an amber-colored
pyramid in the lower sector. Apparently, the aiming point
was the apex of the pyramid, which was located in the
exact center of the field. You could hold over, or anywhere
on the target and nothing would be blocked out. It looked
mighty good to me, but I never had a chance to try it.
Things were popping too fast around that sector in those
days to take time out for any experimenting, so I turned
it in to "ordnance" and had their promise that it would be
fitted with a mounting for use on one of our guns, but it
never materialized and I soon forgot all about it.

All the dope I have written so far has been based upon
my own personal experiences during the years 1915-1918,
using such telescopic sights as were available at that time.
Since then, many qualified riflemen have asked me if I did
not consider the newer and better designed rifle telescopes
to have overcome all of the troubles and faults of the earlier
sights such as we used. It is a bit difficult for me to discuss the merits of these telescopic sights of today, because,
as Will Rogers would say "All I know is what I read in
the papers."

Well, that is not exactly accurate. I have used some of them since the war, but the last time was about 1930 and a lot of improvements have been made since then and all I know about those improved 'scopes is what I have read in the various sporting magazines. However, knowing most of the men who have written up these newer 'scopes I feel safe in taking their word for it that the telescopic rifle sight has finally and definitely *arrived* and is suitable for all-around use—even on running game and in thick woods.

That this was far from the case in 1915—or even in 1918 —is well known to all and sundry who had anything to do with the 'scopes of that period. The ones we then had were as temperamental as a movie actress and had to be babied to about the same extent. We had the Winchester 5-A available, and it was I think, about the best at that time, but just the same they caused us plenty of worry during the time we used them at the Small Arms Firing School at Camp Perry. That was the only type we had there, but prior to that time I had experimented with several others that had been brought out by our Ordnance Department, and during my term of sniping in Flanders I had used the Warner & Swasey prismatic sight of which I have spoken so frequently throughout this story—and found it at least as good as any other I had seen up to that time.

Now I have always contended that, in addition to the 'scope sight, a man should have iron sights on his rifle and ready for use at any time, and I am not going to back out from that statement now, even though the telescope sights are every bit as good as they are cracked up to be. I don't care how good and dependable they are; they are and always will be rather delicate instruments to be hauled and dragged about a battlefield and it is a certainty that they will, at times, become disabled through rough usage.

When this happens, the rifleman will need something to fall back on and if his rear sight has been removed to

make a place for the 'scope mounting, he is going to be
S. O. L., that's all.   For this reason alone, I favor a sight
that is offset so as to permit the use of either the 'scope or
those iron sights at any time.   Theoretically, according to
our experts, there is less chance for error if the 'scope is
mounted directly over the bore of the rifle.   Now, will some
of those experts explain to me how it makes any difference
whether the sight is two-and-a-half inches above, or to one
side, or even under the bore?   Do they know of any man
who can hold within that limit at any range from two hundred yards up?   I don't.

In actual sniping—in war—the greatest difficulty is to
locate your target through the sights.   That is why I have
been harping all throughout this book on the necessity of
having a "great big" aperture in the rear sight, if using
the iron sights, or a wide field of view with the 'scope.
The observer (or your own observation) describes the
"target" with reference to some conspicuous nearby object,
and unless the firer can see this object and a considerable
amount of the surrounding territory, he will probably be
unable to locate the said target at all when he looks through
the sights.   Enemy men do not expose themselves any more
than is absolutely necessary when within easy sniping range.
Not after a few of them have been bumped off, anyway.
Whenever, as was the case with us when we first commenced our sniping campaign, they have not been shot at,
they will probably be very careless, but it doesn't take them
very long to learn to keep well under cover.   When we
first started sniping and for several weeks afterwards, we
had many good, open shots every day, but before I quit,
about two months later, we had many days when we never
saw hide nor hair of a German.   When we *did* get a chance
it was usually just at a bit of one of the little round caps
which blended into the surrounding scenery so closely as
to be well-nigh invisible.   Often I have fired simply by

noting, through the big spotting 'scope or my binoculars, certain conspicuous objects near the actual target and "holding off" with reference to them—not actually seeing the "bull's-eye" at all through the sights—and sometimes was successful in hitting the right spot.

After all is said and done—that is another fine sounding phrase, or maybe it's a song, I don't remember which— there remains just one great big handicap to this business of turning out individual riflemen qualified to use all these new and intricate rifle telescopes and mountings, to estimate ranges, to build invisible sniping posts, to clean out enemy machine-gun nests and to otherwise allay, abate and "bump off" the enemy—there is still one great difficulty that is mighty hard to get around and I have long wondered what can be done about it.

The man who has been trained to do all these things turns out to be an invaluable sort of a chap to have around in the company; far, far better than the hundreds of others whom we have hurriedly thrown together in an attempt to form what will be our next wartime American Army. He stands out amongst the rest, being one of the few who knows what to do himself and also knows how to teach that to the others. That's the rub of it right there. Result? These trained riflemen will seldom be permitted to keep on using that rifle, but will be promoted or commissioned and put in charge of more important work or details. For it is an acknowledged fact that the individual who has the brains and ability to learn to do what is required of the modern, individual rifleman is promptly going to be put where that ability is of supposedly more value—in some post of command.

What can be done about it? Well, the only thing I can see to do is to train and develop so damn many of these chaps that there just ain't commissions enough to go around for all of them. Then we may be able to keep a few of them in the ranks—and using that rifle. Not that it is going to work any harm though, to have all that shooting ability and knowledge in the higher ranks—far from it.

Say—here is a thought. In these days of modern warfare we generally find opposing armies about evenly matched in numbers—at least amongst those units which come in actual contact in the field. Have you ever figured out what would happen if in our next war we can put an American Army in the field with its rifle users all sufficiently trained so they can each hit and kill one enemy soldier. Just ONE apiece now. THINK THAT OVER.

Chapter 18

The Emma Gees

(Machine Guns)

UP TO the time of the outbreak of the World War the machine gun had received scant consideration—strange though it may seem in view of the fact that weapons of this character had been in use for some forty or fifty years. I do not know just when the first *mitrailleuse* was tried out, but I do know that Doctor Gatling had perfected *his* gun by the time I was old enough to notice such things, sometime in the early '80's, and that it had been used very effectively during the Spanish-American and the South-African wars.

For some reason or other, whoever wrote the first text-book on the subject injected the statement that: "Machine Guns are Weapons of Opportunity." Just what he meant by that, I do not pretend to know, but the phrase seemed to suit other subsequent authors of such text-books; and the readers thereof, taking their cue from the book, probably figured that these guns were just some kind of a side-issue, anyway, hardly to be taken into serious consideration when it came to a real fight between soldiers—on horse or on foot.

But not so with our Cousin Heinie. He "catchem plenty savvy" on this M. G. business and when Germany went into this last big war she had an adequate number of better machine guns than any of the allied forces were able to devise and build during the whole four years of the conflict. Now, this may raise a howl from someone or other, but there are facts to back up that statement. We did not have, at any stage of the game, as many nor as good machine guns as had the Germans. By *good guns,* I wish it to be understood that I include the mountings as well as the shooting part of the guns. Those thoroughgoing Germans had figured out—sometime before 1914—a lot of things that we never did catch up with. Of course we beat them; but it was not because we had better equipment—not by a long ways and then a long way more.

I don't know such a lot about *all* the various types of machine guns used during the war but I *do* know plenty about some of them. We (my outfit) went in with Colt guns—with the long-legged tripods and everything. Well, of course, the first thing we did was to saw off the legs of the tripods and bring them down to something like a decent level. Then, one of our mechanical geniuses devised a gadget by which the operator of the gun could flip the lever without reaching all the way around in front. Later on we had the Vickers-Maxim, with a much better mount, but never have I seen any machine gun that is as safe for shooting over the heads of advancing infantry as the Colt. In other words, it has less dispersion, vertically, than any gun I have seen—and that goes right down to this day of grace in 1932. That old Colt sure would hold elevations. I have often shot and seen fired by others bursts of as many as ten shots, at the thousand-yard target, where not a single bullet struck outside the limits of the bull's-eye.

And, by the way, lest I forget it, there is another good argument for the Colt gun, and that is that it is air cooled. Say what you want to, the business of getting water where there ain't any and keeping that old condenser and its hose and everything right with you and ready to hook up, when you are crawling through all the litter of a battlefield, is not so easy. And how that water does boil away! In spite

of the most careful use of the condenser, it evaporates at
a rapid rate and then the problem is how to replenish it.
Even though the action may be literally on the bank of a
river it may be an impossible task to go the few feet and
back; and, often, on the soggy, rain-drenched fields of
Flanders, where everything was simply *soaked,* not enough
real water could be procured to fill the jacket. More than
a few times the members of the gun crew have been called
upon to "make water," and there is a sort of grim humor
in the fact that on such occasions few, if any, could produce
the goods: no, not a drop. Another psychological or, possibly pathological, problem.

The German guns of the heavier type—I believe they
were of the Maxim-Nordenfeldt persuasion—had mounts
which included both elevating and traversing arcs, marked
in degrees and minutes of angle. They also had spirit levels
embedded in the frame, exactly as you will find on any sur-
veyor's transit. In addition, they had substantial shields
which afforded considerable protection to the gunners and
still more to the gun itself. Our mounts, even the Mark
IV, which was the latest of which I have personal knowledge, lacked all these refinements and we had to make all
our corrections by using a simple compass, held in the hand
and with a clinometer or quadrant such as was used by
the artillery. As to protection for the gun or gunners, there
was none whatever.

A single stray bullet could—and often did—put the gunner
out of action, but, of course, gunners, like lieutenants, are
"expendable," so that was not so serious, but if that bullet
happened to hit anywhere in the breech mechanism of the
gun, it was just too bad. Even if it only pierced the water
jacket it would effectually put the gun out of action in a
short time. With the German guns, it was impossible for
a shot coming from the front to strike any part of the gun
excepting a few inches of the muzzle. The only way to

abate them by rifle fire was to gain a position on the flank or in their rear.

The Lewis gun is rated, in the United States Army, as a "Light Machine Gun" and I can offer no objection to that designation. We considered them—and called them—automatic rifles, but I am not inclined to quarrel with anyone who prefers to include them in the class of machine guns, proper. They are wonderfully effective weapons, whatever you call them, and we were mighty glad to get them for use with the advancing troops. This left the heavier types— the *real* machine guns—to the work of directing overhead and indirect fire on the lines of enemy communications while the men with the Lewis guns could advance with the infantry.

The only French machine guns I have ever seen were of the Hotchkiss type—*chaut-chauts*—using clips of, I think, thirty cartridges. Some of the lighter German guns, of the automatic-rifle family, were of similar construction, but they had, in addition to these, another one, called a "Parabellum." This one had the barrel covered with a flanged, aluminum casing and an outside jacket of light metal, very much like the Lewis in some respects but longer and slimmer and with holes in this outside jacket. The rate of fire of these guns was above any others that I have ever seen.

As to the Browning, I must confess utter ignorance. So far as I have been able to learn, very few—if any—were used in actual warfare. In general appearance and construction, they closely resemble the various types of Maxims —either the Vickers-Maxim or the light Maxim-Nordenfeldt. Whether they possess any marked points of superiority over those guns, I do not know; and, unless they have stood the test of a long and strenuous campaign under modern war conditions, it is safe to say that nobody else knows. The true test of any *materiel* is possible only under actual service conditions.

Our Machine Gun training in Canada consisted of, first, a very thorough course of instruction in the construction and mechanical features of the guns themselves, the quickest and most efficient methods of replacing broken or damaged parts, the diagnosis and cure of the numerous malfunctions which are enumerated under the all-embracing name of "stoppages;" second, spirited daily drills, which took the form of competitions, in the rapid mounting, dismounting and moving of the guns, accompanied by sight adjustments and aiming drill and, third, many days of actual firing, with service ammunition, on the Barriefield ranges. This was limited to direct fire but, as it included all degrees of slow and rapid fire, at both bull's-eyes and man-targets, at all ranges from two hundred to one thousand yards, and since the supply of ammunition was not limited, every man had ample opportunity to become thoroughly familiar with every phase of the actual handling and firing of the guns and the filling of belts, both by machine and by hand.

A gun crew consisted of six men, numbered from one to six and each with certain specified duties. The Number One man was designated a lance corporal and was the commander of the crew and did the actual firing. During the period of our training, however, positions were changed frequently, so that each man performed, in turn, the duties of every number. No permanent assignments to crews were made until we were about to leave England for the front.

In England the course of instruction was extended to include practice on miniature targets of various kinds with traversing: horizontal, diagonal and vertical. Then we resumed the firing, on the Hythe ranges, first at bull's-eye targets and then at long lines of individual silhouettes set up on the stop-butt and which fell when hit. This was usually in the nature of advancing fire, starting at about six hundred yards and firing a short burst and then moving rapidly forward, setting up the guns and continuing the fire.

Two guns would work together, one of them maintaining a fire while the other advanced, just as is done in the "advance by rushes" of the infantry. We seldom had any difficulty in downing all the targets in short order, but I have seen several other, inexperienced outfits, going through the same performance, on the same range, when they would have to get both guns clear down to the two-hundred yard range before finishing the job.

But the matter of indirect fire was still merely a matter of theory. A few of us had given the matter considerable study but had had no opportunity to give our ideas a practical try-out until, on our last visit to the range, just a few days before we sailed for France, we spent several hours experimenting. Our only "tools," besides map, protractor and compass, were an ordinary carpenter's square and level. With these and by dint of main strength and endurance, we managed to get on the targets at ranges from 900 to 1100 yards. Next day we received an issue of clinometers—quadrants—such as were used by the light artillery. These, together with prismatic compasses, protractors, maps and elevation charts, comprised the firing equipment with which we took the field. There were, of course, numerous and sometimes amazing gadgets being turned out and offered for the purpose of simplifying the problems of the Emma-Gee officer, many of them of no practical use and none of them living up to the expectations of the inventors.

I collected quite a lot of those innovations and still have several. One which is now before me is: "The Machine Gun Officer's Protractor," by Capt. H. K. Charteris, Hythe Staff. It reminded me, very much, of the mil-rule which had been introduced to our (U. S.) army a few years previously. In one respect it is an improvement on the type of mil-rule I had seen in that it has a small metal disc at the end of the sighting string, with a little aperture through which one sights. The graduations are called "graticules" instead of mils but the purpose is the same in that they are supposed to be of use in determining any given range. Theoretically these instruments, including the mil-rule, are all to the good and their use in schools of instruction may be justified because of the mental exercise and training which resulted from picking out and identifying certain visible objects in the landscape; but when it comes to the matter of their practical use in warfare; well, so far as I can see, they are simply excess baggage. Even if it were possible for a man to stand out in the open, during an engagement, long enough to take any careful sights with one of the blamed things, it seems to me that the only thing they do is to substitute a lot of uncertainties for one good guess— in other words, a man has a darn sight better chance to make one good guess at the range, without messing around with one of those things, than he has of getting a reliable answer to all the ifs and maybesos which their use entails. For instance: how tall is a man? (He may be a six foot Guardsman or a member of the Bantam Brigade.) How high is a tree, or a house, or a church? How long is a wagon or a truck or a box-car? How far is it between telephone poles? If you can supply the right answer to any of these questions, then you have to contend with the fact that hardly any two men can sight through the same aperture and see exactly the same thing. The variations in keenness of sight itself, the degree of steadiness with which the instrument is held and the character of the light, shadows, etc., all combine to preclude the probability of uniformity in the results obtained by different persons. This was conclusively proved to me during the Small Arms Firing School, at Camp Perry, in 1918, when, out of a class of thirty-odd officers, it was seldom that one-fourth of them could arrive at the same result, even when sighting on a water-tower, the height of which was known to a foot.

When I went to Canada, I took with me one of the Hitt-

Brown Fire Control Rules, thinking it might be useful. However, I was disappointed, as the printing on it is so fine that, even then, when my eyesight was excellent, I could not read the letters or figures without the use of a magnifying glass. Anyway, all the dope on it was for the U. S. 1906 ammunition, so not adaptable to the British .303. That Charteris gadget did have some useful information inscribed on it—angles of elevation and descent, cones of dispersion, etc.—all of it useful at times, but I soon discarded it, as I had all those tables on a celluloid protractor which I found more suitable for my work of compiling firing data. In all our work, designating targets, making corrections in range, etc., we used degrees and minutes of angle— as did the artillery. I have been acquainted with this "mil" business ever since it was introduced in the U. S. Army, but, up to this present year of our Lord, 1932, I must confess that I have never been able to form the slightest idea as to the *why* of it, and if there is any real and *practical* advantage in its use, the same has never been explained to me or in my presence. Every rifleman in the United States and in the British possessions is familiar with the *minute,* as a measure used for changes in elevation or horizontal deflection. Probably some of them do not know that it is just the sixtieth part of a degree or that an angle of one minute, extended to the distance of one mile, equals eighteen inches, but they all *do* know that a change of one minute is equal to one inch for every hundred yards of range. (The mile being 1760 yards and the minute equaling eighteen inches at that distance, it is plenty close enough for all practical purposes.) And whenever we have to make up a real army, for war, we will take in men from every walk of life; but, no matter what their normal vocation, they will have a general idea of the structure of the circle and its divisions, used by astronomers, navigators, engineers and surveyors, the world over—and really *understood* by the nucleus of shooting men with whom we would have to start out. What is the advantage in trying to make them learn something altogether different and which cannot, in my humble opinion, increase their efficiency in the slightest degree? The time for training and preparation will be all too short, at the best, so why complicate matters any more than necessary?

The ingenuity, the time and the money wasted by educated theorists would, if properly applied, win most any war. I could not attempt to enumerate all the marvelous and amazing devices that came to my notice, both in the British and American services, during the war. Why, they even issued to us a lot of carefully made cloth masks and neck coverings of a similar khaki-colored material—to be used when on night raids. Nobody ever used them, of course, a smear of mud being much better and easier to apply. Then there were the steel shields, mounted on two little truck wheels, which men were expected to push before them when advancing to the attack. I saw them at various places behind the lines but never up at the front, as it was obviously impossible for men to trundle them across the torn ground of no-man's-land. The most expensive of range finders—useful in their proper place—were frequently seen, in all their glittering glory of a meter of bright and shining brass, sticking in the mud alongside the trenches where they had been thrown by the misguided individuals who had laboriously carried them up from the rear.

When we finally got up to the front, opposite Messines, we had a chance to work up some practical dope on machine-gun firing—indirect firing, I mean. The German position was along the Messines Ridge and ours on a similar height across the valley of the Douve River. The range, from crest to crest, was about a mile, but the front line trenches of both sides were advanced so that they were but some three hundred yards apart. From carefully concealed observation posts, along the crest, we were able to locate several important dumps and points of rendezvous within the enemy lines. The machine gun officer of the outgoing Surreys had begun this work and we took it up where he left off. There we used but one strafing gun, located just far enough back from the crest of the hill to be safe from direct enemy observation. Our maps were the accurate, official maps of the district, upon which had been printed a "grid" with squares of 1,000 yards further divided into quarters and these five-hundred yard squares marked with hatch-marks along the lines which were to be indicated by numbers, from one to ten, both horizontally and vertically, when describing the location of a target. By this system we could locate any target within a space of fifty yards and, by using an additional series of numbers, could bring this down to five yards. The contours were in meters.

Before doing any actual firing, we made range charts by using one of the regular maps and drawing on it the lines running from the gun position to the various targets, which were indicated by letters of the alphabet. The lines of sight were determined by compass and checked, whenever possible, by sending a man to the rear, where from some commanding height he could see both gun and target. Then another man, crawling out in front of the gun, drove a stake at the spot indicated by the observer, in a direct line from gun to target, and the letter of the particular target was plainly inscribed on the stake. The outgoing Surreys had already located several important points within the German lines. One of these, which we named "Cooker's Halt," was the place where the field or rolling kitchens came at night with the next day's rations for the men in the front lines and where the ration parties gathered soon after dark every night. This was our first objective, and our initial night's strafing was highly successful, as was evidenced by the dead horses and men and overturned cookers and limbers which were plainly visible there in the morning. That must have been a hot spot for Heinie for a few minutes. The shouting, screaming and general racket was plainly heard by the men in our front line and reported by them. From that time on their cookers never came over the hill, and we had to search for other targets. Occasional working parties were located and dispersed, and this furnished about all the entertainment; until, one afternoon, while scanning the enemy lines from one of our observation posts, I discovered a long string of motor trucks moving into the yard of a farmhouse where they unloaded boxes and bales of supplies, the character of which could not be determined at that distance.

After a little hurried work in figuring the range and direction we opened fire on them at a range of about 1800 yards—and how they did scatter. One truck, probably disabled, was left in plain sight but all the others quickly made their way back and over the hill, leaving some men lying on the ground.

During all the months that followed, both there and at other places along the line, we always maintained one or more strafing guns. Practice with these not only inflicted a certain amount of damage upon the enemy but it qualified the men operating the guns for the more important work of delivering a harassing fire upon the enemy's lines of communication during an engagement.

In connection with this strafing business I recall a funny incident. One day an officer of the Yorkshire Regiment happened to come down the communication trench just as I was entering it from a side trench which led to one of our strafing-gun positions. As I knew him to be the Emma-Gee officer of his unit, I invited him to go back with me and inspect the position, and I there explained to him just what we were doing in that line. Now he was a newcomer, recently out from England, and, while he had heard, in a vague way, of this kind of machine-gun work, he had never seen it tried out. I explained everything to him very carefully, showing our maps, range-charts and instruments. He had, it seemed, all the necessary equipment, and, becoming very enthusiastic, he vowed that he would surprise his commanding officer by starting something of the same kind in his outfit.

Well, he did, all right for that evening, just before dark, as I was passing along the trench which separated their sector from ours, I noticed a group of men mounting a machine gun some fifty yards behind their front line trench. Curious, I stopped to watch, and soon discovered my officer, busily engaged in giving instructions for the mounting and laying of the gun. He soon noticed me and came over. He was fairly bubbling over with enthusiasm and told me that he had received information from the F. O. O. of the local battery that they (the artillery) were going to strafe a certain cross-road at seven o'clock and that he was going to join the party with the gun which was just now being set up. On his map he showed me the location of the target and also all his firing data. I studied it awhile and then took a look at the terrain in the direction of the target, but said nothing. However, I made it a point to be around at seven o'clock and stood by while they fired four belts (1000 rounds) into the side of "Picadilly Hill," about two hundred yards away. In figuring his firing dope he had made no allowance whatever for the difference in elevation. His target was on a high flat, some ten meters above his gun position, and with the edge of the flat—the hill mentioned—directly in front of the gun. With the gun and ammunition he was using it would have been a physical impossibility to hit the designated target from that point. *Our* guns, that is, our strafing guns, were located from three to five hundred yards behind our front line and on ground nearly or quite as high as that occupied by the enemy.

This machine-gun strafing was but one of the many innovations introduced by the Canadians. It was quickly taken up by all the others and soon became an established practice. Some units only used it occasionally, but we (of the 21st Battalion) made it a regular part of our business, and, having six guns instead of the regulation four, we were able to man all the usual front line positions and still have two guns left for strafing work. I hope that these lines may come to the notice of some of the men who were instrumental in providing those two extra guns, that they may know that their gift was a direct and important contribution to the fighting strength of the battalion.

All our original guns were Colts. I imagine I can hear some sniffs and horse-laughs. *You* think the Colt is a poor weapon, eh? Well, just let me tell you something for your information and instruction. That gun is the best and safest ever invented for firing, at a low elevation, over the heads of your own troops, probably because of the heavier barrel. Whatever the reason, it will fire bursts of ten to twenty shots with less dispersion on the target than any other gun which I have seen. It has its faults—they all have—but to offset them it has a lot of good points. For instance, you don't have to lug around a condenser, to say nothing of the difficulty of finding water when it is most needed. Many a gun jacket has been filled with the individual and personal contributions of urine by members of the crew, just as a sock saturated with the same liquid has done duty as a gas-mask, but dependence on this source of supply is not recommended. The comparatively slow rate of fire of the Colt is not, in my opinion, a serious detriment. It will rarely happen that troops will advance in masses, and for the scattered and loosely-connected groups which usually make up the modern battle line an exceedingly high rate of speed in firing is not only unnecessary but means merely a waste of ammunition. One bullet is quite enough to stop a man—and I have seen some hit by five or more before they had time to fall. Often we used our Colts for firing single shots—sniping—and that is practically impossible with any of the other and faster kinds. From many tests on the ranges, in both Canada and England, we found that we could sight in by firing single shots and then leave the gun in position and go back later and fire a burst which would split the bull's-eye. This proved to be an important point when we had the gun mounted in some position which was within view of the enemy, because we could sight in with single shot and no one would think it was anything but a rifle.

We had breakages, of course, but probably no more than the fellows who were using the Vickers. Most of these troubles were caused, I believe, by faulty ammunition. Cartridges developing an excessive pressure will nearly always break something, and when you are using stuff which has been made in a hundred different little and hastily equipped factories and by girls who never before knew the difference between a bullet and a bodkin, why, what the hell can you expect? By experiment you adjust the retracting springs for some well-known and reliable brand of ammunition and the first thing you know, right in the midst of a fight, you get a bunch of the phoney stuff, and all at once something goes "flooey" and it's a case of blow the whistle and take time out for repairs. Even the difference of a small fraction of an inch in the thickness of the rim of the .303 cartridge would break extractors as fast as they could be replaced. Various other irregularities, so small as to be undiscoverable with the naked eye, would cause stoppages and breaking of small parts. For the first few months, spare parts were practically unknown, and it required the utmost ingenuity on the part of the gun crew to improvise—and with what materials could be found on the spot—or replace some of the small but essential parts that went to make up the mechanism of the gun.

We utilized parts of cream separators, sewing machines,

baby carriages, bicycles and parts of farm machinery found abandoned and lying around those Belgian farms. A bit of work with hacksaw and file and there was our spare part; the members of the gun crew put in many long hours filing out those parts which experience had taught would likely break, and it soon became common belief that we could make any part of a machine gun except the barrel. The French had a great many military bicycles in their organization and these were fitted with a rifle carrier. There was a certain bolt on this carrier which was an exact duplicate of an important part of our guns, so whenever we found one those old broken bicycles which had been abandoned, we would take the time to remove this bolt and carry it along for emergencies. I remember a few bolts which were taken out of bicycles not broken, also.

All automatically operated firearms are naturally very delicately balanced mechanisms, whether gas or recoil operated. The ammunition used must give just the proper power to overcome the normal friction of the working parts, eject the empty cartridge case, reload the chamber properly, fire it and continue the cycle as long as the trigger is kept pressed. Ammunition which does not give the proper pressures, or cartridges which through faulty manufacture cause undue friction either in being seated or ejected, will soon cause a "jam." Also, ammunition which develops too much pressure or creates too little friction will cause breakages on account of the excess jar and hammering.

Hence we soon learned to test out all ammunition and find just how it was going to work before anything important was pulled off, either by ourselves or by the Germans. We would load up a few belts of a certain lot of ammunition and fire them at comparatively unimportant targets such as sweeping the top of the German trenches at morning stand-to, or a short burst in strafing work at night. This soon gave us the number of that particular batch of cartridges and if they were good we promptly took the necessary steps to obtain a reserve supply of that ammunition and store it away for use during the prolonged firing of a drive against us, or for covering fire over our own troops during an advance.

No, I'll tell you fellows: we just had to make up this game as we went along. It was not easy either. Many better men than I am, spent their lives in trying to teach the rest of us how to do it. I wish I could remember the names of some of those men of the Twentieth Canadian Battalion Machine Gun Section; you know they alternated with us—relieving one another—all through that winter of 1915-16. The machine guns always went in ahead of their infantry. Well, anyway; we "Emma-Gees," as they called all the machine gunners in the British service, went in and learned the game in the only way any game can properly be learned—*by playing it.*

During the war we used all kinds of ammunition. That loaded in England and (most of it) in Canada, was loaded with cordite, but most of the product of the factories in the United States used one or the other of the nitro-cellulose or pyro-cellulose powders manufactured by the duPont Company. Of course they were all designed to give the required initial velocity of 2440 f. s. and I suppose they actually did approximate that standard, but we found a vast difference when it came to machine-gun work where we were required to fire over the heads of our own troops.

Naturally we blamed the ammunition for all our troubles but, since I have had time to think about it, I am inclined to believe that part, at least, of the trouble, was due to worn-out barrels.

We went in with two barrels for each gun and so long as we were able to change barrels after each two belts (500 rounds) and thoroughly clean the used barrel, we had no difficulty in holding elevations within the limits required for safety, but there were times when this changing was impossible and many thousands of rounds would be fired through the one barrel without cleaning. Now, it seems to be pretty generally believed by civilians—and some soldiers, too—that a machine gun just shoots and shoots and shoots, that all the gunner does is to squeeze on the trigger and run out belt after belt, without any intermission. Of course this is all wrong. The really efficient machine gunner will fire short bursts with corresponding pauses between. On rare occasions, when the action becomes hot and the enemy is advancing in overwhelming numbers, he may have to simply "pour it into them," but when he does he knows full well that he is sacrificing his gun.

From time to time we received new barrels and the old ones were sent back to "Ordnance" where I suppose they were tested or, perhaps, just calibrated, to see how badly they really were worn. We tried always to have at least one good one for use in our strafing work where accuracy at long range was essential.

There is one phase of machine-gun work which I have never seen mentioned in print and that is wire-cutting. When a raid was contemplated or even a minor attack on a limited bit of front, it was customary to have certain men delegated to go out ahead and cut lanes through the enemy wire. The British even had several varieties of gadgets which fitted on the muzzle of the rifle for wire-cutting purposes. One was something like the extended pruning shears which gardeners use, but this was not strong enough for some of the heavier wires. Another had two "horns" which brought the wire directly across the muzzle of the rifle where a shot would sever it. But where a general advance was in preparation and it was desirable to keep some semblance of a line, it was necessary to cut up, roll up or blow up as much as possible of the entanglement.

For a long time this work was done by the artillery—

mostly light, field batteries. Given time they could certainly make a mess of things and would usually flatten out the barricades so that men could work their way through. Then some bright "Emma Gee" discovered that bullets would cut wire, and, from that time on, it was one of the functions of the machine gunners to do this work. By mobilizing a group of guns—anywhere from four to a dozen, they could rip lanes through any barbed-wire defense in a few hours.

We Canadians of the Second Division were originally equipped with Colt guns. We afterwards—at various times—learned to use others, all of the Maxim persuasion. The machine gunner's business, so far as I learned it, was either to keep the infantry out of trouble, or get 'em out of it after they had over-estimated their own ability.

At the time of the beginning of the war, in the British as well as in the United States Army, the machine gun had been considered—and so described in their textbooks—as a "weapon of opportunity:" something to fall back on or to use when conditions appeared to be favourable. Evidently they did not look for the opportunity to occur very often, because each regiment had but two machine guns issued them. In visiting various army posts and from conversations with officers of the regular establishment during the years prior to 1914, I got the idea, and I think it was well founded, that the machine-gun section was a place to send undesirable individuals from the various companies or troops—just a convenient dumping ground for all the no-account soldiers and bums who did not seem to fit into the spick and span ranks of the regular units. I had occasion to observe the same feeling during my training period with the Canadians.

I suppose my own gang, in the Emma Gee Section of the Twenty-first, harbored more of the happy-go-lucky and devil-may-care individuals than all the rest of the battalion. Some of them were transferred to us because their company commanders had become tired of having to gloss over their insubordinate and utterly undisciplined actions; but many others had voluntarily—even eagerly—sought this service because it offered the best chance for more excitement than the monotonous routine of the infantry companies. However that may be, it is just such a mixture of adventurous spirits, disdaining personal danger and ever on the lookout for a chance to stir up a scrap, that makes a good and efficient machine-gun organization. Hard swearing, hard fighting and, yes, on occasion, hard drinking men; it is no place whatever for the sissy or the mollycoddle.

Lest some of my readers may infer, from the above, that the machine-gun men were just naturally a depraved and unregenerate lot, I hasten to deny any such allegation. Among them were to be found many of the highest type of "gentlemen and scholars"—men of education and refinement, who harbored, under the surface, an intense and burning desire for high adventure. Others, perhaps, denied even the most elementary schooling, were possessed with the same undefinable urge for the excitement of primitive combat. A few months of association under the stress of actual warfare and it was difficult for an observer to detect any material difference. All had been fused into a perfect, synchronized unit to which might well be applied the slogan: "one for all and all for one." Tough? Yes, indeed; I'll say they were tough, but, by the same token, they were not *mean* or "ornery." Their toughness was of the case-hardened nature which is absolutely necessary if men are long to endure the frightful horrors and desperate, relentless ordeal of furious life and sudden death which is their daily portion. Hard indeed, on the surface, but underneath this artificial veneer was hidden a generous store of the milk of human kindness. The Oxford graduate and the homeless hobo met on common ground, where the only thing that counted was innate courage and honest friendship.

Chapter 19

The Soldier in Battle

THERE is a universal curiosity about war. Of the great primary human impulses constantly manifested in the will to live, it is rather curious that this one, the impulse to kill, is the only one that is highly organized. In the matter of eating and mating we pursue our individual ways; but war is the most stupendous business on earth; it is the most highly organized and the most lavishly financed; it takes precedence over every other social activity, and women who have never done anything in their lives except to attend teas and entertain week-end guests turn out *en masse* to raise funds and stimulate patriotic fervor. It is a well known quirk of human nature that we like to do what is forbidden, and when it comes to defying the commandment which says that "Thou shalt not kill," our efforts are set to martial music and the national tempo undergoes remarkable changes.

But it was not speculations of this sort that induced me to undertake this book. I don't know just why I began it; but once I was setting about it, I was aware of a desire to answer a lot of questions, mostly those asked by soldier-friends who got to see little or nothing of the conflict. These questions were evidence of a practical sort of curiosity. I can best be regarded as a practical sort of soldier, not concerned with the moral or ethical aspects of war, but with the fact that it *is*. What about the Ross rifle? Did it fail you? What about these automatics that are to put it out of business? Did excitement or fright threaten to make worthless your ability to hold, to score with each shot? Where do pistols come in, anyway? It was questions of this sort—numbers of them, and not only about rifles—that I set out to answer. I am not a professional story-teller. I know that the foregoing chapters do not make a smooth-running story; but I hope that, somewhere in them, may be found the answers to some of these questions—and the provocation to ask, and honestly try to answer, a great many more; for national defense is still an important matter. For the rest, the story might well close anywhere. It is at best but a diffuse and disjointed record of the observations and experiences of a rifleman who went to war. There have been many books about the war; yet it remains as something of an anomaly in human experience, its interest never satisfactorily summarized or epitomized, even for themselves by those who took an actual and active part in it.

I have, of course, not attempted this. I shall be satisfied if I have answered a few questions to the partial satisfaction of a lot of men honestly interested in them. Yet what I have written is so fragmentary and incomplete that some summing up is necessary; for in answering these questions I have frequently emphasized one point; the value of rifle-training. With another word about the rifleman here, I shall go on to the larger implications of this sort of training. I think it will appear that the emphasis was justified.

Riflemen are not born, they are made. In the early stages of American history, they were made by the sheer necessity of providing food for themselves and their families and of protecting themselves from the savage and war-like owners of the land they, the intruding white men, were determined to possess.

All the time the youth of that day were learning to shoot straight they were also learning the arts of concealment and of woodcraft that enabled them to steal upon their prey, whether it be human or four-footed, without being detected.

The riflemen of Morgan, of Marion and "Nolichucky Jack," the men who followed John Rogers Clark to Kaskaskia and thence through the indescribable hazardous journey which won Vincennes—and, with it, the whole Northwest; the men who won the battle of King's Mountain from the best rifleman officer who ever wore the King's uniform, Captain Patrick Ferguson, all had their initial training in performing the ordinary routine work of their daily lives. Deer, turkeys and, in the very early days, buffalo and elk, furnished a large part of their larder. To successfully stalk and kill this game they must, inevitably, learn the stealth of the Indian or of the game itself. From those men and their achievements, came the slogan, "The Americans are a Nation of Riflemen."

Yes, that's right. They were. But, how about now?

Those men, with their woefully inadequate weapons, as measured by modern standards, successfully vanquished their human adversaries, largely because *everybody* was a rifleman; and their ability was not only in their marksmanship, but in their knowledge of woodcraft, their alertness, initiative and self-reliance under all circumstances. How many Americans, today, can even approach the state of perfection reached by those—our forefathers—in the rifle shooting game. (We call it a game. With them it was a business —a vocation.)

We are training men in the art—or, should I say, science —of rifle shooting. We train them on a range where everything runs on a hard and fast schedule. At eight o'clock, we know we can go to the six-hundred yard range and, upon reporting to target No. 69, will find a scorer and a range officer who will issue ten rounds of ammunition and tell us that we have just ten minutes to get rid of them. The target is fixed—in the same place it was yesterday; it won't move

—it will stay right there until we finish the ten shots and, moreover, someone down there will tell us just exactly where each bullet strikes.

Well, that's fine. It is a great game, and we can learn a lot from it. We can learn just what we may expect from these rifles—at known ranges—and we can learn how to sight and hold and squeeze the trigger and all that.

But—and of all the BUTS in the world, this is the most serious—but when we go to war? What do we do then? There is no scorer or range officer or fixed target. Just a hell of a lot of other fellows shooting at us. Don't know just where they are—somewhere over yonder—in that woods I guess.

Unless the rifleman has learned, in addition to his ability to hit a clearly visible target at an approximately known range, how to take advantage of all the available protective cover, he is surely out of luck (SOL, in short). It is up to him, personally and individually, for the protection of his own hide, to be able to locate the enemy and to place himself in a position where he can deliver effective fire upon said enemy. Failing in this, he can say his prayers, secure in the knowledge that his grateful country will put a nice little white cross over his grave.

What with tanks, machine guns, trench mortars, grenades —both hand and rifle—automatic rifles *et cetera,* it does seem that the rifleman has been driven back into his last ditch, the one he came from in the days when America *was* a "Nation of Riflemen." If he is to survive at all, it must be because of his ability to go into battle *as an individual,* even though surrounded and flanked by thousands of other fighting soldiers. To be of any practical service whatever, he must be able to take advantage of cover, able to search out individual *men* of the enemy and, in the midst of all the turmoil of battle, to shoot *and hit* these individual targets.

It is not easy. Having tried it, I know.

But, by all the Gods of war, it can be done—and it is up to the riflemen of America, the real riflemen, who are really and truly endeavoring to fit themselves for war service, not only to qualify themselves, but to encourage a system that shall make available to as many men as possible, training that fosters the growth and development of the basic qualities that go into the making of a real rifleman.

Then, no matter how thorough this training and how well designed to approximate the conditions of warfare, the soldier will still be woefully unprepared for battle. I had had many years of it, and I was not prepared and just here, before going on to justify this insistence upon training in the effective use of the rifle under all conditions, I may as well say something about this inevitable unpreparedness. This involves not only the reaction of men to fatigue and discomfort and imminent death under all sorts of fantastic and gruesome conditions (all the "horrors of war" stuff)—not only this; but also the purely practical matter of our inability to know in advance the manner and methods that will suddenly develop in another war.

The first of these considerations is of course largely psychological; but the two are closely related, and the emphasis in another war may well be upon methods of instilling "psychological horror." But it is all but useless, and certainly not my intention here, to attempt to say what the next war will be like. No one has yet told us what the last one was like. The strategists and tacticians will study it; and the rank and file may well do so.

What *was* it like? A number of my friends who have read extracts from these pages have criticized me for being so "cold-blooded," as they phrased it, and have insisted that I should elaborate on the mental and physical sufferings of the actors. They—both men and women—have harped on this subject until I have come to dread having any of them visit me. But, just a few minutes ago, one of my good friends put it into new words. "Hell, Mac," he said, "that's fine, but you ought to put more misery into it." As he was a soldier and went through several major battles, he probably has a vague notion of what he is talking about; but that phrase doesn't define it at all. Misery wasn't the dominant note for either of us. There was no dominant note. It was an incredible symphony, beginning in a tedious, endless and uncertain overture, mounting through countless variations, and ending, for many of us, not in a final, crashing crescendo, but in nothing. We were picked up and thrown out and we can't even recall what it was like. I should like to hear a barrage again, a real decent barrage.

I might well have been considered an old soldier (on the range and parade-ground) when I began. I was equipped to act and shoot, and I was eager for the fray. After the long preliminaries, I soon got into it, and I found no trouble in being of service. But I didn't have time—or capacity— to see what was happening. (The High Command didn't either.) We were all enthusiastic and purposeful. We went in with our rifles and machine guns and fought, and had a great time. Then suddenly, we didn't know just what we were doing. The war was a good deal bigger than any one of us. Well, I know when this reaction struck me. It was during one of the periods of inaction in London. Prior to that time, I had never given a serious thought to the matter of surviving—or of dying. I didn't then. But I was not keen as I had been. The war was not staged for my entertainment. But I had had, largely, entertainment out of it. There was something else—a great deal more. I didn't analyze it, but just sort of collapsed under it.

Now, I find the same sort of lethargy assailing me when it comes time to relate the incidents leading up to my final months of war.

Coming back from England and walking right into that Somme fight, I tried to, and think that I did, do some of the best and most useful work that was permitted me during the whole period of my service. The fight at Combles, alone, was just about the best. Just a scratch crew; made up of volunteers of the Ox and Bucks—and some few of the War-wicks—with me, a rank outsider—a Colonial—well: the French appreciated it, anyway, and several of our crowd received individual medals for it, whether or not our own people ever made it a matter of record. The Frenchmen, with their 37 mm guns, shooting right into the port-holes of the German M. G. emplacements, while, at the same time, we were working around the left flank and pouring bullets into the back door. That's what took Combles and don't you ever let anyone try to tell you differently.

But, I found that I was weakening. Not that I allowed anyone else to see it but, right down in my heart, I felt that the game was over, so far as I was concerned. And, right here, before I forget it, I want to rise up and propose three rousing cheers for those who stuck it out and played the game all through the full four years. They are better men than I am and I take off my hat to them.

During those last few months, the whole world took on, for me, a grotesque and bizzare appearance. Nothing was normal: we were all just living in some peculiar place, out-side the pale of the commonly-accepted conventions. What we did, when back of the lines, was probably contrary to all the generally-accepted rules and regulations of ordinary hu-man intercourse. I make no apologies—not for myself or any of the others—for I feel that none is needed. Men and women were either uplifted to a higher plane of thought or dragged down to a lower—you may take your choice—but the result was just exactly the same, in either case. We were just human beings, endeavoring to enjoy the pleasures and passions of the human race for the short time allotted us before we, too, were cut down by the scythe of the gaunt old spectre—Death.

As a rifleman, I did exactly nothing during the months in between the end of the Somme battle and the time when I was finally discarded as "no longer fit for duty," in 1917, but I hope that, as an officer, I did manage to do a little good.

For more than a year I had managed to keep out of hospitals. Though several times hit, sustaining injuries which would have been considered good "Blightys," I just had a notion that I could hang on until the one came along that would finish the whole business for me. Please do not mistake me. This was not any particular bravery on my part— I went back to war to get killed, if you want to know the low-down on it—never had the slightest idea that I would not "go West." But the joke was on me. It didn't happen that way and, after taking seven clips on the jaw, I finally found myself in the custody of the R. A. M. C. No, that does not mean "Rob All My Comrades," as some would have you believe: it is just the "Royal Army Medical Corps"—God bless 'em.

I got to know the hospitals pretty well. From the North Chimneys (dressing station), in Albert, through the Field Hospital at Brickfields, thence through Warloy, Frevent, St. Pol, on to Le Treport and, eventually, to England— Queen Alexandra's Hospital, Miss Pollack's—yes: I was quite a well known case. Seemed like, when you got the first one, you were bound to get some more. However, I got back in time to do my little bit in getting the boys ready for the Vimy Ridge affair. On the day they won that fight, I was aboard a ship, sailing for New York. All I did after that time was to mess around a lot of camps—Ft. Benjamin Harrison, Camp Shelby and Camp Perry most of the time —trying to do some good but still laboring under the curse of infelicity that did not leave me for several years after peace had been declared.

I am just a plain, ordinary Hoosier. I do not recall that I had any particularly intense inner feelings while under fire.

I was always busy and managed to keep my mind concentrated on the work in hand. There were numerous occasions, however, when the actions of others did awaken within me a feeling—well, I can't describe it but it is just the same feeling I now experience when I hear a fife and drum corps and see the old flag coming down the street, followed by the straggling remnant of the *real* "old soldiers": the veterans of the Grand Army of the Republic. One such occasion was when the Gordons came in with their pipers; another, during the battle of Sanctuary Wood, when our artillery drivers were thundering down the road past our trenches, in plain sight and under direct fire of the German guns. Oh, man! that was a sight to do your heart good. It was just like the pictures of artillery going into action in the old days and, I suppose, very much like many of the things that really happened during the retreat from Mons.

We were right in front of an old chateau—Chateau Segard it was called—just a little way from the road crossing at Kruisstraathoeck, and the Germans had the range perfectly. They would make a hit now and then, and horses, men and limbers went into the ditch, but that never made any difference with the rest. They continued to "carry on." Hell bent for 'lection, they went: shells bursting all around them; drivers, standing in the stirrups and lashing the horses and the limbers bouncing up and down over the shell-torn road. We forgot everything else and jumped up out of the trenches and cheered and cheered as they went by. All day that Sunday they kept it up, taking ammunition to the guns that were now far advanced beyond the usual artillery positions due to the fact that the enemy had forced our front line back some seven hundred yards and we were backed up against our G. H. Q. line. (We took it all back a week or so later.)

For my friends, as they fell, I sincerely did grieve but I am afraid that it was mostly a selfish feeling. I grieved at my own loss, not for them. Many times, since the war, have

I been sorry that I did not "get mine," so I could rest peacefully with them under the poppies. This was the old feeling —of being spent. I begin to see, now, what it was about: When the excitement was over, there remained the serious business of winning the war; we had had our fun and I began to see what we were paying for it. How much of the business was bungling—and how many lives sacrificed to it?

Well, this is *post mortem*. To get back to our feelings at the time: I have said enough of mine. There were some millions of others. They fall, of course, more or less into types: from the naturally nervous member who was probably considerately dropped as "shell-shocked" or, as they had it in the Canadian service, "on compassionate grounds," to the stolid, phlegmatic individual who never bats an eye or shows any visible evidence that he "cares a damn" what happens to him. Between these two extremes are the great number who, in one manner or another, for one complex reason or another, "carry on" with the work in hand.

Recently there has been published a story in *Adventure,* written by a member of the Mounted Rifles, which I consider the very best and most vividly realistic war story I have read. However, I must emphatically disagree with the writer regarding one matter. He dwells considerably upon his mental anguish and all that and takes the ground that those who do not feel—and who do not show, by visible signs that they feel—the same way, are more or less dullards, devoid of the finer instincts that sway him. If his story is a true one and he was only sixteen when he enlisted, we can set it down to youthful inexperience.

I have known many men of the very highest mental calibre and fine sensibilities who have gone through the hell-fire of many battles without showing, by word or act, the slightest sign of mental perturbation. In memory of a good friend and a gallant officer, I mention one by name: Lieutenant-

Colonel Elmer Watson Jones, D. S. O., killed in action, August 8, 1918, in the Battle of Amiens, after having been previously wounded during the attack on Vimy Ridge, in April, 1917.

To understand anything of the individual reactions of the soldier it is necessary to have lived with him, to have drunk and talked with him in barracks and billets, to have known him in the mass; and then to have experienced the conditions under which he lives—and dies—as he moves toward the front—and takes the front with him. It would be fine to stay in billets for a week, but let us hurry on toward the sound of shells, observing him in the mass as we go.

A very sensitive and active pen long ago wrote the last word about "that man who hath no music in his soul." The psychologists and psychiatrists who have lately been probing into this universal and little known realm will probably add a great deal to our understanding of it and not much to the truth, save in the way of substantiation; not by condemning, as "fit for treason, stratagem, spoils," a great many men now considered non-musical, but by disclosing a trifle of music in their souls. They may even succeed in enabling them to liberate it, not audibly, perhaps, but essentially. That is what the band does, quickening it into rhythm that makes the step as well as the heart lighter. It means a great deal thus to awaken the inner man and bring his strength into unison with the outer on a long march.

And when there is no band, a lilting song will do it—and did do it. I doubt if there was a single company that did not have at all times the necessary two or three men, at least one of whom was ready when the time came to start a song. And it was not always the songster who did it. Some hard old mug who bore every appearance of having long ago soured on the world might suggest it, or manage to have it done.

"How about a little song there, Scotty," he would say to the next man.

Scotty, he knew, didn't sing much, but he would instantly raise his voice: "How about a little song?"

Maybe it came to nothing, then. The time wasn't quite ripe. There was neither that ebullience of spirit which demanded an outlet in song nor that weariness or monotony which required a song to dissipate it. Perhaps some one would start, but finding no response, he quickly gave up. Had he been articulate, he might have explained the failure of the pious sing-songsters to impose their pretty patterns or to palm off the products of Tin-Pan Alley when that center became active in the military ballad business. All credit to the wise and subtle ones who trained what they found. Songs must be spontaneous.

Half an hour later someone raised his voice:

"Keep your head down, Allemand—"

With the second measure a dozen voices had taken it up. The wise platoon commander stepped out of line and reviewed his straggling platoon. By the time he had fallen in at the rear, nearly everyone was singing, the files had closed up, the straggler had pulled himself together. When the song was over, a ripple of bantering conversation ran up and down the column. Then another song.

"Madamoiselle from Armentieres, parlez-vous—"

I have sometimes encountered the notion that this one came with the United States troops. I suspect it originated with the Canadians. Armentieres was in their territory. It is certainly much older than United States participation. There must have been hundreds of stanzas set to this measure and they sprang from as many *estaminets,* billets, brothels and dugouts, from Frenchmen, Yankees and Englishmen. It may be that the true origin was known to Frenchmen before the war.

The authorship of many of the most popular songs, I am sure, could not be traced. There was none. An incident was remembered for a phrase. The phrase became a jest;

the jest was mended and grew and became a song. I should like to tell you of one called *Souvenir*. It seems never to have got very far; but it was good, though the words which suited it never found the satisfactory music—at least for marching—and it did not survive. It was a charming bit, and I hope that somebody will let us have it as it ought to be.

It is difficult to say what decided the acceptance or rejection of a song. Some from this side—those inspired by the same sentiment that placed stars in the windows—became popular. Others were adapted, satirized, vulgarized or scorned. *God Save The King* was frequently heard on the march, largely, I sometimes thought, for the satisfaction it gave the grousing soldier to punctuate it with appropriate remarks. But let me add that His Majesty was popular and respected.

There was a song called *West Sandling,* by which I best remember singing in England. It is, I suspect, one of those that was born on paper. A training camp is not the sort of place that produces soldier's songs. And the efforts of sing-songsters there were largely futile. A canary sings when he wishes and when he has something to sing for. In leaving billets, for example, to proceed toward the line, it was as a rule useless to attempt to start a song. There might be a spurt at the beginning, celebrating events, amorous, convivial and otherwise, of the past few days, and sort of shaking things down. Then, for a time, marching took care of itself. When things became monotonous the songs commenced.

"Sing a song of bonnie Scotland,
Any old song will do—"

And most any song would do—unless it was one of those definitely rejected importations. So far as the rhythm went, it could nearly always be brought to the proper swing. There was one, I remember, which was popular, but which, as I first heard it, seemed far removed from a marching song, though it exactly suited the steps of the singer at that time— if steps they were. He was drifting about in leisurely search, it appeared, of a fair tide that should take him to his billet; and mumbling in a thin and vague falsetto:

"What a blow to Rotten Row when I go over the sea!
I know I can do without London; but can London do
   without me?"

It was a sure sign that there was not a place open where one might get another drink. It was the final curfew, the last lugubrious good-night, and it took a long time in the saying. It was a genial proclamation to all that Dad had had a successful evening. He had had many of them, in many parts of the world, and they had left their mark on his gray old face, bleached his hair and removed most of his teeth. But he was happy in the morning when somebody picked up his song, quickened its movement, and kidded him about it a little.

Occasionally a man returning from leave would bring something current in the London Music Halls. Of one such, I remember the injunction:

"Don't pity a man disabled, find him a job."
and again
"He's a father for your children, give him a job."

This came about the time I left, so I don't know if it was kept alive.

The French national anthem was a good one, but most men had to resort to wordless sounds in lieu of words. Other popular ones were: *There's a Long, Long Trail a-Winding; Pack Up Your Troubles in Your Old Kit-Bag; I Want to Go Home,* with interesting and infinite variations; *John Brown's Body,* or, rather, its illegitimate sister, *Mary Ann McCarthy, She Went Out to Gather Clams;* also *The Pride of Dundee.* The endless verses that celebrate the rambling of the bull should not be forgotten; nor, perhaps,

should *Bang Away My Lulu*.   The tragic, somewhat sorry,
but highly esoteric and agreeable adventures of *Christopher
Columbo*, not commonly known to school-children, are
doubtless immortal.   Anyone may add a few of the hymns
that are his favorites.   Then there are *Loch Lomond* and
Annie Laurie and *The Irish Jauntin' Car*.

I am always forgetting the best jokes.   Possibly I have
forgotten the best of these songs.   I think they are worth
remembering.   They have no value, perhaps, to the military
strategist; but they make the cobblestones softer for the man
with the rifle who wins the wars.

The songs die out when the battalion has reached the
vicinity of the G. H. Q. Line, which they do, generally, as
soon as possible after dark.   If they were early, they have
halted at some point beyond observation and waited for
darkness.   If they have marched very far, the field kitchens
will be here and the men fall out and have a hot supper.
While, if they are going in on their old front or for any
other reason have been billetted nearby, they have had their
last meal at the field-kitchens before leaving.   The men
sprawl about on the sides of the road in comfortable atti-
tudes, chatting indifferently about nothing, much as might
a group of them at home awaiting an inter-urban train.   If
it is raining, some of them pull out their ground-sheets for
use as ponchos; others do not.   The principal indication that
they know that there is a war going on is in the brief remarks by which they take note of the nature of the shelling:
"Oh, oh! What the hell's he after? We must have a battery
stuck in the side of that pile of plaster over there."

The pile of plaster is the remains of the familiar quad-
rangle which was once a French farm-house.   It is about
the level of a man's waist, with a timber sticking up here and
there.   It is a singular fact that almost no one ever voices
any wonder as to where the owners are, or how they live.
They do not even think of it as a home, or as having been a

home. This illustrates better, than anything I know, the strange impersonality of war, its complete severance from everyday experience, a severance so subtly made that no one knows how or when it was made. In the most advanced "borderland" villages, the strange thing is not that there are soldiers here, in this town which doesn't belong to them, but that there are a few civilians poking about. A woman or an old man has opened a little shop in the corner of a ruined building. A soldier goes in for a bar of black chocolate or a few candles for use in the trenches; and it is much as if an explorer had come upon a tiny trading-post far beyond the Arctic Circle in a land where nobody, except explorers, belongs. No; this is a land of men in uniform, and guns and rifles, shells and bullets; there is nothing puzzling about it; but there is something puzzling about coming upon an old woman prodding with a stick among the shell-holes, just beyond a little grayish patch sprinkled with a few red tiles. (This was her vegetable garden, and she has come up to see if she can find a bit of garlic or a bunch of leeks.) There is something funny, incongruous, about this apparition who presently hobbles on to the road and takes her way back to the nearest village still whole enough to shelter her from the rain.

But there is nothing incongruous about the scene a short time later, when the battalion has ceased to move as a battalion;—headquarters has gone to its position and the various companies or platoons are on their several ways to theirs, led by guides, and under conditions and over distances that vary a great deal. The area may be perfectly quiet, or mildly shelled and swept by bullets, much of which they time and localize without difficulty and almost without thinking. But presently there comes an unlucky shell, or, in an overland stretch, someone stops a machine-gun bullet. There is no confusion, no excitement. War is the business here, and death as familiar as it can ever be for the living. It is dark. The few words are spoken quietly, merely for guidance: "This way, stretcher-bearers." "Oh, you're all right. I won't dress it; wait till you get back where they have a light. Tell them to send for him; there is no hurry; half his head is gone." "Who is it?" "Johnson." "Give me those candles out of his haversack."

"Anybody else hurt? All right men, close up. Keep in touch here."

So they go: Step down. Step up. Hole. Wire here; easy in front; all right, go ahead. Dash across here, forty feet, watch out for little holes. Everybody over? Keep in touch.

There is a spurt of orange flame in the darkness at a height of a hundred feet some yards ahead. A leisurely sort of a hiss mounts rapidly and ends abruptly in an explosion: Shrapnel. But they go on, waiting for the next to see whether it is worth while to take cover.

After a while they arrive at their position; which is neither in Berlin nor St. Petersburg, as has been suggested—for the ears of the guide—several times *en route;* it is the front-line trench.

A comparatively quiet sector affords the best opportunity for observing the soldier and noting the little incidents and scraps of conversation which indicate something of his attitude. If these seem quite undramatic, free of excitement, horror and ghastly unreality, you are on the right track. They are concerned with such things as the posthumous career of Adolph. Adolph was once a Bavarian Lieutenant. When I first saw him the insignia of his rank had been stripped off. I was told that he had been cashiered. But that same day there was another court sitting on the case. He was being tried for having been a good soldier. I am sorry that I haven't a complete record of the evidence introduced and of the findings, not only of this but of dozens of other trials which he had undergone—and still continued to undergo, for there was hardly enough of him left now to bury. He had been buried, originally, I understand, shining helmet and all. No one knew when this had taken place. His first appearance, so far as our history went, was on a fine morning in the midst of breakfast, when a *minnie,* evidently intended for the dugout, unearthed him. He was pretty badly scattered about; but when breakfast was over, he was raked together and buried again, the helmet, bearing a suitable inscription and identification as to rank and regiment, being affixed to the top of the grave.

Within a few days he was out again. It seemed hardly worth while to attempt to keep him down. There was not much of him now; a half-dozen bones, a skull, a portion of one leg of his trousers and a fragment of coat with some bits of piping in red. Someone had made him look as tidy as possible, supporting him on a strand of old wire and placing his battered helmet in position. The shells had quite destroyed the parados immediately beside the entrance to the dugout, and it had never been rebuilt; so that he was in plain view—only a few feet away—to all who passed along the trench or paused for a breath of fresh air, or to finish their tea, at the entrance. Most of the men were on familiar terms with him, but with each new trip in the line there were some new men, and these were curious. Their questions resulted, in the end, in quite a long and somewhat contradictory history. He was treated very kindly, and sometimes so brilliantly that he ceased to be a ragged old coat, relict of the comedy of war, and became a splendid young Bavarian with flashing eyes and a quick smile, wearing his nice new uniform with a manner, saying good-bye with a pleasant jest and promising to return soon.

Somebody, seeing his utter defenselessness, had in time supplied him with an old bayonet. In the mornings after stand-to, while waiting for breakfast, they would stop to exchange greetings with him or to congratulate him on being damned well out of it, or to inquire as to what he knew about the plans of the High Command. But there was nothing strange about his fate, and he was not a constant reminder that at any minute a similar fate might overtake one of them. They didn't need such reminders; death was their business; they treated it familiarly because they were familiar with it. They forgot all about it, and waited impatiently the return of the ration party with their oatmeal, bacon and tea.

"Ah here we are fellows; Fritz is sending us a few pineapples for breakfast." The sound was like that of a rifle firing defective ammunition. When the grenade had exploded, near the trench apparently, but thirty yards to the right, there were other reports, and for perhaps five minutes the miniature bombardment continued. Then it tapered off, with one now and then, at long irregular intervals, at the whim, possibly, of some German soldier who had nothing else to do.

"Hey, two of you fellows come along here and help with the rations."

Two men set off without question, first calling down the dugout: "All right down there; you can eat your jam and bread and dig up a can of bully. There's brains in the tea this morning."

But the tea was all right. So was the oatmeal and bacon; though there was a big dent in the side of the dixie: "Who was it?" "Smith and McGregor. Mac is done for. Smith got a knee-cap torn off." "Dammit; why in the hell don't they keep their eyes open!" "All right, fellows, I'm not going to be here all day dishing this out."

Such incidents were not frequent in the quiet sectors after things had settled down into the long siege of trench warfare. During my last few weeks in France it was not unusual for a battalion to make its tour of front-line duty with so few casualties that they went almost unnoticed. But no matter how frequently they occurred, they did not, as a rule, bring death any closer to the survivors. Each one went on with his business in hand as if he were quite certain he would live to see the end of it and return to peace-time pursuits. It was not a matter of *believing* this or knowing it. It may better be called hope; but it was hope without its opposite of doubt or fear. A man might in an odd moment think about it and face quite frankly the possibility that before another day had passed he would be pushing up daisies, but meanwhile he carried on on the very definite assumption that he would not. This was an imperatively necessary attitude. Without it a man could not face a hail of machine-gun bullets and showers of whining shrapnel. With it, he faced them without thinking of the danger. He ducked only to rise again and carry on. But he did not need to remember the casualty list— or look at the men falling on each side of him—to know that it was only an attitude. So in the instant while he waited he faced the possibility of never rising again. This instant might be filled with a thousand reactions, all so brief that perhaps two of them were clear; and these might be, first, a momentary shrinking wonder as to where the damned thing would hit and, second, a dim bitter reflection that this is a godamned fine end for a man. It was only an instant; the ground shook, the fuse assembly of a shell whirred and buried itself in the mud under his nose, and he was up and away, with a queer, excited, short laugh or a shout to his comrades. Maybe, in the next shell-hole, he would say to one of them: "That damned Boche thought he had my number that time."

This came to be a very common expression of that attitude. Sometimes it took a hold so deep that it amounted almost to a superstition; and I can readily imagine how this might come about from watching high-angle shells, at times when a man had nothing to do but watch them, as on an idle afternoon when Heinie decided to liven things up a bit by trying for a machine-gun emplacement or battering down a few yards of trench. He would put a *minnenwerfer* to work. You had to watch them in order to be somewhere else when they came to earth, because if one of the big ones landed within twenty feet of you you were taken directly to the cemetery, unless you were very close, in which case they might have difficulty finding you. You didn't have to be hit; you might be killed without a mark.

To get the full and awesome effect, though, you had to see them at night, sometime when our guns were doing a bit of intensive shelling, for a raid or as a feint when the artillery began preparation of the way for an attack on another front. You needed enough of it so that Heinie got the wind up in proper fashion and sent along a few parachute-lights in addition to the shower from Very pistols. When everything was as it should be, the air above the front-line trenches and all between was lighted like the scene of about twenty particularly elaborate Fourth of July fireworks displays all rolled into one, though there was nothing to suggest that it was not a grim and unearthly business; no bursts of laughter and applause, no smooth, green lawns sprinkled with deck chairs and people in brightly striped jackets. There was only this chasm, born of a thunderous and shrieking uproar, dotted with puffs of black, white or yellowish smoke and the orange glare of bursting shells, and above it the signal flares of the artillery drifting singly or in pairs or threes, white, green, red, and everywhere the trail and burst of Very lights with now and then the white glare of a parachute. A man was fortunate to be able to witness such a display with little to do except witness it; particularly a new man, who could thus get his baptism of fire without also getting a baptism of blood. He had nothing else to do except listen to the hiss and crack of bullets (if you heard them then you could be certain they were close) and dodge the stuff that fell in the trench. There was no fighting, no feverish activity or duties to distract the attention. Some men were quiet, others shouted constantly to men beside them. It was difficult to say what their faces betrayed. It might have been the effect of the lurid light on them.

When such a show was at its height, such small objects as pineapples were frequently visible, if you happened to catch them just right; and the *minnies* could nearly always be seen. They rocketed upward, and before they reached the top of their flight you could spot them. They seemed to be in no hurry. Their sides gleamed like dull copper in the sulphurous light. At the apex, they bundled themselves and turned slowly downward, two hundred pounds of steel and T.N.T., nosing about like something uncannily alive scenting its prey. The old timer or any man in complete control of himself was little concerned with those that were visible broad-side on: "Come on, you dirty bastard; old Lady Krupp doesn't even know my number." But he kept an eye and an ear for those directly in front. These were more difficult to see. Sometimes at the top of their flight they plunged out of sight or became but dim shadows: "All right there, my lad, watch out for this one." If they were long or short they were, generally speaking, much more easily seen than when the angle of descent would bring them to the position of the watcher. But at best, while matching their wits against visible death, there might come a soft, earth-shaking thump at the end of the traverse, and instantly they were down in the mud as deeply as possible, with no chance to do anything about the one on which they had had their eyes and which might be expected any second to land about the small of the back.

After such an experience, it didn't require a nervous or timid man to develop a sort of a superstitious awe of these monsters. Standing again beside the parapet, watching them rocket up into the sulphurous air and slip downward toward the trench, he would suddenly remember the five minutes during which he had done this all unmindful of the one which might have at any time dropped unseen. It was not difficult to imagine his regimental number etched on its sinister surface. But it wasn't on those to either side. It might be on one there in the smoke above him. But none came, and he became aware again of the bullets whistling across, sometimes ending abruptly in a soft *spat*. Anyone of them might have his number. But the one he heard never did have it; for he wouldn't hear the fatal one.

Men got used to them of course. You kept down when it was possible, but when you had to go you might as well go on as though there were no bullets about. You hurried when visible, or over a known danger spot; but at night, walking across the open in support areas or beyond, a man might duck if a gun opened directly to his front when by its sound he knew it was firing toward him; then, when it had swung to one side, he might get up to be stopped by a bullet slipping in at a long angle from a gun which he had hardly heard. Some men always ducked or were inclined to; others paid no attention whatever to traversing guns, walking on as though they were firing blanks. Sometimes it was necessary to travel overland for long distances. Of a file of men coming in under such conditions half of them might drop into each bit of shallow trench they came to, following it as long as possible; the other half stuck to the bank until they reached a real trench. I recall intercepting a water-party one night to get a supply for a gun-crew whose known address was the front-line but which was that night about two hundred yards back. The support trench was hardly more than a crooked muddy ditch, in which no one stayed. I went along this to about the point where the water carriers would reach it coming overland. The area was being swept at intervals by guns from either flank and from the front. The frontal fire was probably safely overhead here, being intended for that vast nightly movement which went on farther back. I sat and listened to the guns and their hissing little slugs until the party showed up—six vague blurs in the darkness somewhat to my right as I sat. Four of them immediately dropped into the little trench, while the other two turned along the bank. They all stopped when I spoke and offered my six empty water-bottles.

"Right-oh," said the first of the two men on the bank. I have forgotten his name, though I remember his build and features very distinctly, and also that he came from some place up in the woods of Ontario, around Cochrane. I waited for him to get into the trench, where the others had already leaned against the bank, content to rest for a few minutes and pass the time of day. But he didn't come down.

"Let's have one," he said. I passed the bottles out, giving him one of them. And just at that minute, almost as if the gunner had seen the man stop there, a gun opened up with the sharp distinct report which told that the muzzle was not pointed the other way. I noticed at once that it was not the gun I had been hearing from that quarter, the one which I thought was firing overhead. I noticed, too, that he was traversing, while the other, I thought, had been fixed.

"You damned fool," somebody said, "you had better get down."

"Hell, they won't hurt you if they don't hit you." Then, turning to me he added: "Did you ever see that well where we've been getting water? There's a little piece of brick wall there, and they've just about cut it down with machine-gun bullets. You have to wait off a little distance to keep from getting brick dust in your eyes; and then while you are awaiting some other damned party gets in ahead of you."

In the meantime they had begun filling my bottles. The man on top had picked up one of his petrol tins, caught it between his knees and, bending over, held the bottle to catch the water. This necessitated putting his head down fairly close so that he could see a little of what he was doing. Then the gun opened again. The first burst had been a short one. It seemed now to have got down to business, and the bullets were ripping across at a slow rate of fire some distance to our right, and the rising report of the gun told us that it was coming our way.

"Aw, shoot, you damned squarehead," the man said. Then "Well, I'm a—Hey you fellows; fill the bottles out of this tin; it's got two extra holes in it."

Trench warfare soon became routine stuff, though each new sector offered its little variations in the matter of living conditions, supplies, communications, machine-gun and artillery activity, facilities for observation, etc.; and each day, almost, brought to light some strange incident or quirk of fate or insignificant circumstance which decided between life and death. Some of these came to hold in trench gossip a place comparable to many of our traditional superstitions; but they were never superstitions; they were never held for more than they were worth. The best known example, perhaps, is the pocket testament which turned aside the bullet aimed for the heart. Another favorite talisman was the steel pocket mirror. A man would transfer it from his haversack to his pocket with every indication of grave concern that he was about to forget it: "Hell, man, this damned thing will probably save my life; not that I give a damn; I'm simply looking out for a good woman back in Medicine Hat."

"Medicine Hat, my eye! You'll be growing poppies in Ballieul when another spring-time comes around."

No; they didn't worry much about it; and anyone who was inclined to do so couldn't very well keep it up. Another thing; I don't think we ever took God into the trenches with us. The Germans have been known to carve over the entrance to their dugouts such inscriptions as the "Gott mit uns," on their belt buckles. This is well enough, perhaps; but I think most of us left God out of it. Those of us who were very religious had a better God than that; we might in a pinch call on him to get us out of it; but we didn't charge him with partiality in the affair.

Of the more exciting business of actual battle it is not so easy to write. In the first place there are battles and battles. There is a vast difference between such a nasty business as the St. Eloi affair—insignificant though it was —and that of the Somme, which was significant. Of the two, I think anybody would choose a half-dozen Sommes rather than one St. Eloi. On the Somme we went somewhere, got it over with, consolidated, and were relieved. At St. Eloi we crept or were blasted back and forth over the same area daily and nightly for some weeks. There were some splendid moments, but there is something depressing and pathetic about splendid moments that end repeatedly in nothing but more blood and mud. How did the men behave? They carried on.

But there is a vast difference in conditions even when considering those battles which resulted in real advances, as planned. And in the same battle, much depends upon whether you started it or ended it, or came in at the middle. Frequently those troops who launch the assault and gain the first objectives fare better than others who take up the advance on subsequent days. Usually the first assaulting troops leave from fairly comfortable positions which become untenable only about the time they are leaving them for the German front line and points East. They may see as hard fighting as anybody, but they are usually in better shape at the beginning. They have come in after less hard marching and with less harassing delay; and this little matter of waiting is usually more trying than fighting. They know exactly when they are to start and that they needn't, usually, worry about exposure on either flank. They have only to wait for the barrage to lift, and this interval is usually utilized in checking up and reviewing any special instructions that may have been considered. Generally, however, conditions do not favor talk of any sort; and when the enemy puts down his counter-barrage, conversation becomes almost impossible. Men will shout now and then into the ears of those near them, and sometimes in the course of these words there may be brief mutual reminders to see that those back home are informed that there was nothing particularly distressing about the end; for most men face at this time the possibility that their remaining time on earth may be numbered by minutes. I have seldom noticed any evidence of particular concern about it. There is nervous tension, of course, a greater strain than most men realize; though it is not induced by the imminence of death, in itself; but only because it is in terms of death that results of the next throw of the dice are to be stated; the tension differs only in degree from that to be noted before any event on which much depends, which is final, after which no mistakes can be rectified.

The wise ones are calmly considering the practical aspects; they have already noted the nature of the enemy barrage. Picking out the gaps in it, they point them out to others as favorable places to go over. If conditions favor it, all of them have already been taken out to an advanced position, where they lie low, awaiting the final word. This does not, then, offer a particularly fertile field for psychological analysis. It is largely a simple matter of a feeling of fitness amongst the men, of their being up to scratch. And although this is a simple matter to state, it is a difficult condition to achieve and maintain.

And just that is the burden of my song about riflemen. When you have a good rifleman you have a man who is confident of his ability to take care of himself; the quality pertains not to the rifle, but to himself; so you have a man who can quickly be turned to doing anything. No one can say what another war will be like, what conditions will develop and what weapons will be devised to meet them; but it is certain that men will be required, and it will be more important than ever that these men be highly trained. The rifle, of course, is the primary arm. It belongs peculiarly to the individual soldier; it goes wherever he goes; it is not spent, put out of action, or impossible to get into action in time. The man who most thoroughly understands its use and appreciates its possibilities will be the first to recognize its limitations and adapt himself to something else when needed. He is not trained to win the war with the rifle, but to win the war. He is a hunter and fighter; not a specialist who is at a loss when his specialty fails him.

Such a man was about as well prepared for the developments of trench-warfare as was the keenest strategist and student of military affairs; for these were not at all prepared for it, though, in two nations at least, they had been forty years tuning up for the conflict. The legions of Germany were shot forward smoothly, according to plan, and swung out along the arc which in six weeks was to bring them victory. The French armies were set in motion. Britain sent out her handful. Belgium defended her forts gallantly and fell back. Presently somewhere northeast of Paris an entire British army passed between two German armies without either of the three knowing what was happening. Then they sorted themselves out and we had a battlefield five hundred miles long, siege warfare of a novel sort. And while the proper siege guns were being devised and supplied the rifleman was on the job. When he couldn't use his rifle, he was making grenades out of bean-tins to meet the emergency.

He had played a main part in preventing that retreat from Mons from being a disaster. And he remained on the job. It is always impossible to know what would have happened if something else hadn't happened, but it is none the less interesting to speculate upon the number of times that a simple emergency promptly met forestalled an emergency that might have been far from simple. These little things may develop suddenly, in the advanced stages of a battle, on the third gray morning, before sunrise, communications bad, observation zero. A thin line of men has just got into a trench, not yet in possession of it, when some alert eye discovers the enemy debouching in mass for a strong counter attack, pouring through an ample communication trench or along a sheltered defile. Nobody knows it but the man who sees it and the half-dozen whom he can quickly command. It is not only the expert marksman who is needed, but the hunter, whose instinct, or soundly instilled training, is to outwit and overcome, to take care of himself. He fights with sandbags, wire, enemy machine-guns, enemy grenades, and a quiet summons for help; but most of all with resourcefulness and confidence. This is what justifies the insistence upon rifle training, for the rifle is the individual arm and the emphasis is upon the man; in other things the emphasis is upon the specialty and the proper time and manner of its use.

I wish it understood that this is not to be regarded as the viewpoint with which I went into the war. It is that, and a good deal more. I was a rifleman, but I had not thought much about the larger and practical implications of what sound and thorough training as a rifleman means. Now, when I try to assort and set down some of my experiences and observations I find that the significant thing which emerges is the demonstration of the value of this sort of training. If these remarks have any interest at all, it is intended to be a practical one. I have not been concerned with shadows, but with the objects which cast them. I have not been concerned with patterns, but with the forces which make them. I have not been concerned with theories, but with experiences which test them or dispense with them.

I was, most of the time, a machine-gunner. Whatever excellence I may have had with this arm was due largely to my previous training and experience as a rifleman. No amount of special instructions could have taken the place of this training. The same thing holds true in my observation of others. This chapter began with a vague intention of saying something about the reactions of the soldiers to the conditions of the modern battlefield. This is a field for the dramatist, and a fine one it is, too. The net result of my observations, for practical purposes, may be reduced to a single remark: That men behaved well in proportion as they felt themselves equal to the occasion—again, the rifleman. The man who *knows* he can *shoot* and *hit* will get himself out of a bad hole. And if he can't get out he can die fighting. There is not that final despairing consciousness that his death is futile; for I know that men died uncomplainingly and splendidly in proportion as they had failed to discover that their death might have been avoided by more adequate training and preparation. If you think this is attributing too much to the last-minute insight of the average, not over-intelligent soldier, you are wrong. Under critical circumstances there was a revelation in every dying face. It didn't require a mystic to read it.

Retrospect

FIFTEEN years. It is a long time; yet it seems but yesterday. How readily they come back to mind the old faces, the old voices, the old distinguishing characteristics—so readily that one does not at once realize that most of them come back from beyond the beyond. This one lives, perhaps, somewheres, a middle-aged man; and that one, now almost old; but for each one of them a half-dozen are gone where they will grow no older.

Where did they go, and how? Casualties of war.

Of a few we know—all the details, the last words. Of others we remember first-hand accounts—a bullet, a whining fragment of steel, a trench-mortar projectile falling unnoticed in the general uproar. But the great majority— merely casualties, attested by figures.

How gaily they marched and sang over the snow-covered roads of Canada! And in England they marched some more, with enthusiasm unsubdued, but rebelliously impatient to get into action. Then—ah then! Parade hours were behind; it was night in the trenches; some were dead. The transition from the training-ground to the battlefield was so readily made that suddenly the interminable delay seemed a thing of the far past and war was an old game. The first shell-torn house was a tragic curiosity; but shortly they moved among them as quite natural phenomena. The first dead left a strange gap; but the others simply faded away.

The Battalion went in—and some did not come out. And again.

One did not realize the total effect unless, by some chance, one happened to be at the transport lines when the battalion got together again. It was "closed up." One had perhaps planned a dinner of "eggs and chips" with a bottle of *vin ordinaire* to celebrate this brief return to civilization. One of the proposed party was missing.

But not until one returned from leave was there anxious scanning of the ranks for familiar faces. With this perspective, they seemed changed. Then, one understood that they were changed, that there were many new faces. One waited uncertainly for this platoon or that, to pick out one or another to share talk of the visit to London: "He's out of it, Mac." "Dead" "No; Blighty; but good for the duration, and then some—leg gone."

A score or so of others, also just returned, were having similar experiences: "where's Red?" "Gone West." "Say, Signaller, your long friend's off on the long trek." "Aye; I can tell you all about it if you want to write his wife."

It was quite simple. In a day or two the ranks were filled up. And now and then an old face would reappear, a trifle white and awkwardly fresh in a new uniform. It was the slow business of war. In the end, perhaps two hundred of the "originals" returned to Canada. Something more than a thousand had gone out.

But at no time was there sign of concern, or even awareness, as to the ultimate end of this gradual decimation. They carried on with the work in hand. The Battalion was but one—and not the first. These men would never have to endure what the First Division had endured, unprotected and without warning.

* * * * * * * *

Readers of history are familiar with the stories of human fortitude as exemplified by the Greeks at Thermopalye and we all have read of "Horatius at the Bridge" and other similar legendary tales of stark courage.

Far be it from me to dispute or to endeavor to disparage the exploits of those ancient heroes, but I most humbly submit the opinion that the stand of the Canadians at Ypres, when subjected to the ordeal of poison gas—the hellish concoction, conceived by that utterly unfathomable thing, the German mind—must take first rank as an epic of human courage and devotion to duty.

There, outnumbered more than four to one, with weak artillery support and but few machine guns, they met and stopped the advance of the enemy horde.

And they did it with rifle fire.

There, during those momentous days from April 23 to May 8, 1915, died many of the flower of Canadian chivalry, among them that gallant gentleman; that sterling rifleman, Lieutenant Colonel Hart McHarg; who had come over with the invading Canadian rifle team to Camp Perry in 1913, and captured the Individual Palma Trophy from the best shots we could pit against him.

To the men who fought under the Maple Leaf of Canada, the story of the achievements of those immortals of the first Division is as sacred as the Gospels. During the succeeding years of the war, each Division, as it came to the front, tried to emulate the exploits of the First.

Ypres: The Somme: Vimy Ridge: Passchendaele: Amiens: Arras: Cambrai: Valenciennes: Mons:—all are emblazoned in letters of gold on the Canadian escutcheon—but the greatest of these is YPRES.